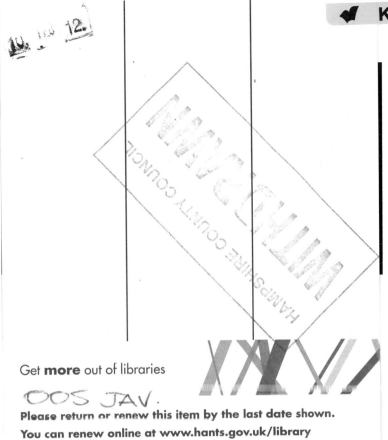

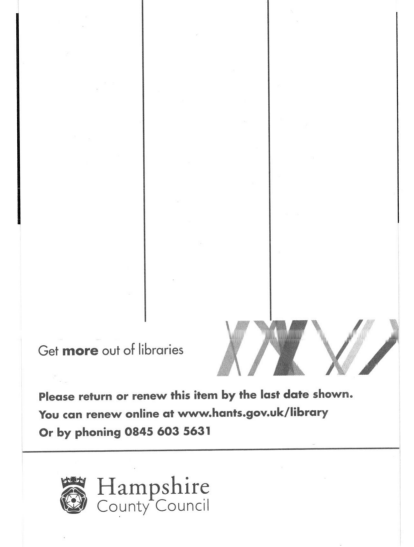

Get **more** out of libraries

Please return or renew this item by the last date shown.
You can renew online at www.hants.gov.uk/library
Or by phoning 0845 603 5631

Hampshire
County Council

Wiley Publishing, Inc.

Best-Selling Books • Digital Downloads • e-Books • Answer Networks • e-Newsletters • Branded Web Sites • e-Learning

Java™ & XML For Dummies®

Copyright © 2002 by Wiley Publishing, Inc., Indianapolis, Indiana

Published by Wiley Publishing, Inc., Indianapolis, Indiana

Published simultaneously in Canada

For general information on our other products and services or to obtain technical support please contact our Customer Care Department within the U.S. at 800-762-2974, outside the U.S. at 317-572-3993 or fax 317-572-4002.

Wiley also publishes its books in a variety of electronic formats. Some content that appears in print may not be available in electronic books.

Library of CongressControl No.: 2002106037

ISBN: 0-7645-1658-2

1B/RZ/QW/QS/IN

Wiley Publishing, Inc. is a trademark of Wiley Publishing, Inc.

About the Author

Dr. Barry Burd received an M.S. degree in Computer Science at Rutgers University, and a Ph.D. in Mathematics at the University of Illinois. As a teaching assistant in Champaign-Urbana, Illinois, he was elected five times to the university-wide List of Teachers Ranked as Excellent by their Students.

Since 1980, Dr. Burd has been a professor in the Department of Mathematics and Computer Science at Drew University in Madison, New Jersey. When he's not lecturing at Drew University, Dr. Burd leads training courses for professional programmers in business and industry. He has lectured at conferences in America, Europe, Australia and Asia. He is the author of several articles and books, including *Java 2 For Dummies,* published by Hungry Minds.

Dr. Burd lives in Madison, New Jersey with his wife and two children. In his spare time, he enjoys being a workaholic.

Dedication

```
<Dedication>
   <For>
      <nuclearfamily>
         <wife> Harriet </wife>
         <kids> Sam, Jennie </kids>
      </nuclearfamily>
      <parents> Sam, Ruth </parents>
      <grandparents>
         <maternal> Jennie, Benjamin </maternal>
         <paternal> Katie, Abram </paternal>
      </grandparents>
   </For>
</Dedication>
```

Author's Acknowledgments

```
<Acknowledgments>
   <ThankYou>
      <Family>
         <who>Jennie, Sam, Harriet</who>
         <why>
            For being loving, supportive, patient and
         helpful; for under-
            standing when I'm too busy to do my share
         at home; for lending
            clever ideas for the book; for putting up
         with my messiness
         </why>
      </Family>
      <Wiley>
         <ProjectEditor>
            <who>Paul Levesque</who>
            <why>
               For applying just the right mix of
            toughness, encourage-
               ment, and good judgment; for helping
            me feel good about my
               work as an author; for making
            decisions that I'm too wimpy
               to make myself
            </why>
         </ProjectEditor>
         <AquisitionsEditors>
            <who>Steven Hayes, Jill Byus Schorr</who>
            <why>
               For giving this project the jumpstart
            that a project needs
```

```
            </why>
        </AquisitionsEditors>
        <TechnicalEditor>
            <who>Namir Shammas</who>
            <why>For keeping me honest</why>
        </TechnicalEditor>
        <CopyEditor>
            <who>Barry Childs-Helton</who>
            <why>
                (What can I say? We "Barrys" have to
        stick together.)
            </why>
        </CopyEditor>
    </Wiley>
    <StudioB>
        <Agent>
            <who>Neil Salkind</who>
            <why>
                For doing something that I hate doing
                (negotiating the contract)
            </why>
        </Agent>
        <ManagingPartner>
            <who>David Rogelberg</who>
            <why>
                For doing something else that I hate
        doing
                (reviewing the contract)
            </why>
        </ManagingPartner>
    </StudioB>
    <NewYorkJavaSIGmembers>
        <who>
            Nancy A. Beck, Shuang Chen, Tek N.
            Dhital, Cristian Georgescu,
            Mary Ann Hays, David B. Herst, Rajiv
            Kewalramani,
            George Natalino, Oleg Shteynbuk
        </who>
        <why>
            For excellent technical advice
            (often on short notice)
        </why>
    </NewYorkJavaSIGmembers>
    </ThankYou>
</Acknowledgments>
```

Publisher's Acknowledgments

We're proud of this book; please send us your comments through our online registration form located at www.dummies.com/register/.

Some of the people who helped bring this book to market include the following:

Acquisitions, Editorial, and Media Development

Project Editor: Paul Levesque

Acquisitions Editor: Steve Hayes

Copy Editor: Barry Childs-Helton

Technical Editor: Namir Shammas

Editorial Manager: Leah Cameron

Permissions Editor: Carmen Krikorian

Media Development Manager: Laura Van Winkle

Media Development Supervisor: Richard Graves

Editorial Assistant: Amanda Foxworth

Production

Project Coordinator: Jennifer Bingham

Layout and Graphics: Joyce Haughey, LeAndra Johnson, Jackie Nicholas, Brent Savage, Betty Schulte, Ron Terry, Julie Trippetti, Jeremey Unger, Mary J. Virgin

Proofreaders: Andy Hollandbeck, Susan Moritz, Angel Perez, Linda Quigley, Dwight Ramsey, TECHBOOKS Production Services

Indexer: TECHBOOKS Production Services

General and Administrative

Wiley Technology Publishing Group: Richard Swadley, Vice President and Executive Group Publisher; Bob Ipsen, Vice President and Group Publisher; Joseph Wikert, Vice President and Publisher; Barry Pruett, Vice President and Publisher; Mary Bednarek, Editorial Director; Mary C. Corder, Editorial Director; Andy Cummings, Editorial Director

Wiley Manufacturing: Ivor Parker, Vice President, Manufacturing

Wiley Marketing: John Helmus, Assistant Vice President, Director of Marketing

Wiley Composition Services for Branded Press: Debbie Stailey, Composition Services Director

Wiley Sales: Michael Violano, Vice President, International Sales and Sub Rights

Contents at a Glance

Cartoons at a Glance

By Rich Tennant

page 355

page 7

page 285

page 39

Cartoon Information:
Fax: 978-546-7747
E-Mail: richtennant@the5thwave.com
World Wide Web: www.the5thwave.com

Table of Contents

Introduction

* *

1 thought they were crazy. They wanted a *For Dummies* book about Java and XML. "What about *Neurosurgery For Dummies*?" I asked. And they said, "Save your wisecracks for the book."

So I started writing, and I discovered that they weren't crazy after all (at least not that way). I can write a simple, readable book about Java and XML. All I have to do is keep asking myself what readers want to know, and what they don't want to know. I have to proofread each of my explanations, looking for fuzzy spots, loopholes, and other ambiguities.

Yes, I can do it. I can write a clear, helpful Java and XML book without butchering the subject matter.

How to Use This Book

I wish I could say, "Open to a random page of this book and start writing code. Just fill in the blanks and don't look back." In a sense, this is true — but I'll be honest: If you don't understand the bigger picture, then working with Java and XML is difficult. That's true of XML processing in any computer programming language — not just in Java. If you're typing code without knowing what it's about, and the code doesn't do exactly what you want it to do, then you're just plain stuck.

That's why this book divides the subject into manageable chunks. Each chunk is (more or less) a chapter. You can jump in anywhere you want — Chapter 5, Chapter 10, or wherever. You can even start by poking around in the middle of a chapter. I've tried to make the examples interesting without making one chapter depend on another. When I use an important idea from another chapter, I include a note to help you find your way around.

In general, my advice is as follows:

- ✔ If you already know something, don't bother reading about it.
- ✔ If you're curious, don't be afraid to skip ahead. You can always sneak a peek at an earlier chapter if you really need to do so.

Conventions Used in This Book

Almost every technical book starts with a little typeface legend, and _Java & XML For Dummies_ is no exception. What follows is a brief explanation of the typefaces used in this book.

- New terms are set in _italics_.

- If you need to type something that's mixed in with the regular text, the characters you type appear in bold. For example: "Type **java CallSAX** at the command prompt."

- You'll also see this `computerese` font. I use computerese for Java code, XML tags, filenames, Web page-addresses (URLs), on-screen messages, commands, and such. Also if you have to type something that's longer than a word or two, it appears in computerese font on its own line(s):

```
<Remark>
    Say you've got an XML file or a Java File
    to type. The file's lines step out on their
    own like this.
</Remark>
```

- I use _`italicized computerese`_ font to indicate things that you'll change when you type them on your own computer keyboard. For instance, I may ask you to type

```
public class Anyname
```

which means you should type **public class** and then some name that you make up on your own.

What You Don't Have to Read

This book isn't like a novel. You can skip all around, reading a section here and a chapter there, without getting lost at all. Many of the chapters are completely self-contained; most discussions have helpful pointers to what you need to know.

Each chapter is divided into sections and subsections. In some places, an example takes up an entire section, so you can become confused if you jump into the middle of a section. That's okay; I've marked the dependent subsections with phrases like "Continuing the example, . . ." and "The next step in this process . . . ." If you read any such phrase and suddenly get reader's vertigo, you'll know you have to backtrack a bit.

I assume you won't be reading everything in order. So, if you know all about the material in (or just aren't interested in) a chapter, you can skip to more exciting stuff. Of course, you may be perplexed by references to ideas in the chapters you missed, but you'll understand the relevant technical points.

Foolish Assumptions

In this book, I make a few assumptions about you, the reader. So, read about these assumptions, see whether you fit the mold, and kindly make allowances wherever you don't.

✔ **I assume you can navigate through your computer's common menus and dialog boxes.**

You don't have to be a Windows, Linux, or Unix power user, but you should be able to start a program, find a file, put a file into a certain directory . . . that sort of thing. Most of the time, when you practice the stuff in this book, you type code on your keyboard. You don't point and click your mouse.

Certain Java housekeeping tasks occur frequently in this book, and some tasks are crucial in getting your Java code to run. For these tasks, I provide step-by-step instructions. When I write the instructions, I imagine that you're a Windows user who's learning to use Linux, or a Unix user thrust into a Windows environment.

Of course, your computer may be configured in any of several billion ways, and my instructions may not quite fit your special situation. So, when you reach one of these platform-specific tasks, try following the steps in this book. If the steps don't quite fit, consult a book with instructions tailored to your system.

✔ **I assume you can read and understand Java code.**

In a few spots, I explain obscure (or infrequently used) Java features, but for the most part, I leave Java and its syntax to other books. Anyway, most of my Java code is self-documenting and reader-friendly.

Of course, if your knowledge of Java is weak, then there's an excellent book to help you get going. It's called *Java 2 For Dummies*, and it's available in your local bookstore.

✔ **I assume little or nothing about your experience with XML.**

If you can read words, then you can make sense of the tags in an XML document. It's not very tricky. Here and there I explain a few lesser-known XML concepts; most of the stuff is self-explanatory enough to pick up as you go along.

Besides, you don't need to compose XML documents by hand in order to follow the examples in this book. In many examples, I give you a document, and your Java code processes the document. All you have to know about XML tags is how to read them and nod politely.

In other examples, you start with a Java program, and the program creates an XML document for you. It helps to understand the structure of XML documents in general, but to write the program, you don't need to know the details of XML syntax.

Of course, if you want to learn more about XML, then you can rush to the bookstore and buy *XML For Dummies* by Ed Tittel. For every hundred people that buy this book on my recommendation, I get a friendly pat on the back.

If you write XML documents by hand, or you need an editing tool that analyzes existing documents, then try XML Spy from Altova. It's expensive, but for working with XML files, there's nothing else like it. (For more info, visit www.xmlspy.com.)

How This Book Is Organized

This book is divided into subsections, which are grouped into sections, which come together to make chapters, which are lumped finally into four parts. The parts of the book are listed here.

Part 1: Getting Started

This part is your complete executive briefing. It includes a tour of the major technical concepts, along with the reasons for using Java with XML. It also includes a complete set of instructions for configuring your computer.

Part II: General-Purpose Tools

The tools in this part apply to any problem that involves an XML document. You can write code to do financial processing, system planning, genealogy, literature searching, or any other task that uses structured, self-describing data.

Each tool in this part views XML documents in its own unique way. For instance, the first tool works with tags, and the second tool works with entire XML elements. All the tools have roughly the same processing power, with some important differences that I mention in the chapters.

Part III: Special-Purpose Tools for the Web-Services Revolution

Some say that it's a new paradigm in computing. Others call it a giant leap in the evolution of the Web. Who knows? Maybe it's a big boondoggle. One way or another, the Web-services model is having an enormous impact on software development. As I write these words, Microsoft is pulling out all the stops to promote Web services with its .NET Framework.

So there's no doubt about it: For the next few years, lots of XML-related activity will focus on Web services. Millions of XML documents will search for services, describe services, and call methods offered by services. It's a very important trend.

That's why Part III deals with Web-services tools. In Part III, you use some specialized packages that target XML and Web services. If you're maintaining an XML grocery list, and you have no plans to share with other computers, then the chapters in Part III aren't for you. But if you have any interest in using a network, then these chapters are great reading.

Part IV: The Part of Tens

The Part of Tens is a little candy store. In the Part of Tens, you can find lists — of tips, resources, and all kinds of other interesting goodies — ten per chapter.

Icons Used in This Book

If you could watch me write this book, you'd see me sitting at my computer, talking to myself. I say each sentence in my head. I mutter every sentence several times. When I have an extra thought, a side comment, something that doesn't belong in the regular stream, I twist my head a little bit. That way, whoever's listening to me (usually nobody) knows that I'm off on a momentary tangent.

Of course, in print, you can't see me twisting my head. I need some other way of setting a side thought in a corner by itself. I do it with icons. When you see a Tip icon or a Remember icon, you know that I'm taking a quick detour.

Here's a list of icons that I use in this book.

A tip is an extra piece of information — something helpful that the other books may forget to tell you.

Everyone makes mistakes. Heaven knows that I've made a few in my time. Anyway, when I think people are especially prone to make a certain mistake, I mark the mistake with a Warning icon.

Question: What's stronger than a Tip, but not as strong as a Warning? *Answer:* A Remember icon.

Occasionally I run across an interesting technical tidbit. The tidbit may help you understand what developers were thinking when they created a particular feature. You don't have to read the technical tidbit, but you may find it useful. You may also find it helpful if you plan to read other (more geeky) books about Java and XML.

Where to Go from Here

If you've gotten this far, then you're ready to begin the journey. Think of me (the author) as your guide, your host, your personal assistant. I do everything I can to keep things interesting and (most importantly) help you understand. If you like what you read, then send me a note. My e-mail address, which I created just for comments and questions about this book, is JavaXML@ BurdBrain.com.

Part I
Getting Started

The 5th Wave   By Rich Tennant

VISUAL WEB DEVELOPMENT TEAM

"Give him air! Give him air! He'll be okay. He's just been exposed to some raw HTML code. It must have accidently flashed across his screen from the server."

In this part . . .

Where I come from, we have a saying: "If you don't know where you're headed, then you'll probably mistake New Jersey for your final destination." At least, I think that's how the saying goes.

Anyway, this part of the book explains where you're going with Java and XML. The part includes an overview of the book's main points, and an example to get your computer humming. I think you'll enjoy it.

Chapter 1

Java and XML: Joining Forces in Search of the Holy Grail

At my home, we celebrate every year on the tenth of May. That's because May 10, 1869 was the day of the "Golden Spike" — the driving of the final stake into the Transcontinental Railroad. The completion of this nineteenth-century engineering miracle — connecting the two ends of the continent by rail — was an event of enormous importance.

Of course, miracles don't come easily. This miracle faced some serious stumbling blocks along the way. As late as April 1869, the two railroad companies (one working from the west coast, and the other from the east coast) were competing for big government subsidies. The top dogs in each company wanted to lay more track than the people from the other company. So the two companies didn't agree on a common meeting point for the tracks.

Both companies laid tracks along their preferred routes and, instead of meeting, the routes actually passed one another. Imagine two stretches of railroad tracks, covering an overall distance of three thousand miles, and then missing one another near Promontory, Utah. The companies' work crews were close enough to fight with one another while they both laid track over the same two-hundred-mile stretch.

At this point, you may be asking yourself what this railroad story has to do with Java and XML. Well, many of my stories travel long journeys before they turn around and go home. But this railroad story isn't such a stretch. For me, the story illustrates the most blatant lack of standards in history.

It wasn't the absence of insight that kept these people from setting a standard. Quite the contrary, the whole point of the endeavor was to join the tracks. It wasn't a lack of communication, or a shortage of funds. These people simply refused to agree. And because they refused, their workers laid two hundred miles of parallel track. What a waste!

Well, if this story has a point, it's that standards are important. (Notice that I said "if.") Without standards, the modern world would be a no-tech zone. We'd be lighting candles because Brand A's bulbs didn't fit Brand B's sockets. And, if we could muster the know-how to build two computers, then one computer's software wouldn't communicate with the other computer's software.

That's good. I've finally reached a relevant point. Software standards are important. That's what a book on Java and XML is all about.

Why Software Doesn't Work

Long ago, in a mythical village named Philadelphia, some people named Mauchly and Eckert developed the first general-purpose, all-electronic computer. The computer weighed over 30 tons, and consumed enough electrical power to run 150 present-day homes. Some folks say that inventing a computer was the easy part. The hard part (a job that consumed peoples' time and energy for the rest of the millennium) was creating software that runs effectively on this modern marvel.

I don't want to bore you with historical details. (Well, actually, I'd *like* to bore you with 'em, but my editor won't let me!) Anyway, the problem with software is threefold:

- ✔ **There's always more than one way to express a solution to a programming problem.**

  Forget "skinning the cat" — how do you give someone instructions to clean a cat box? You could say, "First scoop the litter, then add more litter." You would start with imperative statements.

  But when you write a computer program, you don't necessarily start with imperative statements. In Java, for example, you start by constructing the *objects* — as in, "Create instances of the `CatBox` and `CatLitter` classes" — before you tell it what to do with them. Such is the approach used in object-oriented programming.

  It's taken decades for the world to understand the benefits of object-oriented programming. We've seen FORTRAN, C, and many other languages get pushed into the background as newer, more usable languages come to the fore. The ultimate challenge — finding the *best* way to issue instructions — is a never-ending battle. It's one developer against another, one company against another, one passionate believer against another.

✔ **Software is virtual, not physical.**

That means you can build, rework, replace, and destroy it at lightning speed. If we could build bridges as quickly as we build computer programs, then we'd have billions of miles of shore-to-shore spans. The average hobbyist would build a bridge in minutes — and most of the world's bridges would be completely unusable — a vast tangle of kludges.

Easily built structures tend to be complex and unwieldy. When you work hard to piece together a physical system (a real bridge, for instance), you're constrained by nature to make the system as simple and (we hope) reliable as possible. But when you piece together a large system with no physical effort, the system can sprout complexities till you don't fully understand its parts. Interactions among the parts become less predictable, the system becomes unreliable, and that's why so much software is so brittle.

✔ **Without rigorous standards, software isn't useful in more than one context.**

In the olden days, every computer had its own, private version of FORTRAN or COBOL. This didn't work well, because one person's program couldn't run on another person's computer.

Along came standard FORTRAN and standard COBOL, and the software world rolled along nicely for a while. But then other languages came on the scene and muddled it up again. Your machine ran only FORTRAN or C, while my machine ran only Algol, PL/1, or COBOL. If you wanted to share a FORTRAN program with me, then I'd have to spend time and money configuring a FORTRAN compiler to run on my computer. Of course, no one worried too much about this problem because the notion of sharing code seemed like sharing profits with competitors — not a very popular idea.

These days we have the Internet, and open-source software is all the rage; everyone wants to run everyone else's code. The more you share, the more your paid services become desirable. But with half a million programmers in the United States alone, each one writing code in his or her own way, how do you coordinate all that programming activity?

At the start of the third millennium, we've found partial solutions to each of these problems. Here's what we know so far:

✔ **On expressing a programming solution:**

Some programming languages are better than others. Some ways of representing data are better than others. For many applications, object-oriented programming is better than straight procedural programming. Everyone has his or her favorite language, and everyone has his or her favorite programming style. While no one is rational and unbiased, everyone is ready to fight for his or her choice.

✔ **On software's being virtual, complex, and generally unreliable:**

The people who study software engineering have some clever tactics for tackling this problem. According to these folks, the answer lies in a standardized discipline for analyzing, designing, coding, and maintaining a software project, with attention to every detail in the software life cycle.

The promise of software engineering has had mixed success. Some people swear by it, some cast asparagus on it, and others ignore it. One way or another, software engineering is a worthwhile and noble effort.

✔ **On standards and portability:**

As offensive as it may be to the freethinkers of this world, experience has shown that industry-wide standards make life easier.

If everyone uses a standard programming language, then your code has a fighting chance of running on my computer, and vice versa; code has become *portable* from platform to platform. Maybe you want to sell your code to me, or maybe you realize that, when I run your code, I can build on top of it, make enhancements to it, and eventually make your code more salable.

If everyone uses a standard format for representing data, then my programs can read your data, and your programs can read mine — the data has become portable. Sure, this situation isn't always desirable, but with sharable data, the potential benefit is mind-boggling. Share product information with visitors to your Web site. Share the terms of a financial agreement with partners and clients. Share tidbits with friends using Comics Markup Language.* The possibilities are endless.

Portable Code and Portable Data

Java is portable, XML is portable — so what's the big deal? Well, in the realm of portability, the chain is as strong as its weakest link. Take, for instance, the following scenario:

Your company forms a partnership with Joe's Hardware — a company with roughly five thousand employees. The two companies' products complement one another, so an increase in either company's sales will benefit the other company. For as long as you've been in business (two whole years, including the dot-com downturn), you've been storing your data in your company's homegrown format. Now it's time to share data with your partner Joe.

Fortunately, your homegrown data format is based on XML. Getting Joe's computers to read your data is easy. You just juggle some XML elements.

*For information on ComicsML, visit `www.xml.com/pub/a/2001/04/18/comicsml.html`.

Anyway, you and Joe agree on a procedure for transforming data. You send representatives to work on a pair of transformation programs. One program transforms your data into an intermediate format, and then another program transforms the intermediate data into Joe's format. The intermediate format is encrypted for safe passage across public Internet lines. (The encryption process is a resource hog, but it's a necessary component to ensure the data's safety.)

Your transformation program is written in Java for a Unix machine, and Joe's program is written in C++ for a Windows machine. That's okay, because each program runs in its own environment.

Everything is rosy until Joe sends you a memo. The memo reads as follows:

To: You, CEO

   Your High-Rolling Company

From: Joe

   Your Not-So-Esteemed Partner

My assets are sinking,

Of merger I'm thinking

A marriage! Yes, that would be nice.

With champagne a-flowing,

And bridesmaids all glowing,

And shareholders throwing the rice.

Sincerely,

Poor, Undernourished Joe

Suddenly, the bits hit the fan. You'll have one company, with one information-technology department, and one set of computers. The combined company will run your Unix-based computers. But what about all that data? Remember the costly intermediate format used to transfer encrypted information across the Internet? All the data will be transferred internally. You can save a bundle by eliminating that transfer step. (Two can live cheaper than one. That's what mergers are for.)

But the two programs to blend the companies' XML formats aren't compatible. Your code is written in Java; Joe's code is written in C++. Melding the two programs to eliminate the bottleneck in the middle will be a living, breathing nightmare. Try compiling the Windows C++ code on your Unix machine. What do you get? You get one warning after another. Try running the C++ code on your Unix machine. What do you get?

```
Bus error (core dumped)
```

What an unpleasant situation! What was once beneficial data compatibility has turned into a long-term maintenance headache. And why did things turn out so badly? Because Joe's C++ code isn't portable, that's why. Joe's *data* is portable, but his *code* isn't.

Consider the facts

In case you're not convinced that both XML and Java enjoy cross-platform portability, look over these facts about the two technologies:

- **In its brief lifetime, XML has become the worldwide standard for representing structured, self-describing data.**

  The XML registry, housed at www.xml.org, lists over one hundred XML data formats. They include formats for financial data, healthcare, arts and entertainment, human resources, multimedia, and many other domains. The XML standard encapsulates almost any kind of data in a way that's flexible, extensible, and easy to maintain.

- **Java runs as bytecode on a virtual machine.**

  A "compiled" Java class file that runs on Windows will run the same way on Linux, on Windows, or on whatever platform supports the Java Virtual Machine.

  With Java, there's no such thing as platform-specific code. When you go from a .java source file to a .class bytecode file, you don't lose portability. To run the .class file, all you need is an operating system that can support a Java Virtual Machine. And versions of the Java Virtual Machine are available for at least twenty different operating systems.

- **Java is based on object-oriented programming technology.**

  Java code is reusable. You can call methods from existing classes, extend classes, or stretch and bend classes to meet your specialized needs. If someone writes a wonderful XML-handling package in Java, and the package has bits and pieces that you can use in your own work, you can import the package and extend the classes to solve exactly the problems that you need to solve.

  This cooperative model works both ways. When you create a package for your own anticipated needs, other developers can adopt your package, enhance your package, and spread the good word about your code.

Taken together, these factors eventually ensure that software written in one environment can run in all other environments. Instead of reinventing the wheel, programmers reuse the wheel. This ideal — the seamless integration of parts from many sources to build large, reliable software systems — has been the Holy Grail of computing for the past several decades. Now portable code and portable data put the ideal within reach.

The partnership between Java and XML

Java and XML work well together. Taken together, Java and XML form the virtual equivalent of a well-oiled machine. Why do I say this?

Well, for starters, much of the code created for processing XML *is written in Java.* I have no hard statistics to prove this, but I visited the utilities page at www.xmlsoftware.com. On that page, I found references to 79 utilities, of which 10 were written in C++, 7 were written in Python, 6 were written in Perl, and 9 were written in other non-Java languages. A whopping 47 utilities were written in Java. Clearly the XML developer community has an investment in Java — for many good reasons, of which the likely best one is that both Java and XML are streamlined for the Internet.

Since its humble beginnings in the 1990s, Java has been an Internet-ready language. When it first hit the scene, Java was viewed primarily as a tool for building applets and other Web-client applications. Java's core *API* (*Application Programming Interface*) included a package named java.net. This package contained support for URLs, sockets, authentication, and other necessities of network coding.

As time went on, people saw more and more uses for server-side Java.

- ✔ The first big push came in 1997, when Sun released the Java Servlet API. With a servlet, you respond dynamically to a request for your Web site's services. (For instance, you can build a customized Web page on the fly to accommodate a particular visitor's needs.)
- ✔ In 1998, Sun Microsystems started developing the JavaServer Pages specifications. With JavaServer Pages, you create a Web page that includes both HTML tags and Java program logic.
- ✔ In 1999, Sun announced support for JavaServer Pages as part of the ever-popular Apache Web server.

XML was developed (in part) to address the weaknesses of HTML, the lingua franca of the Internet. The whole push for XML has been based on the desirability of sharing of data. Company A's software examines the data made public by Company B. Company A's software can read Company B's data because the data is stored in an XML document. The infrastructure for the exchange of data becomes the entire Internet.

Starting with version 1.4, Java's core API includes packages devoted exclusively to the processing of XML documents. These packages help solidify the bond between Java and XML.

Java Tools for XML Processing

In this section, you get a ten-cent tour. The tour includes descriptions of several useful Java APIs. Each API is freely available for download and use. (Most of them can be downloaded from java.sun.com/xml.)

✔ **JAXP: the Java API for XML Processing**

The name JAXP is a catchall term for several of Java's XML tools that form the backbone of the Java XML strategy. JAXP is the most mature of all the toolsets described in this book.

JAXP is actually a collection of APIs — in particular, SAX, DOM, and XSLT:

• **SAX: The Simple API for XML**

SAX represents a general-purpose approach to the handling of XML documents. Using SAX, you can do almost anything with an existing XML document, because the SAX approach to XML is very low-level. (This API has a nickname. It's QDAX — the Quick-and-Dirty API for XML.)

SAX views an XML document as a sequence of tags. You assign an action to each kind of tag, and perform the appropriate action for each tag in a document. This tag-hunting approach makes SAX a real speed demon. If you have lots of work to do, you can count on SAX to do the work in record time.

You'll find material on SAX in Chapters 3 through 6.

• **DOM: The Document Object Model**

Like SAX, the DOM API is an all-purpose tool. You can perform almost any XML task with DOM, because DOM isn't targeted toward specific XML applications.

DOM doesn't view a document as a collection of tags. Instead, DOM works with XML *elements*. To do this, a DOM program makes a big copy of a document, and stores the copy in the computer's memory. So DOM isn't fast. If you run DOM on a large XML document, then the run takes a long time. That's the price you pay for dealing with elements instead of tags.

In this book, Chapters 7 through 9 cover the DOM API.

• **XSLT: Extensible Stylesheet Language Transformations**

With XSLT, you can turn any XML document into almost any other form. You don't have to get lost in *procedural* (do-this-and-then-do-that) code. Instead, you create templates. If part of a document matches a template, then the computer uses that part of the document to compose its output.

In this book, I cover XSLT in Chapters 12 and 13.

You can get JAXP on your computer in one of two ways:

✔ You can visit `java.sun.com/xml/jaxp` and download the JAXP API on its own.

✔ You can get JAXP as part of the Java 2 Platform Standard Edition, version 1.4 or later. The last time I looked, this was a 40MB download — but it's worth every byte. The link to the download is at `java.sun.com/j2se`.

SAX, DOM, and XSLT are all included in Sun's JAXP pack. The next two items are not:

✔ **JDOM: The Java Document Object Model**

Neither SAX nor DOM is specific to Java. You can write DOM programs in C++, in Perl, and in a number of other programming languages. When you write DOM programs in Java, the core Java API gets rusty from disuse. DOM is all things to all languages, so DOM can be awkward and cumbersome to use.

To remedy this and other DOM shortcomings, two guys named Jason Hunter and Brett McLaughlin created JDOM. In many respects, JDOM is a reworking of the ideas behind DOM. The big difference is, JDOM takes full advantage of the power of Java, and uses a sleek intuitive tree structure that's missing from DOM.

Yes, JDOM is streamlined for Java. But no, JDOM isn't part of Sun's Java toolset. Instead, you download JDOM by visiting `www.jdom.org`. (To learn about JDOM, visit Chapters 10 and 11 in this book.)

✔ **JAXB: The Java API for XML Binding**

The first time I saw some JAXB code, I was jealous. Why didn't I think of that? With JAXB, you take an XML document, and turn it into a Java class. If the document has a `Sale` element, then your Java code can have a `Sale` class. If the `Sale` element has a `quantity` attribute, then the `Sale` class has methods `getQuantity` and `setQuantity`. What could be simpler?

JAXB is part of Sun's XML suite, but it's not currently bundled with JAXP or with the Java 2 core API. So, to get JAXB, you have to do a separate download. The home page for JAXB is `java.sun.com/xml/jaxb`. For your reading pleasure, I cover JAXB in Chapters 14 and 15.

I have three more APIs to tell you about. But first, I have to introduce you to the star of the show — Web services.

Web Services (Hot Stuff)

The Internet era is marked by several stiff competitions, all going on at roughly the same time. One competition was called the "Browser War."

It was Netscape versus Microsoft, and everyone knows who won. Later came the brawl between Microsoft and the U.S. Department of Justice. This brawl raised the possibility that Microsoft holds an unfair monopoly in the software market. (Well, that issue seems to have been settled.) These days, another competition is vying for center stage — the scramble for pieces of the Web-services-software pie — potentially a big, big deal.

So what's the fuss all about? What are Web services, and why do they concern XML hounds like you and me? Well, the answer is illustrated in Figure 1-1.

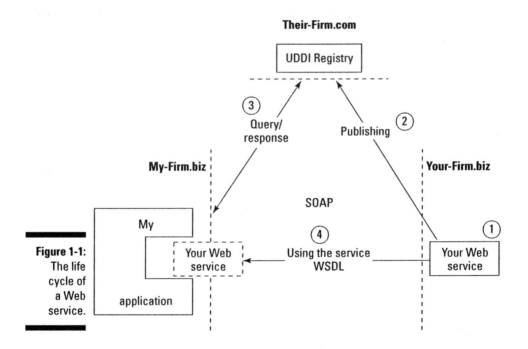

Figure 1-1: The life cycle of a Web service.

Of course, I have a story to go with Figure 1-1.

Your company creates software

You write a useful piece of software. (See the bubble numbered 1 in Figure 1-1.) Your software is so useful that you decide to offer it to others. (You offer it for a fee.)

You want to tell the world about the availability of your software. How can you do that? Well, you can take an ad out in the local newspaper, create a commercial for night-owl TV, or wear a sandwich board around town. But it's better to put information about your company and its software on the Internet. A place to deposit such information is called a *registry*.

How do you get information about your company into a registry? Once again, there are clunky alternatives. You can write a nice letter to the registry manager, or spend hours online filling out cumbersome Web-based forms. But the best procedure is one that's completely automated. You need a standardized protocol for describing things about your company. You use the protocol to describe your company and its software. Then you automate the sending of the description to the registry. (This sending of information is called *publishing* to the registry. If you're following along in Figure 1-1, we're up to the bubble numbered 2.)

Well, there just so happens to be a standard protocol for describing companies and their services. That protocol is named *UDDI* (*Universal Description, Discovery, and Integration*). So now this thing we've been calling a "registry" has a more specific name. It's called a *UDDI registry*. In case you haven't guessed, UDDI is based on XML.

In fact, at this point in the story, XML is useful on two different layers. On an upper layer, you describe your company and its services with XML based UDDI. On a lower layer, you need a standard for transporting this UDDI document to a registry on a remote computer. That standard has to work with Windows, Unix, Java, C#, Fred's Private Programming Language, or anything else that's at the other end of the Internet pipe.

Well, you're in luck. There's a standard for sending information, and it's called *SOAP* — the *Simple Object Access Protocol*. Of course, SOAP is based on XML. The idea behind SOAP is to wrap a message in an XML envelope. Then you send this envelope across the Internet, and have the receiver unwrap the message. With the SOAP standard, a Java program on a Windows computer can send stuff to a Perl program on a Linux box. The underlying platform is irrelevant.

My company gets wind of your software

You've published information on a UDDI registry. Now you wait while others visit the registry. In the meantime, my firm develops a very specialized need. I've developed software that has a big, fat gap in the middle of it. I suspect that some pluggable components can fill that gap. (For instance, I may have a Web site that's crying out for a currency converter. I know there must be currency converters that I can use.)

To help me fill the gap, I send an automated query to the UDDI registry. This query can be automated because the query/response mechanisms are part of the UDDI specification. Anyway, I send a query to the UDDI registry and what do I get as part of the response? I get information about your software. (See step 3 in Figure 1-1.)

In an ideal world, I would skip immediately to the next automated step. But in the real world, I probably hold six or seven boring meetings. My associates compare alternatives, schmooze with people over lunch, and spend money on expensive consultants. When all is said and done, we decide to plug your software into my system. This is Step 4 in Figure 1-1.

By now, it's safe to stop calling your stuff "software," and start calling your stuff a *Web service*. After all, you're making your stuff available through Web-based protocols, and my firm will avail itself of your firm's service.

So to make your service work with my software, we use XML tools. One of the tools is called *WSDL* (the *Web Services Description Language*). WSDL is an XML standard for describing the way in which your software can get called into action by my software. (Like UDDI, a WSDL description draws a picture of the service that you're offering. But unlike UDDI, the WSDL description goes into detail about under-the-hood software interfaces.)

On the registry, you've posted a WSDL document describing the technical details of your Web service. My software can download the WSDL document, and decide on its own how to mesh with your software. Because my software configures itself, fewer people need spend hours reinventing wheels.

I use your software

The day for deployment has finally arrived. To use your service on my Web site, I have to call your class's methods. I call methods that run on your computer, and the end result is no different from calling methods on my own computer. This is Bubble 4 in Figure 1-1. It's where your Web service plugs seamlessly into my company's application.

As usual, the process needs rules and regulations. Exactly how do these method calls work? The answer brings us back to SOAP. With SOAP, we transport UDDI documents, WSDL documents, method calls, and many other things. So, you see, it all comes down to SOAP. And SOAP is an incarnation of XML.

That's the Web services story in 1000 words or less. That's what all the fuss is about.

More Java Tools

Earlier in this chapter, I described some Java APIs for use with XML. Now, with a basic understanding of Web services, you're ready to read about three additional APIs.

✔ **JAXM: The Java API for XML Messaging**

A SOAP message is an ordinary XML document with some special demands on the kinds of elements that it contains. For instance, a SOAP message has envelope and body elements. So some people working with SOAP messages asked themselves an important question. "Why don't we create an API that has classes and methods just for envelope and body elements?" As a result, they created JAXM, with classes and methods that target all the special features of a SOAP document.

Sun's Web page for JAXM is java.sun.com/xml/jaxm. I cover the JAXM API in Chapter 16 of this book.

✔ **JAXR: The Java API for XML Registries**

Let's face it. Everything in this world is becoming highly specialized. We have pills to make us happy, pills to make us happy without making us drowsy, and pills to make us happily drowsy (without making us drowsily happy).

Well, the Java tools for XML are also becoming specialized. Take, for instance, the API for XML Registries. With this API, you do some of the things shown in Figure 1-1. You publish services on registries, and you query the registries. In essence, you send SOAP messages, but your program doesn't have to concern itself with envelopes and bodies. In fact, you can write JAXR programs without knowing squat about SOAP elements. With JAXR, you call methods named findOrganizations and createService. The JAXR API composes SOAP messages behind the scenes.

You can read the official story about JAXR by visiting java.sun.com/xml/jaxr. You can read the unofficial story by visiting Chapter 17 in this book.

✔ **JAX-RPC: The Java API for XML-based Remote Procedure Calls**

To bring a published Web service into my own software environment, I call procedures that live somewhere else on the Internet. (And these days, the gold standard for reaching another place on the Internet is to communicate using SOAP.) If I need prices, weather information, or song titles, then I use SOAP to reach out and call your getPrice, getRainfall, or getSongTitle methods.

I can compose SOAP messages from scratch, but it's better to use an API that can call remote methods on my behalf. That API is called *JAX-RPC*, and it's described in Chapter 18. (The home page for this API is java.sun.com/xml/jaxrpc.)

I've made a decision: When I finish this book, I'm going to retire my computer's "J" and "X" keys. I'll work with pencil and paper to create something the world really needs — a *triple*-nested acronym. I'm thinking about integrating SAX and DOM. It'll be called "DSDA," which stands for "Dummies SAX and DOM API," which stands for "Dummies Simple API for XML and Document Object Model API," which stands for "Dummies Simple Application Programming Interface for Extensible Markup Language and Document Object Model Application Programming Interface." People will call it the "DSDA API" (right before they start gibbering helplessly) — but I'll remind them that the "A" in "DSDA" already stands for "API," and that'll probably put 'em over the edge. After all, nature abhors redundancy.

Chapter 2

Try This!

The goal of this chapter is to give your fingers some exercise. The chapter is dedicated to addicts — the ones who can't keep their hands off of the computer keyboard. You know the kind.

"It's midnight. I must stop working and go to bed soon."

"It's 12:30. The faucet is dripping. I should get up and turn off the faucet."

"It's 1:00 a.m. I forgot about the faucet. I'll shut the faucet in a minute."

"It's 1:30. I'll get up and shut the faucet when this program starts running."

"It's 2:00 a.m. I must stop working and go to bed soon."

Nuts and Bolts

In this chapter, I don't explain much about Java and XML. Instead, I get you started running some XML-oriented Java code. You'll just copy the code from this book without worrying about the statements in the code. (In Chapter 3, you'll start worrying about statements in the code.)

You don't have to retype any of the code in this book. You can download the code by visiting this book's Web page at www.wiley.com/extras. You can also find the code at my Web site — users.drew.edu/bburd.

System Requirements

Does your system meet the *minimum* requirements to run this book's examples? The answer is probably "yes." The code in this book was tested with the Java 2 Platform Standard Edition, Version 1.4. This version requires a Pentium

166MHz or faster processor, and at least 32 megabytes of RAM. You can also run the code on a SPARC processor from Sun Microsystems.

Java 2 version 1.4 can run on Microsoft Windows — all versions from Windows 95 onward. If you use Linux, then you need the Linux kernel v 2.2.12 and glibc v2.1.2-11. You can also run the code on Solaris 7 or Solaris 8.

 For more details on the requirements for running Java 2 Version 1.4, visit the following Web pages: java.sun.com/j2se/1.4/install-windows.html, java.sun.com/j2se/1.4/install-linux.html, java.sun.com/j2se/1.4/install-solaris.html.

Get Going with Java

To run the examples in this book, you need a Java development kit (software that goes by several aliases — including Java Software Development Kit, JDK, and SDK). There are several variations on this theme:

✔ **You can download the Java 2 Platform Standard Edition from** java.sun.com/j2se.

I recommend Java 2 version 1.4 or later. Starting with version 1.4, Java comes with *JAXP* — the *Java API for XML Processing*. If you have JAXP, then you can compile and run most of the code in Chapters 2 through 10. (For the code beyond Chapter 10, you'll have to do more downloading. The only reason you can't run the code in Chapter 1 is pretty simple: There's no code in Chapter 1.)

Java 1.4 is available for the Windows, Linux, and Solaris operating systems.

✔ **You can use an older version of Java.**

Perhaps you like your older version of Sun's Java 2. Or you downloaded Java 2 version 1.3 a while ago, and your Internet connection isn't fast enough to download a new version every week. (I'm kidding. Sort of.) You can enhance your existing Java software by downloading the XML packages separately. The JAXP-only download is available at java.sun.com/xml/jaxp.

✔ **You can use a Java development kit that's built into your favorite integrated environment.**

You're running Borland JBuilder, Sun Forte for Java, Metroworks CodeWarrior, IBM VisualAge for Java, or some other development environment. If the environment doesn't use Java 1.4, then it's not a problem.

The JAXP-only download at java.sun.com/xml/jaxp isn't specific to a particular operating environment. You can download JAXP, look for the .jar files that you've downloaded, and add these .jar files to your system's classpath. When you compile this book's code, your development environment should have no trouble finding the classes in these .jar files.

If this talk about .jar files and the classpath gives you the willies, have no fear. Just read on.

Opening a command-prompt window

Go ahead; call me a reverse snob! I look at folks who use fancy, integrated development environments and say, "Hey, whatever happened to typing commands and code?" You may not agree with me, and that's okay. If you like to use a handy Java IDE tool, then please feel free. On the other hand, if you're tough like the old-timers (who used to program uphill both ways in the snow), you can use your system's command line.

The specific technique varies by platform, so here's a list:

- ✔ In Windows 95, 98, or Me, choose Start➪Run. Then, in the little Run dialog box, type **command**, and click OK.

- ✔ In Windows NT, 2000, or XP, choose Start➪Run. Then, in the little Run dialog box, type **cmd**, and click OK.

  In Windows NT, 2000, and XP, typing **cmd** and **command** will start two different kinds of command-prompt windows. The **cmd** window is better.

- ✔ In the Linux KDE panel, click the icon with a picture of a screen and a shell on it.

- ✔ On the Gnome desktop, click the icon with a picture of a screen and a paw on it. (If you hunt around a bit, you can find the screen with a shell on it too.)

Tinkering with Your Classpath

From time to time in this book, you have to tweak your computer's classpath by editing the CLASSPATH variable (whose value is known to the operating system). You may already be familiar with the PATH variable. Well, the CLASSPATH is the same kind of thing. The big difference is, the entire operating system uses the PATH variable; only Java uses the CLASSPATH variable.

There are several reasons to mess with your classpath:

- ✔ The first time you install Java on a particular computer, you have to set the classpath.

- ✔ On subsequent installations, you should check to make sure that the classpath contains an entry that's a just a dot (a period, that is).

✔ To run some of the examples in this book, you need to add additional entries to the classpath.

My goal is to describe two things — what value the CLASSPATH variable should have, and how you can set the value of that variable.

The value of the CLASSPATH variable

The classpath is a collection of locations. A typical location is a directory on your computer's hard drive, but other kinds of locations are possible. When you compile or run a Java program, the computer looks in these locations for some of the files it needs. (Depending on what you're trying to do, the computer may look in these locations for .java files, .class files, or both.)

For instance, the CLASSPATH string

```
.;C:\JavaPrograms;C:\JARS\xerces.jar
```

lists three locations:

✔ **The first location, denoted by a dot, points to a user's current working directory.**

If you're using a command-prompt window, and you see the C:\Author> prompt shown in Figure 2-1, then the classpath's dot stands for the C:\Author directory. When you issue the java command, the computer looks in the C:\Author directory for any .class files it needs.

✔ **The second location is the directory C:\JavaPrograms.**

Let's say that, to run CallJDOM, the computer needs an additional .class file named MyContentHandler.class. If the computer can't find this .class file in the C:\Author directory, then the computer looks next in the C:\JavaPrograms directory.

✔ **The third location is a Java Archive file (a .jar file).**

A *Java Archive* (*JAR*) file contains .class files and other interesting things. With a JAR file in your classpath, Java programs can look inside the JAR file to find classes that they need.

Figure 2-1:
Working
in the
C:\Author
directory.

```
C:\Author>java CallJDOM_
```

A JAR file is really a collection of files, compressed in ZIP format. If you copy a file named xerces.jar, and change the name of the copy to xerces.zip, then you can examine the file with your favorite unzipping program. You can also use the jar command that comes with the Java 2 Platform.

Starting with Java 2, you don't need to include files that come with the Java download in your classpath. These files are included in your classpath automatically.

Remember, the classpath is a collection of locations.

✔ In Windows, you separate the locations from one another with semicolons.

```
.;C:\JavaPrograms;C:\JARS\xerces.jar
```

✔ If you run sh, ksh, or bash in Unix or Linux, then you separate the locations from one another with colons.

```
.:/home/bburd/JavaPrograms:/usr/share/xerces.jar
```

✔ If you run csh, then you separate the locations from one another with spaces.

```
(. /home/bburd/programs /usr/share/xerces.jar)
```

Classpath examples

Before I tell you how to set your classpath, I want to go over a few classpath examples. Just look at each example, and say "That's nice." Don't do anything on your computer until you reach the next section.

One location: The working directory

You just downloaded the latest Java 2 Platform Standard Edition from java.sun.com/j2se. Your system has no CLASSPATH variable.

In this case, you should put the working directory in your classpath. You'll make the value of the variable be a single dot. For an illustration, see Figure 2-2. (I hope you can see the tiny dot in the figure.)

Figure 2-2:
Putting the
working
directory
in the
CLASSPATH.

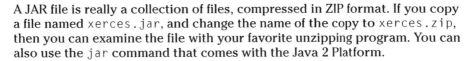

Several locations, including the working directory

You just downloaded a new version of the Java 2 Platform Standard Edition. When you check for a lone dot among the entries in the classpath, you don't find one. You add the dot to the beginning of the classpath. (See Figure 2-3.)

Figure 2-3: Adding the working directory to the CLASSPATH.

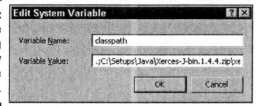

Several locations, including a JAR file

You just downloaded the JDOM API. Because JDOM isn't part of Standard Java 2, you have to add the JDOM `.class` files to your Java environment. Among other things, you add `jdom.jar` to your classpath. (See Figure 2-4.)

Figure 2-4: Adding jdom.jar to the CLASSPATH.

Setting the classpath

The way you set the classpath depends on a few different things. Mainly it varies from one operating system to another. If you're running Unix, it varies with your choice of shell.

This section has instructions for setting the classpath in several different operating systems. (If you've done this kind of thing before, and you're comfortable setting environment variables, then just do it without reading the rest of this section.)

Windows 2000

1. **Choose Start⇨Settings⇨Control Panel⇨System.**

   The System Properties window appears.

2. **In the System Properties window, select the Advanced tab. Then click the Environment Variables button.**

The Environment Variables window appears.

3. **In the Environment Variables window, check to see if there's a variable named** CLASSPATH.

The name is not case-sensitive. It could be classpath, cLaSsPaTh, or anything spelled that way.

a. If there's a variable named CLASSPATH, then select the CLASSPATH line in the Environment Variables window. Click the Edit button that's below the CLASSPATH line.

An Edit Variable dialog box opens. (See Figure 2-5. Depending on your configuration, and the alignment of planets, the dialog box may be titled Edit Variable, Edit System Variable, Edit User Variable, or something like that.) First, make sure the little Variable Name field has the word CLASSPATH in it. Then, in the Variable Value field, type whatever you need to add to the classpath. To separate your new addition from what's already in the Variable Value field, type a semicolon.

You may have a choice between editing a system variable and editing a user variable. The deal is, a Windows computer can have several different users. (If you set things up a certain way, then you get prompted for your username when you start the computer.) A system variable's value applies to everyone who uses the system, but a user variable's value applies to only one user on the system. If this confuses you, then you're in luck! It means you don't have to worry about this issue. Either the system variable or the user variable will probably work for you.

For instance, in Figure 2-5, I need to add a dot (meaning the current working directory) to the classpath. So, in the Variable Value field, I type a dot, followed by a semicolon.

Figure 2-5:
Adding a dot to the classpath (Windows 2000).

Edit System Variable	? X
Variable Name:	classpath
Variable Value:	.;C:\Setups\Java\Xerces-J-bin.1.4.4.zip\xe
	OK Cancel

b. If the Environment Variable window doesn't already have a variable named CLASSPATH, then click either of the New buttons. (One New button creates a variable for you alone. The other New button, if it's available, creates a variable for all users on the system.)

A New Variable dialog box opens. (Maybe the box's title is New System Variable or New User Variable.) For the variable name, type

CLASSPATH. For the value, type whatever you need in the classpath. (To find out what you need, read the previous section.)

In Figure 2-6, I put a dot in the window's Variable Value field.

Figure 2-6:
Creating a
CLASSPATH
variable
(Windows
2000).

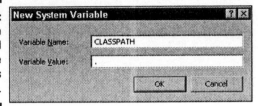

4. Click OK in every window that's been opened.

Click OK in the Edit Variable or New Variable window, in the
Environment Variables window, and in the System Properties window.

Windows NT

1. Choose Start⇨Settings⇨Control Panel⇨System.

The System Properties window appears.

2. In the System Properties window, select the Environment tab.

**3. In the Environment pane, check to see if there's a variable named
CLASSPATH.**

The name CLASSPATH is not case-sensitive.

    a. If there's a variable named CLASSPATH, then select the CLASSPATH
line. In the Value field near the bottom of the Environment pane,
type whatever you need to add to the classpath. (To find out what
you need, read the previous section.)

    For instance, in Figure 2-7, I need to add a dot to the classpath. So,
in the Value field, I type a dot, followed by a semicolon.

    b. If the Environment pane doesn't already have a variable named
CLASSPATH, then type the word **CLASSPATH** in box labeled Variable
(near the bottom of the Environment pane). In the Value box, type
whatever you need in the classpath.

    In Figure 2-8, I put a dot in the window's Variable Value box.

**4. In the System Properties window, click the Set button, then click the
OK button.**

It's easy to forget to click the Set button in step 4. If you don't click the Set
button, then any changes that you enter have no effect. This can drive you
crazy. (I ought to know. I'm crazy.)

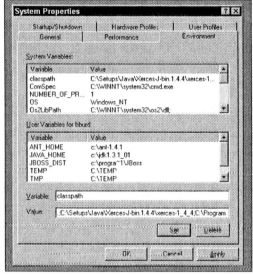

Figure 2-7:
Adding a
dot to the
classpath
(Windows
NT).

In Windows NT or 2000, the change described previously doesn't affect any command-prompt windows that are already open. You should close any command-prompt windows after you follow the previous steps. Then, when you open a brand-new command-prompt window, the change of classpath will have taken effect.

Figure 2-8:
Creating a
CLASSPATH
variable
(Windows
NT).

Windows XP

1. **Choose Start▷Control Panel▷Performance & Maintenance▷System.**

   The System Properties window appears.

2. **Follow the previous instructions for Windows 2000 (starting with item 2).**

   The Windows XP Environment Variables box is just like its counterpart in Windows 2000. The only difference is that Windows XP has dazzling colors instead of neutral blues and grays. (To protect your eyesight, please wear sunglasses.)

Windows 95, 98, or Me

1. **Choose Start▷Programs▷Accessories▷Notepad.**

   This sequence of clicks opens Windows Notepad.

2. **Choose File▷Open. In the File name box, type \autoexec.bat, and click the Open button.**

   This little ritual opens the \autoexec.bat file. (See Figure 2-9.)

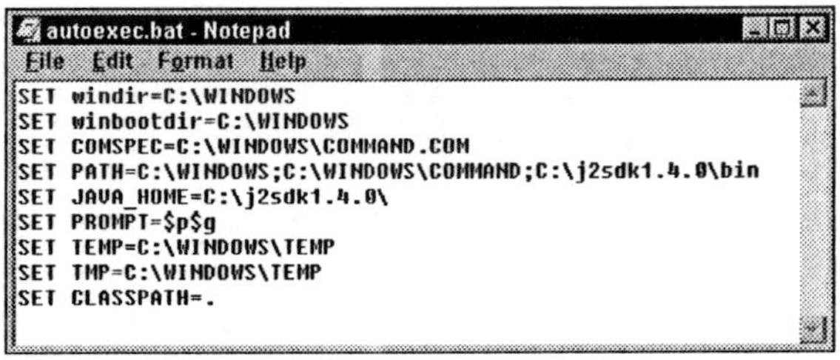

Figure 2-9:
Editing the
\autoexec.
bat file
(Windows
95, 98, or Me).

```
autoexec.bat - Notepad
File  Edit  Format  Help
SET windir=C:\WINDOWS
SET winbootdir=C:\WINDOWS
SET CONSPEC=C:\WINDOWS\COMMAND.COM
SET PATH=C:\WINDOWS;C:\WINDOWS\COMMAND;C:\j2sdk1.4.0\bin
SET JAVA_HOME=C:\j2sdk1.4.0\
SET PROMPT=$p$g
SET TEMP=C:\WINDOWS\TEMP
SET TMP=C:\WINDOWS\TEMP
SET CLASSPATH=.
```

3. **Edit the \autoexec.bat file.**

   If the file has a line that starts with CLASSPATH or SET CLASSPATH, then make changes to that line. (To find out what changes you need to make, read the previous section.)

   If the file has no such line, then add a SET CLASSPATH line to the \autoexec.bat file. (It doesn't matter if you put the line in the beginning, the middle, or the end of the file.) For instance, if you're installing Java for the first time, then add the line

   ```
   SET CLASSPATH=.
   ```

   to the \autoexec.bat file.

4. **Choose File▷Save.**

   Congratulations! You just saved your \autoexec.bat file.

5. Choose Start➪Shut Down➪Restart.

The changes don't take effect until you reboot your system.

Unix and Linux

What you do to set the classpath in a Unix-like operating system depends on several things, including the kind of command shell that you're using. For instance, if you're using `sh` or `ksh`, then add a line of the following kind to your `~/.profile` file:

```
CLASSPATH=.; export CLASSPATH
```

If you're using `bash`, then add a line of that kind to either your `~/.bashrc`, `~/.bash_profile`, `~/.bash_login`, or `~/.profile` file. Your choice of file depends on the way in which you use the command shell, and on which of these files already exist. (For more details, check the `bash` man pages.)

If you're running `csh`, then add a line like the following to the `~/.cshrc` file:

```
set CLASSPATH=.
```

On some versions of `csh`, you use a `setenv` command in the `~/.cshrc` file:

```
setenv CLASSPATH .
```

Setting your classpath on the fly

There must be dozens of ways to set your classpath. For instance, you can set the classpath for one invocation of the `javac` or `java` command. To do this, you type something like the following in your computer's command-prompt window:

```
java -classpath .;C:\JavaPrograms CallJDOM
```

This command runs the `CallJDOM` class's main method using classpath `.;C:\JavaPrograms`.

If you're running Windows, you can type a line like

```
set CLASSPATH=.;C:\JavaPrograms
```

in the command-prompt window. This modifies the classpath for any commands that you issue in that particular command-prompt window.

The `set` command holds for only one copy of the command-prompt window. When you open a command-prompt window and type this `set` command, then none of your other open command-prompt windows use that modified

CLASSPATH value. When you close the window in which you typed the set command, then that modified classpath value goes away. If you want the modified classpath again, you have to type the set command in another command-prompt window.

Running Some Code

This section encourages you to put down the book. Put your fingers on your keyboard, and get some Java code running. The code counts elements in an XML document. How the code works is not important. What's important is that you can run the code on your computer. (If you can run this code, then your computer is set to run many of the examples in this book.)

Creating a place for your files

Our immediate goal is to put three files on your computer's hard drive. You should put files into specific directories. For instance, I like to create a directory for all my Java programs.

I also think in terms of projects. All three listings in this chapter work together as one unit, so I think of the three listings as parts of one project. When I start a new project, I create a new subdirectory within my Java programs directory.

You can use the same sequence of commands in almost any operating system to create a directory and a subdirectory. The following procedure works even with the Wxroogtz 8270 operating system used by aliens on the planet Glanxblag 7 Prime Prime:

✔ **Open a command-prompt window.**

See the system-specific instructions earlier in this chapter. (For example, you open a command-prompt window in the Wxroogtz 8270 operating system by applying your seventh tentacle to the icon labeled hShee~Ght~zaH.)

✔ **Create a directory for your Java programs.**

Type the command

```
mkdir JavaPrograms
```

The directory name that you use (in place of the name JavaPrograms) is entirely up to you.

✔ **Make the new directory be your working directory.**

Type the command

```
cd JavaPrograms
```

✔ **Create a subdirectory for a particular project.**

With JavaPrograms as your working directory, type a command like

```
mkdir Chapter02Project
```

Now you have a directory (a folder) named \JavaPrograms\
Chapter02Project. You can put the code from Listings 2-1, 2-2, and 2-3
into this new directory. For details, read on.

Creating the files

The files that you need to run this chapter's example are reproduced in
Listings 2-1, 2-2, and 2-3. Two of the files are Java source files, and one is an
XML file. Remember, in this chapter, you don't need to understand any of the
stuff inside the files. You just need to get these files onto your computer's
hard drive.

Listing 2-1: CountSheep.java

```java
import javax.xml.parsers.*;
import org.xml.sax.*;
import java.io.*;


class CountSheep
{
  static public void main(String[] args) throws Exception
  {
    SAXParserFactory factory =
      SAXParserFactory.newInstance();
    SAXParser saxParser = factory.newSAXParser();
    XMLReader xmlReader = saxParser.getXMLReader();

    xmlReader.setContentHandler(new MyContentHandler());

    xmlReader.parse
      (new File("Sheep.xml").toURL().toString());
  }
}
```

Listing 2-2: MyContentHandler.java

```java
import org.xml.sax.helpers.DefaultHandler;
import org.xml.sax.Attributes;


class MyContentHandler extends DefaultHandler
{
  int count=0;


  public void startElement(String uri,
              String localName,
              String qualName,
              Attributes attribs)
  {
   if (qualName.equals("sheep"))
     System.out.println(++count + " sheep");
  }


  public void endDocument()
  {
   System.out.println("Sleep tight!");
  }
}
```

Listing 2-3: Sheep.xml

```xml
<?xml version="1.0" encoding="UTF-8"?>

<Sheep>
  <sheep/>
  <sheep/>
  <sheep/>
</Sheep>
```

You have a choice. You can type your fingers to the bone, or you can down-load all the code in this book, including the code in Listings 2-1, 2-2, and 2-3.

✔ **To download the code, visit** users.drew.edu/bburd **or** www.
  hungryminds.com/extras.

  After downloading the code, copy Listings 2-1, 2-2, and 2-3 to the
  Chapter02Project directory that you created previously. If you're a
  Windows person, then you can copy the files using Windows Explorer.

✔ **To type code on your own, use a plain old text editor.**

  Type the stuff in Listings 2-1, 2-2, and 2-3. Name these files CountSheep.
  java, MyContentHandler.java, and Sheep.xml, and save them in the
  Chapter02Project directory that you created previously.

Windows Notepad can add the `.txt` extension to the name of a new file that you save. You think you're saving `CountSheep.java`, and instead, you save `CountSheep.java.txt`. To keep this from happening, enclose the filename in double quotes. (See Figure 2-10.)

Figure 2-10:
Saving a file
in Windows
Notepad.

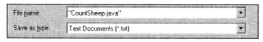

It's not a good idea to use a word processor (such as Microsoft Word) to edit your Java and XML files. You can get away with it, but *you must save these files in plaintext format.* In Word, you may see a dialog box like the one in Figure 2-11. Click Yes when you see the box.

Figure 2-11:
Say "Yes"
to plain text.

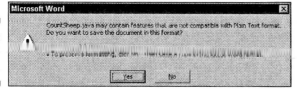

I don't get any kickbacks for putting this tip in my book. There's a great text editor with Java syntax highlighting, XML syntax highlighting, and tools for compiling and running Java code. It's called TextPad, and you can find it at `www.textpad.com`.

Running Java programs

Once you've saved the files in Listings 2-1, 2-2, and 2-3, you can run the code on almost any operating system by issuing the following lines in your command-prompt window:

```
javac CountSheep.java
java CountSheep
```

When you issue the `javac` command, you type the `.java` file extension. Then, when you issue the `java` command, you *don't* type a `.java` file extension.

When you successfully run the code in the `CountSheep` class (Listing 2-1), you should get the output shown in Figure 2-12.

Figure 2-12:
Running the
program in
Listing 2-1.

If you get this output, then you can move on to Chapter 3. If you don't get this output, then double-check the instructions in this chapter. (If necessary, send e-mail to me at JavaXML@BurdBrain.com. I like hearing from readers!)

Part II
General-Purpose Tools

The 5th Wave — By Rich Tennant

"The kids are getting up right now. When we wired the house we added vibrating pager technology to their bunkbeds."

In this part . . .

This part of the book is for control freaks. You dissect an XML document until every little piece of it is exposed. You examine each piece, and do whatever you need to do with it. Then you put the whole thing together again, and make yourself something new. This new thing can take any form — XML, HTML, plaintext, sound, or whatever you want. You're the boss.

Chapter 3

Scanning Data from Top to Bottom (Using SAX)

In This Chapter

▶ Handling events
▶ Using the Simple API for XML processing
▶ When you should use this API

This chapter is about SAX — the Simple API for XML. SAX is so simple that the essence of SAX can be summarized in just one sentence.

Start at the beginning, and work your way forward until you get to the end.

And, speaking of working your way forward, I hereby dedicate this entire chapter to Zeno of Elea. Zeno was an ancient Greek philosopher. He's best known for having confused people about what it means to work your way from the beginning to the end. Zeno's confounding reasoning goes something like this:

Suppose you're trying to get from one end of a room to the other end. You start at one end, and go half way across the room, to get to the middle. Then you go half way across the remaining half of the room to get three quarters of the way across. But then, you go half way across the remaining quarter of the room to get seven eighths of the way across. One way or another, you'll have to traverse infinitely many lengths to get across the room. But there's no time for you to traverse infinitely many lengths. Eventually, you'll get very tired, and you'll have to stop for a commercial break. So you can never make your way across the room. Sorry!

Zeno was born in 490 B.C. So, back in 472 B.C., when Zeno was eighteen, he had an argument with his father Teleutagoras. He called his father an old geezer and his father replied, "Don't make fun of me, Zeno. You'll be an old geezer some day." But Zeno, like any presumptuous eighteen-year-old, was quick to reply:

Dad, that's impossible. Why, I'll never even reach the ripe old age of 38. To make it to 38, I'd have to become 20 years older than I am right now. To get to be 20 years older, I'd first have to live half that time, and be 10 years older. But then to become 10 years older, I'd have to live half that time, and be 5 years older. The whole process would take infinitely many steps, and I'm too busy enjoying my youth to take infinitely many steps.

Zeno's father, being no philosophical slouch himself, proposed a counter-argument:

As mathematician Leonhard Euler will prove someday, the sum of infinitely many numbers, like 10 + 5 + 2½ + 1¼ + ... adds up to a finite number — a number like 20. If you wait long enough (or even if you keep busy instead of just waiting around) you'll eventually reach the age of 38.

That explanation was fine for Zeno. But, as anyone older than 38 knows, there's a little bit more to the story. In fact, there are infinitely many steps in going from one age to another. In that respect, Zeno was right. But as you get older, each of these steps takes less and less time. Going from 18 to 28 takes ten years. But then, contrary to popular belief, going from 28 to 33 takes only one year. Going from 33 to 35½ takes only a week. From then on, reaching 50 is a matter of minutes, maybe even seconds.

No wonder you can live infinitely many moments and still grow older! The moments shrink more rapidly than nature can stack moments in front of you.

Handling Events

The word *event* conjures up all kinds of images. For a non-programmer, an event is just "something that happens." If you're used to dealing with windows and frames in Java, then you probably think of an event as an occurrence that wakes up a piece of code. For instance, a user's mouse click or keystroke wakes up the code that sets an option and displays an OK box. The click or keystroke itself is called an *event* because it happens independently of the running program. Only the user knows when he or she will press that button. And when the button gets pressed, some part of the Java program just wakes up and deals with the situation. This scenario is called *event-driven programming*.

Event-driven programming

SAX programs are *event-driven*. What does that mean? Glad you asked.

Picture yourself at that most wonderful time of day — getting into bed and getting ready for a good night's sleep. You reach over to set your alarm clock. When the clock has been set, you settle in, close your eyes, and become unconscious for a number of hours. Then an important event happens: A certain time of day arrives. When the event takes place, the alarm clock goes into its "wake the bum up" mode — and makes an awful din to stir you out of your restful sleep.

Here's another scenario. You're a busy executive, scratching and crawling your way to the top of the corporate ladder. You'll be out for several hours, having a two-Martini lunch, but you don't want to miss any important business. Before leaving the office, you tell your secretary, "Call me if anything important comes up." Issuing this order is akin to setting the alarm clock. You're telling your secretary (your alarm clock) to wake you up if an event takes place. Making this request to your secretary (or to your alarm clock) is called *registration*. In either scenario, you're registering yourself with a wakeup service. Once you've registered, you can pursue your leisurely non-activity, ignoring all real business until some event happens. Then . . .

Ring, ring. Your cell phone is hollering at you. "Hello?"

"Hello. This is your secretary. Remember that nine-to-five job you have? Anyway, I have the sales figures for the first quarter. They're one million, four million, and two million."

"Let's see. That's a total of seven million," you say. "I'll note it on my Palm Pilot. Thanks." You hang up.

Several forkfuls later, you get another call. "The president of Big Bucks, Inc. wants to close that deal. They're talking ten million dollars."

"Hmm," you respond. "That'll bring our year-to-date revenue up to seventeen megabucks. I'll store that information in my spreadsheet application. Thanks for calling."

Each of these interactions is known as a *callback*. Earlier in the day, when you registered your wish with the secretary, you requested a callback. Then, whenever an event takes place, the secretary makes a callback to notify you about the event. In Java programming terms, the secretary calls one of your many methods (one of your Java subprograms).

The essence of event-driven programming

Event-driven programming has three parts:

- ✔ **Registration:** You register your wish to be notified whenever an event occurs. You register this wish with another piece of code — another object, usually something you've imported (such as a piece of code that's part of somebody else's API). This object then watches, from behind the scenes, for the occurrence of the event you specified.

- ✔ **Event occurrence:** A specific event happens.

✔ **Callback:** The other piece of code performs a callback. One of your methods gets called.

The action is illustrated in Figure 3-1.

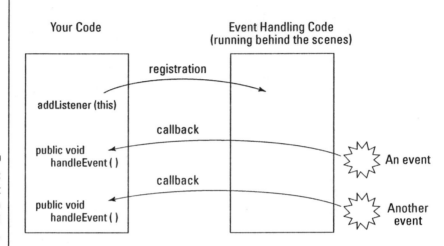

Figure 3-1:
Event
registration
and
callback.

Two kinds of code (a "Barryism")

I make a distinction between *active* code and *passive* code, which, though it's not part of official Java terminology, I still find useful:

✔ **Active code has a main method.** Active code, once it starts running, takes the center stage. Active code contains the thread of execution that controls the whole ball game.

✔ **Passive code just sits there, waiting to be called.** A passive Dice class does nothing until some other code calls Dice.roll().

Now, you may think I'm going to say that passive code is all you need for event-driven programming but I'm not. After all, in the Dice example, you could just write your own main method to call Dice.roll(). Calls would be made regularly and predictably, so no events would be taking place. No, event-handling code involves a little bit more. For event handling, we need this registration step. The passive code starts by getting registered with some other piece of code.

To firm up this notion of registration, think about an example from the on-screen world of mice, windows, and buttons. You create a window or frame. You want your frame to respond to mouse clicks, so you issue the following command:

```
button.addMouseListener(this);
```

This command registers your frame with the button. The command says, in effect, *Whenever a mouse event happens, call one of the frame's mouse-handling methods.* Later, when the user clicks the mouse, the frame gets a callback. The computer calls the frame's mouseClicked method.

SAX events

Sure, SAX is event-driven, but this doesn't mean that a SAX program waits for mouse clicks. Instead, SAX code follows the register-event-callback model that I described in the last several paragraphs. Every SAX program has two indispensable pieces of code:

✔ **A piece of code that you write — called the *handler*.** (Your handler can extend a pre-written DefaultHandler class.)

The handler is like the lunching executive in my earlier anecdote.

✔ **A piece of code that you normally don't write — the *parser*.** The parser plays a role like that of the secretary in my "lunching executive" story. The Java 1.4 API has a built-in parser. You create an *instance* of this parser, and then you register your handler with that parser instance. In effect, you tell the instance to call back your handler whenever an event takes place.

 Anything having to do with XML is new, and is still in a state of flux. Because of this, the terminology is patched together in some peculiar ways. While developing SAX version 2, some techies had a make-up-new-names festival. What's normally called a "parser" is embodied in a Java interface named XMLReader. There used to be a class named org.xml.sax.Parser, but the class got *deprecated* (which means that you should scrape it off the bottom of your shoe). To make things a bit more complicated, there's still another parsing tool, javax.xml.parsers.SAXParser. You use this SAXParser to make yourself an XMLReader. With any luck, you'll quickly become accustomed to this convoluted terminology. For now, remember that what I call a "parser" is usually an instance of XMLReader.

The register-and-callback scenario is what makes SAX event-driven. Now the funny thing is, a SAX event isn't tangible. A SAX event won't remind you of a keystroke or a button click. In SAX, the parser scans an XML document from top to bottom. Whenever the parser encounters something interesting, the parser fires off an event and calls the handler. Then, it's up to the handler to do something about this interesting encounter.

Of course, this talk about events is nice, but all talk and no code makes Java a dull language. So let's dig in and see some code.

Getting Up and Running (Basic Example)

To get up and running, you need two things — an XML document and a Java program. Fortunately, XML documents aren't in short supply; there's a good one in Listing 3-1.

Listing 3-1:   My Three Sins

```
<?xml version="1.0" encoding="UTF-8"?>
<MyThreeSins>
    <Sin rank="favorite">sloth</Sin>
    <Sin>gluttony</Sin>
    <Sin>envy</Sin>
</MyThreeSins>
```

For this Java program, we create two classes. (Strictly speaking, we don't *need* two separate classes, but I think the code is less confusing this way.) The first class — the code in Listing 3-2 — starts SAX and gets the ball rolling. This code creates a parser — and then applies the parser to the document MyThreeSins.xml.

Listing 3-2:   Starting SAX

```
import javax.xml.parsers.SAXParserFactory;
import javax.xml.parsers.SAXParser;
import javax.xml.parsers.ParserConfigurationException;

import org.xml.sax.XMLReader;
import org.xml.sax.SAXException;

import java.io.File;
import java.io.IOException;


class CallSAX
{
    static public void main(String[] args)
        throws SAXException,
                ParserConfigurationException,
                IOException
    {
        SAXParserFactory factory =
            SAXParserFactory.newInstance();
        SAXParser saxParser = factory.newSAXParser();
        XMLReader xmlReader = saxParser.getXMLReader();
```

```
    xmlReader.setContentHandler(new MyContentHandler());
    xmlReader.parse
        (new File("MyThreeSins.xml").toURL().toString());
    }

}
```

Take a good look at the code in Listing 3-2. You'll be using code like this to get each of your SAX programs running. In fact, with slight variations, you can reuse the code in Listing 3-2 for all the examples in Chapters 3, 4, 5, and 6. I'll refer to the code in Listing 3-2 (and to pieces of code that resemble it) as a *SAX-calling* class (or, more succinctly, a `CallSAX` class). From one example to another, I add a few statements to my SAX-calling class, but in its essence, the SAX-calling class will stay the same throughout this chapter and the three chapters that follow.

The CallSAX class

For the simple task that it performs, Listing 3-2 uses up a lot of ink. First, there are the required imports. Then, there's a main method that contains some exception throwing statements. To help you see the code in one gulp, I put all the exception-handling mechanisms into a `throws` clause.

Oh, yes! I can already hear the critics yelling at me: "Your code should be more robust. Use `try` statements instead of a `throws` clause." Well, all right — in practice, a few `try` statements *would* make better Java code. But in this book, I'm sacrificing Java purity to make Java XML techniques as clear as possible. Let some other book teach you how to write great, generic Java code. (Try *Java 2 For Dummies* by yours truly, for instance.) This book concentrates on Java with XML.

Anyway, in Listing 3-2, the real meat is *inside the main method's body*. There are five statements inside the body, and you'll be pleased to know that these statements can be used, reused, and re-reused. Whenever I write a SAX program, I begin by just dredging up an older SAX program and copying these statements from it. I describe these statements in the next several paragraphs.

Three statements create an XML parser

In Listing 3-2, the first three statements in the main method's body define three new objects: `factory`, `saxParser`, and `xmlReader`. Put these three objects into a pot, then just add water, and stir. Presto! You have a SAX parser. If you want more detail, then read on.

✔ The first statement makes a factory object.

Far and wide, throughout the Java universe, you'll find many, many factory objects. A *factory* is an object that's used to create other objects. And why do you need such factories? Why not just call a constructor? You don't call a constructor because you're not always sure which class's object you're constructing.

You see, several teams of programmers have written their own parsers. There's `org.apache.crimson.XmlReaderImpl` and `org.apache.xerces.parsers.SAXParser`, to name just two.

Quick! Which parser do you have on your computer? If you don't know (or if you know, but you want to leave your possibilities open), then you better not write your parser's name into your code. To save you from having to specify the parser's name, you use a factory. The factory will make a parser by fishing around on your system in some of the places where parsers normally hide. That way, you don't have to deal with the question "Which parser should I use?"

For a list of places where the factory looks for parsers, see the `javax.xml.parsers.SAXParserFactory` page in the Java 1.4 API documentation.

✔ The second and third statements build an actual parser (straight from the factory to you!)

The difference between a `SAXParser` and an `XMLReader` has more to do with the Java language structure than with XML processing. The bottom line is, you use both of these things to piece together the thing that I call a "parser." Once you have an actual parser, you're close to doing some real XML processing. In Listing 3-2, the variable *xmlReader* refers to the actual parser.

`XMLReader` is an interface, and `SAXParser` is an abstract class. `XMLReader` lists methods that must be implemented, while `SAXParser` forms the base class for the parser to extend. (Is that technical enough for you?)

If, in your travels, you come across the `org.xml.sax.Parser` interface, then the best thing to do is to ignore it. This may come as a disappointment; it's the only name in the API that matches the kind of thing you're trying to create. The trouble is, the name `Parser` was used back when everybody did SAX version 1. With the namespaces in SAX version 2, the Java folks had to switch things around. They replaced the `Parser` interface with `SAXParser` and `XMLReader`. (For a discussion of namespaces in SAX, see Chapter 5.)

Grabbing the XML document

The code in Listing 3-2 has a long line devoted to the grabbing of a document:

```
new File("MyThreeSins.xml").toURL().toString()
```

Pick your parser

The factory in Listing 3-2 chooses a SAX parser on your behalf. It chooses from among the parsers available on your system. This is fine in many situations, but occasionally, you want to hand-pick your parser. Maybe your colleagues or customers use Jolly Jack's SAX Parser. So, to insure consistency, you want to use Jolly Jack's SAX Parser too.

You can tell your program to use a particular parser. Let's say you want the parser whose code is in class `org.apache.xerces.parsers.SAXParser`. In Listing 3-2 remove the calls to `newInstance`, `newSAXParser` and `getXMLReader`. Then, in place of these statements, add the following code:

```
XMLReader xmlReader = XMLReader
   Factory.createXMLReader

   ("org.apache.xerces.parsers
   .SAXParser");
```

Then, to parse your document, the computer will use the `SAXParser` class, in package `org.apache.xerces.parsers`.

And don't forget! When you name your favorite parser, the parser has to be reachable in your computer's classpath. (For info on setting the classpath, see Chapter 2.)

What does all this mean? Well, some parsers barely tolerate relative filenames (names like `MyThreeSins.xml`, with no directory path). Other parsers choke when you feed them relative filenames. Worst of all, some implementations interpret anything you put between quote marks as a relative filename, even if the name you've supplied isn't relative. (An implementation of this kind will take the name

```
"c:\JavaPrograms\MyThreeSins.xml"
```

and rework it as

```
"file:/C:/JavaPrograms/c:\JavaPrograms\MyThreeSins.xml"
```

which is pure nonsense. You'll get a `FileNotFoundException` message if you try a name like that.)

In most cases, the safest thing to do is to put some intelligence between you and the parser. Let this intelligence figure out what the name of the file should be. Well, in Listing 3-2, this "intelligence" comes from calls to the `File` constructor, the `toURL` method, and the `toString` method. Here's how it works:

✔ The `File` constructor finds the file on your hard drive.

✔ The method `toURL` represents your file as a Web-ready resource — something that all parsers like to have.

✔ The method `toString` turns this abstract URL thing into an actual string of characters. That string of characters gets fed to the parser.

To test this stuff, I ran two slightly different versions of the code in Listing 3-2. One version looks exactly like Listing 3-2. The other version uses an absolute filename:

```
xmlReader.parse(new File("c:\\JavaPrograms\\MyThreeSins.xml")
    .toURL().toString());
```

In both cases, I called `System.out.println` to display the string that got sent to the parser and, in both cases, the string was the same. The string was `file:/C:/JavaPrograms/MyThreeSins.xml`. This string is the URL form of the `MyThreeSins.xml` file.

So, you see, the sequence `File...toURL...toString` takes any reasonable name that you send to it, and figures out the correct way to send that name to the parser. It's great!

In a Java string, you represent one backslash by writing a pair of backslashes. So, when you're hard-coding absolute pathnames in your Java program, a file named `MyThreeSins.xml` in your `JavaPrograms` directory is represented as `"c:\\JavaPrograms\\MyThreeSins.xml"`.

If anything happens, call me

Whew! You have a parser and an XML document. What's next? Well, since somebody else wrote the parser for you (somebody at `apache.org`, for instance), you'll have to write your own XML handling code. Exactly what should happen when the parser encounters a new element? You have to encapsulate your wishes inside a specialized Java class called the *handler class*.

The handler

The handler class contains methods with names like `startDocument`, `startElement`, and `endElement`. In the anecdote several pages back about the busy executive, the executive takes the place of some handler object. This handler object gets registered with the parser (the executive's personal secretary). When an event takes place (for instance, the parser encounters the start of a new element), the handler element (a.k.a. the busy executive) gets a callback. This progression is shown in Figure 3-1.

Registration

In the busy executive story, nothing happens unless the executive registers a request. The request is, "Call me back whenever *blah, blah, blah* happens." In terms of SAX-handler objects, nothing happens unless the handler registers itself with the parser. In Listing 3-2, this registration is done with one line of code:

```
xmlReader.setContentHandler(new MyContentHandler());
```

We're creating a new instance of MyContentHandler. We're also saying, "Whenever something interesting gets parsed, call one of the MyContentHandler object's methods." And what, you ask, is a MyContentHandler? Well, that's up to you to define. So, to see how to define a MyContentHandler, look at Listing 3-3.

Listing 3-3: A SAX Handler

```
import org.xml.sax.helpers.DefaultHandler;
import org.xml.sax.Attributes;

class MyContentHandler extends DefaultHandler
{
   public void startDocument()
   {
      System.out.println("Starting the document.");
   }


   public void startElement(String uri,
                            String localName,
                            String qualName,
                            Attributes attribs)
   {
      System.out.print("Start tag: ");
      System.out.println(qualName);

      for (int i=0; i<attribs.getLength(); i++)
      {
         System.out.print("Attribute: ");
         System.out.print(attribs.getQName(i));
         System.out.print(" = ");
         System.out.println(attribs.getValue(i));
      }
   }


   public void characters
      (char[] charArray, int start, int length)
   {
      String charString =
         new String(charArray, start, length);

      charString = charString.replaceAll("\n", "[cr]");
      charString = charString.replaceAll(" ", "[blank]");

      System.out.print(length + " characters: ");
      System.out.println(charString);
   }
```

(continued)

Listing 3-3:   A SAX Handler *(continued)*

```
public void endElement(String uri,
                       String localName,
                       String qualName)
{
    System.out.print("End tag: ");
    System.out.println(qualName);
}


public void endDocument()
{
    System.out.println("Ending the document.");
}
}
```

The output of the code in Listings 3-2 and 3-3 is shown in Figure 3-2. The program displays the names of elements, the values of attributes, and the characters inside elements. The program does this with methods like startElement, characters, and endElement. As the XML document gets parsed, the parser scans the document from top to bottom. When the parser notices an interesting event (the start of an element, characters within an element, and so on) the parser calls the appropriate method. To be precise, the parser *calls back* the appropriate method.

```
Starting the document.
Start tag: MyThreeSins
0 characters:
1 characters: [cr]
3 characters: [blank][blank][blank]
Start tag: Sin
Attribute: rank = favorite
5 characters: sloth
End tag: Sin
0 characters:
1 characters: [cr]
3 characters: [blank][blank][blank]
Start tag: Sin
8 characters: gluttony
End tag: Sin
0 characters:
1 characters: [cr]
3 characters: [blank][blank][blank]
Start tag: Sin
4 characters: envy
End tag: Sin
0 characters:
1 characters: [cr]
End tag: MyThreeSins
Ending the document.
```

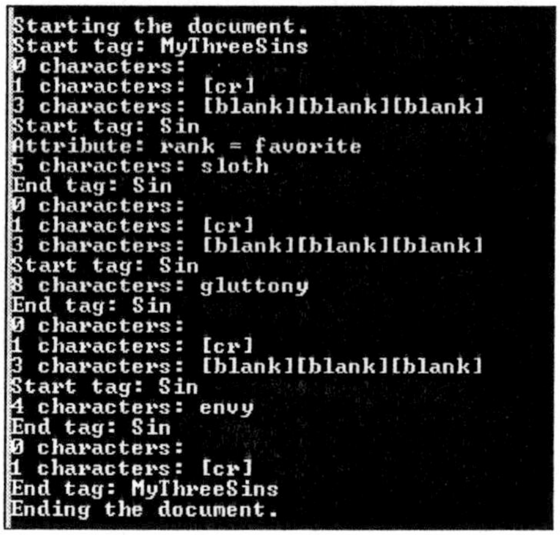

Figure 3-2: Everything you ever wanted to know about an XML document.

Callback methods

Our new MyContentHandler (in Listing 3-3) extends Java's pre-written DefaultHandler class. The MyContentHandler also has five callback methods, each telling the computer what to do when a certain kind of event takes place. For instance, when the parser encounters the end tag `</Sin>`, the computer calls back the `endElement` method.

The next few sections describe the callback methods in Listing 3-3.

The startDocument method

When the parser starts parsing, the parser makes a callback to the `startDocument` method. In essence, a call to this method means *Hey, handler! I'm starting to parse the MyThreeSins.xml document.* In Listing 3-3, the handler does something very simple in response to the callback — the handler displays the words `Starting the document` on the computer screen.

If you're not using a fancy integrated development environment, then a call to `System.out.println` displays text in the computer's command prompt window. In an integrated development environment, such as Forte for Java, JBuilder, or WebSphere Studio, a call to `System.out.println` may display text in a special environment-specific window or pane.

Attributes and the startElement method

The `startElement` method gets called whenever the parser encounters a start tag. For instance, when the parser sees

```
<Sin rank="favorite">
```

in `MyThreeSins.xml`, the parser calls `startElement`.

Although the `startElement` method has four parameters, you need only worry about two of those (`qualName` and `attribs`) in this chapter. Worriment about the other two parameters comes in Chapter 4.

In this example, the `qualName` parameter is just the element's name. The name appears in Figure 3-2 on lines like `Start tag: MyThreeSins` and `Start tag: Sin`.

The `attribs` parameter is of type Attributes (or, more precisely, of type `org.xml.sax.Attributes`). An Attributes object has a whole bunch of useful methods — methods like `getQName` and `getValue`.

- ✔ When you're not dealing with XML namespaces, `getQName` returns the attribute's name, pure and simple.
- ✔ The `getValue` method returns the attribute's value. (No surprise there.)

You can refer to an attribute by number or by name. In Listing 3-3, we refer to an attribute with the index number `i`. But the `Sin` element has an attribute named `rank`. So, if it's more convenient, you can call `attribs.getIndex("rank")` and `attribs.getValue("rank")`. For the first `Sin` tag in Listing 3-1, the value of `attribs.getIndex("rank")` is 0. (Attributes are numbered from 0 onward.) And, for the first `Sin` tag in Listing 3-1, the value of `attribs.getValue("rank")` is "favorite".

The characters method

At some point, you want to do something with characters that come between a start tag and its end tag. That's what the `characters` method is all about. When the parser encounters data between a start tag and its end tag, the characters method gets a friendly callback or two. In Listing 3-3, the `characters` method creates a slightly modified display of whatever it finds in its `charArray` parameter. That's why you see lines like `5 characters: sloth` and `1 characters: [cr]` in Figure 3-2.

The `characters` method in SAX is one of the most complicated in the whole collection. For the unwary user, the method holds about a dozen surprises (mostly unpleasant). Here are a few things to keep in mind:

✔ **Different parsers implement the `characters` method differently.**

Some of the differences are significant — for example, the number of times the `characters` method gets called for the same data, how the parsers handle whitespace, and even how the same parser behaves if you turn validation on or off.

Whitespace includes blank spaces, line feeds, carriage returns, tabs, and form feeds.

✔ **The `characters` method is called more often than you'd expect.**

Notice the first three calls to the `characters` method in Figure 3-2. In the XML document of Listing 3-1, these calls come between the start tag `<MyThreeSins>` and the start tag `<Sin rank="favorite">`.

- The first call sends nothing at all to the `characters` method. (The parser seems to make this call just for the heck of it.)

- The second call sends one carriage return to the `characters` method. In Listing 3-1, this carriage return comes immediately after the `<MyThreeSins>` start tag.

- The third call sends three blank spaces to the `characters` method. In Listing 3-1, these spaces are the indentation for the `<Sin rank="favorite">` start tag.

✔ **The `charArray` parameter contains more stuff than just the characters between tags.**

That's why the `characters` method has parameters `start` and `length`. To show that I'm not lying to you, I did an experiment: I removed the `start` and `length` variables from the `charString` declaration in Listing 3-3. The revised declaration looks like this:

```
String charString = new String(charArray);
```

In this new declaration, I capture all the stuff in the charArray parameter, not just the characters delineated by the start and length values. Well, the resulting output was strange indeed. When I sent this output to a text file, I got the odd-looking gibberish shown in Figure 3-3.

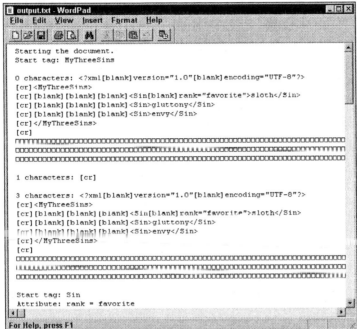

Figure 3-3:
Writing
everything
in the
charArray.

Figure 3-3 shows the first several lines of the revised program's output. Notice what happens in the third call to the characters method. Instead of seeing only the three blank spaces that you see in Figure 3-2, you see the entire content of the MyThreeSins.xml file, and then some. When the parser calls the characters method, the parser puts all this junk into the charArray parameter. Included in the junk are thousands of useless null bytes. (In Figure 3-3, Microsoft WordPad displays a little rectangle in place of each null byte.)

Back in Listing 3-3, the only things that filter out all the irrelevant stuff in the charArray are the character method's start and length parameters.

✔ **A tag within another tag doesn't count as characters.**

Look again at the XML file in Listing 3-1. Using a broad definition for the word *characters*, you wonder whether the stuff between the MyThreeSins start tag and end tag includes characters like <Sin rank="favorite">. But no parts of the <Sin> tag are listed as characters in Figure 3-2.

> The characters method finds only the characters that aren't tracked by any of the other methods. No tags or processing instructions trigger a call to the characters method.

The endElement method

Like the startElement method, the endElement method has a few parameters. The endElement's qualName parameter serves the same purpose as the startElement's qualName parameter. The parameter stores the name of the element that triggered the callback.

In Listing 3-3, notice how the endElement method has one fewer parameter than the startElement method. In particular, the endElement method has no Attributes parameter. That makes sense, because an XML end tag can never have attributes.

The endDocument method

Well, what can I say? When the parser is done scanning the document, the parser calls the endDocument method. That's all there is to it.

Parsers aren't cheap, but . . .

Here's something that programmers tend to forget: Parsers are reusable. Once you've created a parser instance, you can use that instance again and again. For instance, I can rewrite the body of Listing 3-2 as follows:

```
SAXParserFactory factory =
    SAXParserFactory.newInstance();
SAXParser saxParser = factory.newSAXParser();
XMLReader xmlReader = saxParser.getXMLReader();

xmlReader.setContentHandler(new MyContentHandler());

xmlReader.parse
    (new File("MyThreeSins.xml").toURL().toString());
xmlReader.parse
    (new File("SaintlyThoughts.xml").toURL().toString());
```

Having created a single XMLReader object, I can use that object to parse two (or more) documents. This is good, because the creation of a parser can be quite time-consuming.

To test my claim about the creation of a parser, I clocked the milliseconds it takes to perform each of the steps in Listings 3-2 and 3-3. The results were as follows: The creation of a parser in Listing 3-2 takes twice as much time as all the method-calling that goes on in Listing 3-3. (Results may vary. Professional driver on closed course. Data subject to local taxes and restrictions.)

When to Use the SAX API

Some time ago, I was trying to decide what kind of mortgage to take out on my new home. I went to a colleague in the Economics department. "Economics is the science of choices," she said. Well, that certainly straightened things out for me. Anyway, XML is another science of choices. There are so many different packages, proposals, and betas that you can easily get lost in the maze.

And then there's the matter of *application programming interfaces* (APIs). In this chapter (and in Chapters 4, 5, and 6) I use the SAX API to fidget with documents. In later chapters, I use alternative APIs. So how will you choose among all the APIs? Well, case by case — like every other API, SAX is good in some situations and bad in others.

So what's good about SAX? When should you use the SAX API? There are three cases:

✔ **Use SAX when the XML document represents linear data.**

A SAX parser starts at the beginning, and works its way carefully toward the end. The parser sees one tag, then another tag, then yet another. Unlike some other APIs, the SAX parser doesn't view the document as a collection of nested elements. So if you're dealing with a document that involves deeply nested elements, then forget about SAX. For elements within elements within other elements, SAX isn't the right API.

On the other hand, if your document is lightly nested, or if traveling linearly through the document makes sense for your application, then pick up SAX and run with it. SAX is great for processing one item after another, as you'll see in the next couple of chapters.

✔ **Use SAX when you're dealing with every large XML document.**

The SAX API has tunnel vision. When SAX deals with a particular start tag, then all the surrounding tags (including the end tag that goes with that start tag) are invisible. SAX marches along in a document, grabs a tag, processes the tag, and then dumps that tag to go onto the next tag. This short sightedness can be a hindrance, but it can also be an advantage. No matter how large an XML document is, the SAX parser sees only a little piece of the document at once. That saves on memory. (And yes, even with today's cheap prices, memory can still be a scarce resource.)

✔ **Use SAX when you need fine-tuned control.**

As this book progresses, it shows you higher-level ways of dealing with XML documents. In fact, in the last two chapters, you may wonder why all the XML documents have disappeared from view. When you work with specialized markup languages (languages for business-to-business processing, for instance), you use toolsets that deal with big, application-specific ideas. You stop worrying about start tags and end tags, and you start worrying about querying a database of Web services.

As you move to higher levels of abstraction, you can do common tasks more quickly. (For instance, you can query a database with just a few lines of code.) But, at the same time, you lose the ability to do customized tweaking. When you work on the Web-services level, you simply can't handle a start tag without reverting back to something like SAX.

So, if your task isn't mainstream, or your task involves doing something that others haven't done before, you want to rely on a fine-grained toolset such as the SAX API.

Chapter 4

Checking Your Document

* *

In This Chapter

▶ Validating and checking how well-formed your document is

▶ Locating points in an XML document

▶ Doing DTD and schema validation

* *

When Computers Go Bad: A Brief History of Error and Blame

1970: "The computer made a mistake."

1975: "This isn't written in COBOL."

1980: "I can't work with someone else's spaghetti code."

1990: "I don't understand computers."

1995: "I don't know what the Internet is all about."

1996: "My hard drive is too small."

1997: "I don't have enough memory."

1998: "Bill Gates did it."

1999: "That's not Y2K-compliant."

2001: "I don't have enough bandwidth."

2002: "I must have a virus."

2003: "This code isn't portable."

2004: "This document isn't well-formed."

2005: "This document is well-formed, but it isn't valid."

2006: "Bill Gates did it."

2010: "This isn't written in Java, and it doesn't use XML."

2030: "The computer misinterpreted my speech."

2040: "I had to get up from my computer."

2060: "The computer misinterpreted my thoughts."

2100: "Your thoughts misinterpreted my thoughts."

2200: "I'll have my thoughts call your thoughts."

2300: "This time, the computer really did make a mistake."

2500: "I had to get up from my chair."

2900: "I had to leave my virtual-reality universe."

3000: "A long, long time ago, Bill Gates did it."

1 Never Make Mistakes

I'm sure you never make mistakes either. Anyway, when you're processing an XML document, plenty of things can go wrong. Assuming that what goes wrong is the XML document's fault, the nasty things that happen fall into one of two categories.

✔ **The document isn't well-formed.**

The document doesn't use proper XML grammar; in effect, the document doesn't follow the rules that every XML document must follow. No one could possibly understand the document, unless they took guesses about what the author meant to write.

Here's an example of something in English that's not well-formed:

*In make? howdy. ; why for entrance Go tenure *cows*

✔ **The document is well-formed, but it isn't valid.**

Either the document has no DTD (Document Type Definition), or the document's content doesn't match what's described in the DTD. The lines in the document are grammatically correct but, given the rules set out in the DTD (or lack thereof), the lines in the document don't make sense.

Here's an English sentence that's well-formed but not valid:

Delicious makeshift tones, once fraught with dynasty, now endure haughtily.

Checking for a good document

Either kind of mistake (not being well-formed or not being valid) opens its own special can of worms. To help preserve our sanity, we'll take the simpler case first. Let's consider a document that's not well-formed. A horrific document of this kind is shown in Listing 4-1, and some Java code to read this document is shown in Listings 4-2 and 4-3.

Listing 4-1:   A Document That's Not Well-Formed

```
<?xml version="1.0" encoding="UTF-8"?>
<!-- IllFormedDoc.xml -->

<Greeting>
   Hello world!
   <Question>
     How are you?
   <Question>  <!-- Oh, no! This start tag
                    should be an end tag! -->
</Greeting>
```

Listing 4-2:   Calling the SAX Parser

```
import javax.xml.parsers.SAXParserFactory;
import javax.xml.parsers.SAXParser;
import javax.xml.parsers.ParserConfigurationException;

import org.xml.sax.XMLReader;
import org.xml.sax.SAXException;

import java.io.File;
import java.io.IOException;


public class CallSAX
{
   static public void main(String[] args)
      throws SAXException,
             ParserConfigurationException,
             IOException
   {
      SAXParserFactory factory =
         SAXParserFactory.newInstance();
      SAXParser saxParser = factory.newSAXParser();
      XMLReader xmlReader = saxParser.getXMLReader();

      xmlReader.setContentHandler(new MyContentHandler());

      try
      {
         xmlReader.parse
            (new File(args[0]).toURL().toString());
      }
      catch (SAXException s)
      {
         System.out.println("There's been a big mistake!");
         s.printStackTrace();
```

(continued)

Listing 4-2 *(continued)*

```
        }
      }

  }
```

Listing 4-3:   A Simple Handler Class

```java
import org.xml.sax.helpers.DefaultHandler;
import org.xml.sax.Attributes;

class MyContentHandler extends DefaultHandler
{
   public void startDocument()
   {
      System.out.println("STARTING");
      System.out.println();
   }


   public void startElement(String uri,
                            String localName,
                            String qualName,
                            Attributes attribs)
   {
      System.out.print("Start tag: ");
      System.out.println(qualName);
   }


   public void endDocument()
   {
      System.out.println();
      System.out.println("ENDING NORMALLY!");
   }
}
```

Compare the code in Listing 4-2 with the matching code back in Chapter 3. (The matching code is in Listing 3-2.) In Chapter 3, I warned you that all these CallSAX listings would look alike. Well, here we are. Listing 4-2 is almost identical, word for word with the code in Listing 3-2.

Of course, between Chapter 3 and Chapter 4, I couldn't resist making one small improvement. The code in Listing 3-2 works for just one document — the document named MyThreeSins.xml. Now, if your sole ambition in life is to parse that MyThreeSins file over and over again, then the code in Listing 3-2 is exactly what you want. On the other hand, if you'd like your code to be versatile (if you'd like to decide on a different XML file each time you run the program), then the code you should use is in Listing 4-2.

Listing 4-2 uses `args[0]` — commonly known as a *command-line argument*. To run the code in Listing 4-2, go to your command prompt, and type something like

```
java CallSAX MyThreeSins.xml
```

or

```
java CallSAX Gourmet_Foods.xml
```

Whatever you type after the word `CallSAX` will be taken by your program as the value of `args[0]`. So, in the first command given here, the program parses the file `MyThreeSins.xml`. The second command just given tells the program to parse the file `Gourmet_Foods.xml`.

Occasionally, you want `args[0]` to be a string with a blank space in it. If so, then surround the string with double quotation marks. For example, a command such as `java CallSAX "My XML File.xml"` would require quotes (as shown) around the XML filename.

For clarity, I occasionally take shortcuts in the code that I write for this book. For instance, if you run the code in Listing 4-2 without supplying an XML filename, you get a nasty `FileNotFoundException` message. In practice, you should create a Java `try` statement to recover gracefully from errors of this kind. (In real life, people forget to type command-line arguments all the time.) But this book isn't about Java `try` statements, so I'll keep my code as simple as possible. I'll leave it to you to add those extra niceties.

Running the code

The output from Listings 4-1, 4-2, and 4-3 is an error message. (See Figure 4-1.) The message appears because a `SAXException` gets thrown.

To be obsessive-compulsive about it, what the code really throws is a `SAXParseException`. But `SAXParseException` is a subclass of `SAXException`, so everybody's happy.

Figure 4-1:
Parsing a
document
that's not
well-formed.

```
STARTING

Start tag: Greeting
Start tag: Question
Start tag: Question
There's been a big mistake!
org.xml.sax.SAXParseException: Expected "</Question>" to terminate element starting on lin
e 8.
        at org.apache.crimson.parser.Parser2.fatal(Parser2.java:3182)
        at org.apache.crimson.parser.Parser2.fatal(Parser2.java:3176)
        at org.apache.crimson.parser.Parser2.maybeElement(Parser2.java:1513)
        at org.apache.crimson.parser.Parser2.content(Parser2.java:1779)
        at org.apache.crimson.parser.Parser2.maybeElement(Parser2.java:1507)
        at org.apache.crimson.parser.Parser2.content(Parser2.java:1779)
        at org.apache.crimson.parser.Parser2.maybeElement(Parser2.java:1507)
        at org.apache.crimson.parser.Parser2.parseInternal(Parser2.java:500)
        at org.apache.crimson.parser.Parser2.parse(Parser2.java:305)
        at org.apache.crimson.parser.XMLReaderImpl.parse(XMLReaderImpl.java:442)
        at org.apache.crimson.parser.XMLReaderImpl.parse(XMLReaderImpl.java:396)
        at CallSAX.main(CallSAX.java:27)
```

Notice two things about the output in Figure 4-1:

✓ **The program never gets to print the words ENDING NORMALLY!**

When the parser encounters an ungrammatical point in a document, the parser just gives up. After catching the SAXException, the code in Listings 4-2 and 4-3 just stops running.

✓ **The error diagnostics point almost exclusively to code that's behind the scenes.**

You see no reference to the code of Listing 4-3 in the stack trace of Figure 4-1. That's because the methods in Listing 4-3 aren't doing the real parsing. Those handler methods are just responding to parser events. (A method like System.out.println, when called from inside the startElement method, won't be upset by the missing slash in the XML document.)

In Figure 4-1, the stack trace is the stuff with all the fully qualified class names (names like org.apache.crimson.parser.Parser2.fatal).

The missing end tag gets noticed by the parser, and that parser (called by the main method in class CallSAX) is the method that handles the exception.

Creating an error handler

The wimpy error reporting in Figure 4-1 is inadequate for most programming tasks. So what do you do if you want more information? Can you catch a "well-formedness" error in the act? Well, you can give the parser an *error handler* and let the error handler do some reporting.

To give the parser an error handler, you do two things:

✓ **You define an error-handler class.**

There's a sample error handler in Listing 4-4.

✓ **You assign the error handler to the parser.**

To assign the error handler, you add the following statement to the code in Listing 4-2:

```
xmlReader.setErrorHandler(new MyErrorHandler());
```

This new statement goes either immediately before or immediately after the call to the setContentHandler method.

Listing 4-4:   An Error Handler

```
import org.xml.sax.helpers.DefaultHandler;
import org.xml.sax.SAXParseException;
class MyErrorHandler extends DefaultHandler
{
    public void warning(SAXParseException e)
    {
        System.out.println("Warning:");
        showSpecifics(e);
        System.out.println();
    }

    public void error(SAXParseException e)
    {
        System.out.println("Error:");
        showSpecifics(e);
        System.out.println();
    }

    public void fatalError(SAXParseException e)
    {
        System.out.println("Fatal error:");
        showSpecifics(e);
        System.out.println();
    }

    public void showSpecifics(SAXParseException e)
    {
        System.out.println(e.getMessage());
        System.out.println("  Line " + e.getLineNumber());
        System.out.println("  Column " + e.getColumnNumber());
        System.out.println("  Document " + e.getSystemId());
    }
}
```

The result of running the new code is shown in Figure 4-2. When a parsing goof-up occurs, the parser checks to see if an error handler has been assigned to it. If so, then the parser calls a method in the error handler. Depending on the severity of the error, the parser calls the `warning` method, the `error` method, or the (gasp!) `fatalError` method.

Some methods belonging to a SAXParseException

When the parser doesn't like what it sees, the parser calls a method in Listing 4-4. No matter which method gets called, the method gets handed a `SAXParseException`. At that point, you can call the exception's methods to get more information.

For instance, in Listing 4-4, I call methods `getMessage`, `getLineNumber`, `getColumnNumber`, and `getSystemId`.

✔ **The** getMessage **method gives you a capsule summary of the error.**

In Figure 4-2, the capsule summary looks like this:

```
Expected "</Question>" to terminate element
    starting on line 8.
```

You see this message twice in Figure 4-2. The first time you see the message, it's because of an explicit call to the getMessage method. (The call is inside my showSpecifics method.) The second time you see the message, it's because of the call to printStackTrace in Listing 4-2.

```
STARTING
Start tag: Greeting
Start tag: Question
Start tag: Question
Fatal error:
Expected "</Question>" to terminate element starting on line 8.
    Line 10
    Column -1
    Document file:/C:/JavaPrograms/IllFormedDoc.xml

There's been a big mistake!
org.xml.sax.SAXParseException: Expected "</Question>" to terminate element starting on lin
e 8.
        at org.apache.crimson.parser.Parser2.fatal(Parser2.java:3182)
        at org.apache.crimson.parser.Parser2.fatal(Parser2.java:3176)
        at org.apache.crimson.parser.Parser2.maybeElement(Parser2.java:1513)
        at org.apache.crimson.parser.Parser2.content(Parser2.java:1779)
        at org.apache.crimson.parser.Parser2.maybeElement(Parser2.java:1507)
        at org.apache.crimson.parser.Parser2.content(Parser2.java:1779)
        at org.apache.crimson.parser.Parser2.maybeElement(Parser2.java:1507)
        at org.apache.crimson.parser.Parser2.parseInternal(Parser2.java:500)
        at org.apache.crimson.parser.Parser2.parse(Parser2.java:305)
        at org.apache.crimson.parser.XMLReaderImpl.parse(XMLReaderImpl.java:442)
        at org.apache.crimson.parser.XMLReaderImpl.parse(XMLReaderImpl.java:396)
        at CallSAX.main(CallSAX.java:28)
```

Figure 4-2: What can happen when you use an error handler.

✔ **The line number is the place where the parser comes to rest.**

In Listing 4-1, the bad Question tag is on line 8. But, in Figure 4-2, the line number displayed is line number 10. The parser gulps up any surrounding comments before it tries to parse the offending Question tag. So, by the time it notices that the Question tag is bad, the parser has already skipped to line 10.

Notice also, in calculating line numbers, the parser *does* count blank lines.

✔ **A column number of –1 indicates that the column number is unknown.**

A column number of 1 would tell us that the parser has reached the Greeting end tag's open angle bracket (<). Instead, the parser says "I don't know what column I've reached."

The org.xml.sax.Locator page of the Java API documentation has some interesting disclaimers about the fuzziness of these column number and line number values. (As for the Locator interface itself, I have more to say later in this chapter.)

✔ **The method** getSystemId **tells us the name of the document that's causing so much angst.**

If you working with several documents at once, this information can be pretty useful.

A well-formedness error is always bad news

There's one more dire portent you should notice about well-formedness errors: If the parser encounters a well-formedness error, then having an error handler generally doesn't save your neck.

Look again at Figure 4-2, and notice what happens. The parser encounters the bad Question tag, and the error handler's fatalError method gets called. The error handler displays some nice information, but then the parser chokes big time. In the CallSAX class's main method, the parser throws an exception. After my call to printStackTrace, the whole program comes to a screeching halt. (I guess they don't call it a *fatal* error" for no reason at all!)

Validation errors

Having beaten well-formedness errors to death in the last section, it's time to move on to validation errors. The first thing we need is a scapegoat — a document that's clearly and unequivocally invalid. Fortunately, I have just such a document in mind. The document is in Listing 4-5, and the document's DTD is in Listing 4-6.

Listing 4-5:   A bad document

```
<?xml version="1.0" encoding="UTF-8" standalone="no" ?>
<!DOCTYPE Greeting SYSTEM "InvalidDoc.dtd">
<!-- InvalidDoc.xml -->

<Greeting>
    Hello world!
    <Question>        <!-- No Question element in the DTD -->
       How are you?
    </Question>

</Greeting>
```

Listing 4-6:   An incomplete DTD

```
<?xml version="1.0" encoding="UTF-8"?>
<!-- InvalidDoc.dtd -->
<!ELEMENT Greeting (#PCDATA)>
```

Finding normalcy when there is none

Let's start by running the code in Listings 4-2 and 4-3 against our new InvalidDoc.xml file (Listing 4-5). What you get is the output in Figure 4-3. It's pretty unexciting, right? Even if you add the error handler in Listing 4-4, the invalid document shows up as being normal, normal, normal.

Figure 4-3:
Parsing a
document
with
validation
turned off.

```
STARTING
Start tag: Greeting
Start tag: Question
ENDING NORMALLY!
```

Figure 4-3:
Parsing a
document
with
validation
turned off.

Turning on the validation

For the document in Listing 4-5, you don't want the goody-two-shoes output
of Figure 4-3. Instead, you want the computer to recognize the document's
shortcomings. To do this, you have to turn on document validation. It's easy
enough. To turn this feature on, you call one of the parser factory's methods.
(That's right. You don't call a parser method. You call a parser *factory*
method.) You add two statements to the code in Listing 4-2.

✔ After the call to `SAXParserFactory.newInstance`, add a call to
`factory.setValidating`:

```
factory.setValidating(true);
```

✔ Alongside the call to `xmlReader.setContentHandler`, add a call to
`xmlReader.setErrorHandler`:

```
xmlReader.setErrorHandler(new MyErrorHandler());
```

When you run the enhanced code against the document in Listing 4-5 (and
the DTD in Listing 4-6), you get the output shown in Figure 4-4. The computer
generates two error messages — one message when it notices that there's
something illegal inside the `Greeting` tag, and another message when it
notices an undeclared `Question` tag. Of course, both messages are related to
the same mistake — namely, that the `Question` tag isn't declared in the DTD.

Figure 4-4:
Parsing a
document
with
validation
turned on.

```
STARTING
Start tag: Greeting
Error:
Element "Greeting" does not allow "Question" -- (#PCDATA)
    Line 7
    Column -1
    Document file:/C:/JavaPrograms/InvalidDoc.xml
Error:
Element type "Question" is not declared.
    Line 7
    Column -1
    Document file:/C:/JavaPrograms/InvalidDoc.xml
Start tag: Question
ENDING NORMALLY!
```

Damn the torpedoes...

In Figure 4-4, notice that both of the callbacks are errors. They're not warn-
ings and they're not fatal errors. Because the errors aren't fatal, the parser

gets back on its feet and processes the rest of the XML document. You can see that in Figure 4-4 by noticing that the run finishes with the words ENDING NORMALLY.

When you turn validation on, be sure to provide an error handler. If you forget to call setErrorHandler, then the computer will give you a warning message, and Java will use its own default error handler. This default error handler isn't bad, but it's probably not what you want to use.

Using a Document Locator

Earlier in this chapter, I discussed methods named getLineNumber and getColumnNumber. When an exception gets thrown, these methods give you some crude, but useful reports. So my question is, can you get these reports even when no exceptions have been thrown? If something nice happens inside an XML document, and you want to track the location of this nice occurrence, can you do the tracking with methods getLineNumber and getColumnNumber? Well, the answer is yes, you can.

To take charge of this task, SAX has a neat feature called the Locator interface. A locator keeps track where the SAX parser goes during the parsing of a document. Each locator has methods getColumnNumber and getLineNumber. The only thing that's tricky is to locate a locator. Listing 4-7 shows you how to do it.

Listing 4-7:   Creating a Locator

```
import org.xml.sax.helpers.DefaultHandler;
import org.xml.sax.Attributes;
import org.xml.sax.Locator;

class MyContentHandler extends DefaultHandler
{

    Locator locator;

    public void setDocumentLocator(Locator locator)
    {
        this.locator=locator;
    }

    public void startDocument()
    {
System.out.println("STARTING");
        showSpecifics();
        System.out.println();
    }
```

(continued)

Listing 4-7 *(continued)*

```
public void startElement(String uri,
                         String localName,
                         String qualName,
                         Attributes attribs)
{
    System.out.print("Start tag: ");
    System.out.println(qualName);
    showSpecifics();
    System.out.println();
}


public void showSpecifics()
{
    System.out.println
        ("  Line " + locator.getLineNumber());
    System.out.println
        ("  Column " + locator.getColumnNumber());
    System.out.println
        ("  Document " + locator.getSystemId());
}

}
```

You can run the code in Listing 4-7 along with the XML document back in Listing 3-1, and the CallSAX class from Listing 3-2. When you do all this, you get the output shown in Figure 4-5.

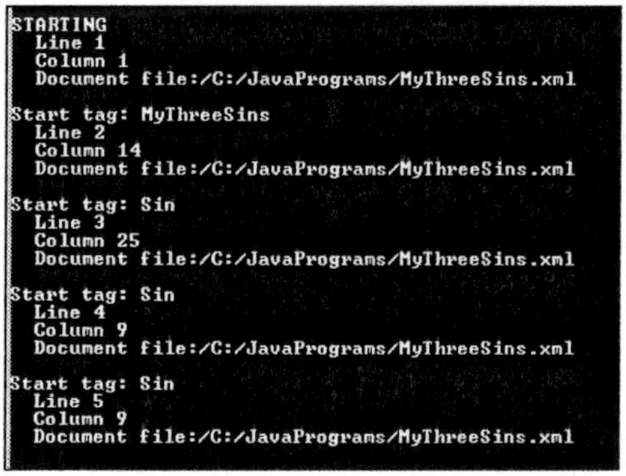

Figure 4-5:
Using a
document
locator.

When you first fire up the parser, the parser makes a locator. The parser uses this locator to keep track of where it is inside the XML document.

Making a locator is considered to be an event. Like other events, this creation of a locator causes a callback. You can take the method that gets called back (namely, the setDocumentLocator method) and use that method to capture a reference to the parser's locator. I do this in Listing 4-7. Throughout the rest of the handler code, I use the locator to tell me where events are taking place inside the document.

Schema Validation

Until this point in the book, we've been validating documents using DTDs. But that old faithful DTD isn't the last word in document validation. There's a new kid in town called the *schema*. With a schema, you define more than just elements and their attributes. You also define value types. For instance, with the schema in Listing 4-8, you say that the characters between the Children start and end tags must represent an integer.

Listing 4-8:   Sorry, No Half Children Allowed

```
<?xml version="1.0"?>
<!-- Children.xsd -->

<xsd:schema xmlns:xsd="http://www.w3.org/2001/XMLSchema">
<xsd:element name="Children" type="xsd:integer"/>
</xsd:schema>
```

According to the schema in Listing 4-8, the document in Listing 4-9 is bad, bad, bad. The number 2.5 isn't an integer.

Listing 4-9:   How Many Children Do You Have?

```
<?xml version="1.0" encoding="UTF-8" standalone="no"?>
<!-- Children.xml -->

<Children
    xmlns:xsi="http://www.w3.org/2001/XMLSchema-instance"
    xsi:noNamespaceSchemaLocation="Children.xsd"
>2.5</Children>
```

To make your program cry out against Listings 4-8 and 4-9, add the following lines to the code in Listing 4-2:

```
factory.setValidating(true);
factory.setNamespaceAware(true);

SAXParser saxParser = factory.newSAXParser();
saxParser.setProperty
    ("http://java.sun.com/xml/jaxp/" +
    "properties/schemaLanguage",
    "http://www.w3.org/2001/XMLSchema");
```

In these lines, the call to `setValidating` works the same way as the `setValidating` call for DTD validation. (It's described earlier in this chapter.) The whole `setNamespaceAware` business is covered in Chapter 5. And I cover the `setProperty` method in the next section.

With these new statements added to Listing 4-2, you get the output shown in Figure 4-6.

Figure 4-6:
Sorry! The
document
doesn't
match its
schema.

```
STARTING

Start tag: Children
Error:
cvc-type.3.1.3: The value '2.5' of element 'Children' is not valid.
    Line 7
    Column 16
    Document file:/C:/Book/Author/Chapter04/Listing0411/scratch/Children.xml

ENDING NORMALLY!
```

Features and properties

A few paragraphs ago, I conjured up the schema validation spirits by calling a method named `setProperty`. In general, every XML parser has certain options that you can set. These options are divided into two types — *features* and *properties*. In general, a *feature* is something that can be either on or off (that is, true or false), and a *property* is something that has a more general value. (A property's value is of Java type `Object`.) Both features and properties give you fine-grained control of the parsing process.

Like most things in life, each feature or property has a name and a value. A typical name is a URI, like the name `http://java.sun.com/xml/jaxp/properties/schemaLanguage` for schema validation. Another example is

```
xmlReader.setFeature
    ("http://xml.org/sax/features/namespaces", true);
```

The acronym *URI* stands for *Uniform Resource Identifier*. Every URL is a URI, but some URIs aren't URLs. For more details, visit `www.w3.org/Addressing`.

Some features and properties come standard with all parsers. Other features and properties are special to certain parser implementations. To see a list of the standard features and properties for SAX parsers, visit `www.saxproject.org`.

Chapter 5

Useful Tools in the SAX API

In This Chapter

▶ Working with whitespace

▶ Using namespaces

▶ Dealing with processing instructions

*B*eing a college professor has its ups and its downs. One of its ups is the work schedule. During the school year, I work 55 hours a week, but I have no classes to teach from mid-May to the end of August. I can spend the whole summer making up silly remarks to put into my *For Dummies* books.

Another one of the ups is the working environment. With the exception of a few faculty members (they know who they are) almost everyone at work is sensible and courteous. Of course, not everything having to do with faculty members is an "up." Most of these people are so smart that you can go crazy just chatting with them.

Over lunch the other day, someone said, "Did you read that fascinating Op-Ed article in this morning's *New York Times*?" And I replied, "No, my family gets the local New Jersey newspaper." So the other fellow said, "The article was about the town of Puerto Casado and the sale of land near the Paraguay-Brazil border. They sold 400,000 hectares to the Reverend Sun Myung Moon."

"Think quickly, Barry," I said to myself. "What's a hectare? Is 400,000 hectares a lot of land, or can you build only a modest swimming pool on it?" So then I remembered the word "Brazil" flying by. I recalled that, contrary to popular North American belief, the largest nation in South America speaks Portuguese as its native language. So I said, "All those hectares in Brazil! I wonder if Sun Myung Moon speaks Portuguese."

After a deafening silence, a woman at the other end of the table said, "Portuguese? Why would Sun Myung Moon need to speak Portuguese? The town of Puerto Casado is on the Paraguayan side of the border. In Paraguay, they speak Spanish."

If you're going to join in at lunch, you need to have a head for details. So this chapter is about details — the details of using SAX.

Whitespace? What Whitespace?

This section is about the effect of a DTD on *whitespace* characters — blanks, tabs, line feeds, and so on. Wait! Don't start yawning yet! The story isn't that boring.

As fate would have it, the availability of a DTD changes the way the parser views whitespace. Here's a summary:

- ✔ If an XML document has a DTD, then the parser views some whitespace as being "ignorable."

- ✔ If an XML document doesn't have a DTD, then the parser views no whitespace as being "ignorable."

Are you baffled? Well, let's start with the notion of *ignorable whitespace*. White-space that comes between tags, and isn't accompanied by any non-whitespace characters is potentially ignorable. Look, for instance, at Listing 5-1. The carriage return after the MyThreeSins start tag can be ignored, and so can the three blank spaces before each Sin start tag. The carriage return after each Sin end tag can be ignored also. These characters don't contribute to the data. They just fluff up the XML document and make it easier to read.

Listing 5-1: Sins with Whitespace

```
<?xml version="1.0" encoding="UTF-8"?>
<!DOCTYPE MyThreeSins SYSTEM "Sins.dtd">
<!-- MyThreeSins.xml -->

<MyThreeSins>
    <Sin rank="favorite">sloth</Sin>
    <Sin>gluttony</Sin>
    <Sin> Writing non-portable code </Sin>
</MyThreeSins>
```

Of course, you don't want to ignore words like sloth and gluttony in Listing 5-1. These words are really part of the data. But what about the blank spaces inside the last of the three Sin elements? In fact, these blanks are also part of the data.

(Youwouldn'tlikeitifIleftnospacesbetweenwordsinmysentences,wouldyou?)

So blanks accompanied by non-blank characters are not considered to be ignorable.

Whitespace with a DTD

To see the difference between the two kinds of whitespace, we can run some code. Let's look at a content handler that distinguishes between ignorable and non-ignorable whitespace. A handler of that kind is shown in Listing 5-2.

Listing 5-2:   I'm Trying to Ignore You

```
import org.xml.sax.helpers.DefaultHandler;
import org.xml.sax.Attributes;

class MyContentHandler extends DefaultHandler
{

    public void characters
        (char[] charArray, int start, int length)
    {
        System.out.print("CHARACTERS: ");
        myWriteString(charArray, start, length);
    }


    public void ignorableWhitespace
        (char[] charArray, int start, int length)
    {
        System.out.print("IGNORABLE WHITESPACE: ");
        myWriteString(charArray, start, length);
    }


    void myWriteString
        (char[] charArray, int start, int length)
    {
        String charString =
            new String(charArray, start, length);

        charString = charString.replaceAll("\n", "[cr]");
        charString = charString.replaceAll(" ", "[blank]");

        System.out.print(length + " characters: ");

        System.out.println(charString);
    }
}
```

To call the new content handler into action, you need a SAX-calling class. That's easy to find. Just dredge up the code in Listing 4-2. You also need a DTD because the document in Listing 5-1 has a DOCTYPE declaration. So, to keep things running smoothly, I put a fine-looking DTD in Listing 5-3.

Listing 5-3:   What, Exactly, Are Sins?

```
<?xml version="1.0" encoding="UTF-8"?>
<!-- Sins.dtd -->

<!ELEMENT MyThreeSins (Sin+)>
<!ELEMENT Sin (#PCDATA)>
<!ATTLIST Sin rank CDATA #IMPLIED>
```

With all these files, you can run the code in Listing 5-2 against the XML document in Listing 5-1. The output you get is shown in Figure 5-1.

Figure 5-1:
Characters
versus
ignorable
whitespace.

```
IGNORABLE WHITESPACE: 0 characters:
IGNORABLE WHITESPACE: 1 characters: [cr]
IGNORABLE WHITESPACE: 3 characters: [blank][blank][blank]
CHARACTERS: 5 characters: sloth
IGNORABLE WHITESPACE: 0 characters:
IGNORABLE WHITESPACE: 1 characters: [cr]
IGNORABLE WHITESPACE: 3 characters: [blank][blank][blank]
CHARACTERS: 8 characters: gluttony
IGNORABLE WHITESPACE: 0 characters:
IGNORABLE WHITESPACE: 1 characters: [cr]
IGNORABLE WHITESPACE: 3 characters: [blank][blank][blank]
CHARACTERS: 27 characters: [blank]Writing[blank]non-portable[blank]code[blank]
IGNORABLE WHITESPACE: 0 characters:
IGNORABLE WHITESPACE: 1 characters: [cr]
IGNORABLE WHITESPACE: 0 characters:
```

Look at the stuff in Figure 5-1, and notice how the parser calls the methods in Listing 5-2. For things like `Writing non-portable code`, the parser calls the familiar characters method. But for the blanks that indent the `Sin` elements, the parser calls `ignorableWhitespace`. As you'll see in a moment, this happens only because the parser finds the DTD in Listing 5-3.

When a parser finds an XML document's DTD, then the parser can call the `ignorableWhitespace` method. It doesn't matter if the parser is, or isn't, asked to validate the document. Even when there's no call to the `setValidating` method, or when there's a call to `setValidating(false)`, a parser with a DTD can call `ignorableWhitespace`.

Whitespace without a DTD

A parser that doesn't find a document's DTD does not call the `ignorableWhitespace` method. To bring this point home, we do another experiment. We remove the `DOCTYPE` declaration from the file in Listing 5-1. We can leave the `Sins.dtd` file (Listing 5-3) right where it is. (It doesn't matter if the DTD file exists. All that matters is if the DTD is associated with the XML document.)

With the `DOCTYPE` declaration removed from Listing 5-1, we run the code in Listing 5-2, and get the output shown in Figure 5-2. The output has no calls to the `ignorableWhitespace` method. All whitespace is handled by the `characters` method.

Figure 5-2:
Running
the code in
Listing 5-2
without
a DTD.

```
CHARACTERS: 0 characters:
CHARACTERS: 1 characters: [cr]
CHARACTERS: 3 characters: [blank][blank][blank]
CHARACTERS: 5 characters: sloth
CHARACTERS: 0 characters:
CHARACTERS: 1 characters: [cr]
CHARACTERS: 3 characters: [blank][blank][blank]
CHARACTERS: 8 characters: gluttony
CHARACTERS: 0 characters:
CHARACTERS: 1 characters: [cr]
CHARACTERS: 3 characters: [blank][blank][blank]
CHARACTERS: 27 characters: [blank]Writing[blank]non-portable[blank]code[blank]
CHARACTERS: 0 characters:
CHARACTERS: 1 characters: [cr]
```

Not valid? Not a problem!

Okay, here's a quiz. What happens if you add `factory.setValidating(true)` to the SAX-calling code in Listing 4-2, and you feed the program an invalid document? Take, for instance, the document in Listing 5-4.

Listing 5-4: An Invalid Document

```
<?xml version="1.0" encoding="UTF-8"?>
<!DOCTYPE MyThreeSins SYSTEM "Sins.dtd">
<!-- InvalidSins.xml -->

<MyThreeSins>
    <Sin rank="favorite">sloth</Sin>
    <Sin>gluttony</Sin>
    <Sin>envy</Sin>
    <Vice> Writing non-portable code </Vice>
</MyThreeSins>
```

Remember, the DTD for the document in Listing 5-4 is the file in Listing 5-3, and the DTD in Listing 5-3 has no `Vice` element (it's as pure as the driven snow). With this combination of DTD and misfired validation, what kind of whitespace will the parser see?

The answer is, the parser will see both characters and ignorable whitespace. Why? Because validation, and the parsing of a valid or invalid document, has little to do with the ignorable whitespace issue. The crucial thing is whether the XML document has, or doesn't have, a DTD. If the document is associated with a DTD, then the parser can call the `ignorableWhitespace` method.

Using Namespaces

If you've been gazing endlessly at the code in Chapters 3 and 4, then you may have noticed that I've been ignoring two parameters in the `startElement` and `endElement` methods. These parameters — `uri` and `localName` — make sense only when you're dealing with *namespaces*.

Namespaces qualify elements and attributes. For instance, with namespaces, you can have two different kinds of person elements. You can have goodGuys: person and badGuys:person.

What do you do about XML namespaces? If you use them, then you'll need some way to track them in your Java SAX code. Of course, some folks avoid namespaces, and you want to keep those folks happy too.

So the big question is, what happens when the parser sees a little colon in an element or attribute name? For example, what does the parser do with an attribute named Ohio:Akron? There are at least two possibilities:

✔ **The parser can treat the name as having two distinct parts, and work with each part separately.**

 • The first part, Ohio, is called the *prefix*.

 The prefix is actually the "name" of the namespace. Along with an xmlns attribute, the prefix points to a place where more information about this element or attribute lives.

 • The second part, Akron, is called the *local name*.

 And why is this called *local*? Well, when you're visiting Wyoming, you're likely to refer to the rubber capital of the United States as "Akron, Ohio." On the other hand, if you're living in Ohio (that is, if you're *local* to Ohio), then you won't say "Akron, Ohio." Instead, you'll just say "Akron" because Akron is the local name.

 Before namespaces were invented, you'd probably have given this attribute the simple name Akron.

 • Taken together, the two-part name Ohio:Akron is called a *qualified name*. In the two-part name, the word Ohio qualifies the word Akron.

 A parser that sees a two-part name is called a *namespace-aware* parser.

✔ **The parser can treat the colon as any ordinary character in an element name.**

 • So what if I call my attribute Ohio:Akron? Who's going to stop me from using colons in an element or attribute name? I can use underscores in an attribute name, right? Well, then why not use colons?

 • Taken as a whole, the name Ohio:Akron is called a *qualified name*.

 A parser that sees a one-part name is *not* namespace-aware.

Namespaces weren't in the original XML specification, and lots of code was written when namespaces didn't exist. When namespaces finally came along, it was important to keep the old non-namespace code from crashing. The whole namespace routine had to be added in a way that would look grammatically correct to the old programs. That's why a namespace-unaware parser thinks that Ohio:Akron is just one big name.

An example with namespaces

Up to this point in the book, I've been settling for the Java SAX default — the default in which the parser is not namespace-aware. That's why none of my code has dealt with the uri and localName parameters in the startElement method. In this section, we'll finally use those two lonely parameters. Listings 5-5, 5-6, and 5-7 have all the stuff we're going to need.

Listing 5-5:   A Document with Namespaces

```
<!    GOURMET_FOODS.xml  -->

<GOURMET_FOODS
 xmlns="http://www.burd.org/ns/foods/1.0"
 xmlns:health="http://www.burd.org/ns/health/1.0">

   <FOOD name="PhillyCheeseSteak">
      <INGREDIENT content:grease="super"
         xmlns:content="http://www.burd.org/ns/content/1.0"/>

      <health:CALORIES>2530</health:CALORIES>
   </FOOD>

</GOURMET_FOODS>
```

Listing 5-6: Setting namespace awareness

```
import javax.xml.parsers.SAXParserFactory;
import javax.xml.parsers.SAXParser;
import javax.xml.parsers.ParserConfigurationException;

import org.xml.sax.XMLReader;
import org.xml.sax.SAXException;

import java.io.File;
import java.io.IOException;


class CallSAX
{
    static public void main(String[] args)
        throws SAXException,
               ParserConfigurationException,
               IOException
    {
```

(continued)

Listing 5-6 *(continued)*

```
SAXParserFactory factory =
        SAXParserFactory.newInstance();
    factory.setNamespaceAware(true);

    SAXParser saxParser = factory.newSAXParser();
    XMLReader xmlReader = saxParser.getXMLReader();
    xmlReader.setContentHandler(new MyContentHandler());

    try
    {
        xmlReader.parse
            (new File(args[0]).toURL().toString());
    }
    catch (SAXException s)
    {
        s.printStackTrace();
    }
  }

}
```

Listing 5-7:   A Fancier Content Handler

```
import org.xml.sax.helpers.DefaultHandler;
import org.xml.sax.Attributes;

class MyContentHandler extends DefaultHandler
{
    public void startElement(String uri,
                             String localName,
                             String qualName,
                             Attributes attribs)
    {
        System.out.println("Start element:");
        System.out.println("\tURI: " + uri);
        System.out.println("\tlocalName: " + localName);
        System.out.println("\tqualName: "  + qualName);

        for (int i=0; i<attribs.getLength(); i++)
        {
            System.out.println("\tAttribute:");
            System.out.print("\t\tURI: ");
            System.out.println(attribs.getURI(i));
            System.out.print("\t\tLocal name: ");
            System.out.println(attribs.getLocalName(i));
            System.out.print("\t\tQualified name: ");
            System.out.println(attribs.getQName(i));
            System.out.print("\t\tType: ");
            System.out.println(attribs.getType(i));
            System.out.print("\t\tValue: ");
            System.out.println(attribs.getValue(i));
        }
```

```
    }

    public void startPrefixMapping(String prefix, String uri)
    {
        System.out.println("Start prefix mapping:");
        System.out.println("\tPrefix: " + prefix);
        System.out.println("\turi: "    + uri);
    }


    public void endPrefixMapping(String prefix)
    {
        System.out.println("End prefix mapping: ");
        System.out.println("\tPrefix: " + prefix);
    }
}
```

Figure 5-3 shows how the output would start if you omitted the call to
setNamespaceAware in Listing 5-6. There would be no such thing as a URI or
a local name. When combing for names, the parser would see xmlns:health
and think, "Ah-hah! The XML programmer made up a name with a colon in it.
The whole thing, xmlns:health, is nothing but one big name."

In XML, a colon is treated as if it were an ordinary letter. An element like
<:::>colons</:::> is legal. The element's (funny-looking) DTD entry is
something like <!ELEMENT ::: (#PCDATA)>.

```
Start element:
        URI:
        localName:
        qualName: GOURMET_FOODS
        Attribute:
                URI:
                Local name:
                Qualified name: xmlns
                Type: CDATA
                Value: http://www.burd.org/ns/foods/1.0
        Attribute:
                URI:
                Local name:
                Qualified name: xmlns:health
                Type: CDATA
                Value: http://www.burd.org/ns/health/1.0
Start element:
        URI:
        localName:
        qualName: FOOD
        Attribute:
                URI:
                Local name:
```

Figure 5-3:
Gourmet
foods
without
namespace
awareness.

On being namespace aware

With the call to setNamespaceAware in Listing 5-6, the parser learns some
new tricks.

- ✔ The parser recognizes element names and attribute names as having
  two parts (a part before the colon, and a part after the colon).
- ✔ The parser makes callbacks when it enters and exits a namespace.

Look at the output in Figure 5-4, and you'll see what I mean.

The parser starts at the top of the document in Listing 5-5. The parser sees two xmlns attributes — one for the document default, and another for the health namespace. In response, the parser does some *mapping*. That is, the parser makes itself an internal roadmap. Instead of mapping Interstate 80 to a thick red line, the parser maps the name health to the URI http://www.burd.org/ns/health/1.0.

Because the start of a mapping is an event, the parser calls the handler's startPrefixMapping method (Listing 5-7). This startPrefixMapping method displays some stuff on the screen.

Once the parser reaches the GOURMET_FOODS element, the effects of the mapping become visible. At last, the uri and localName parameters become useful. In Figure 5-4, the element's URI is http://www.burd. org/ns/foods/1.0 and the element's localName is no longer empty. For this element, the local name is the same as the qualified name (namely, GOURMET_FOODS.) The names are the same because, in Listing 5-5, there's no colon before the word GOURMET_FOODS. The URI http://www.burd.org/ ns/foods/1.0 has been assigned to GOURMET_FOODS by default.

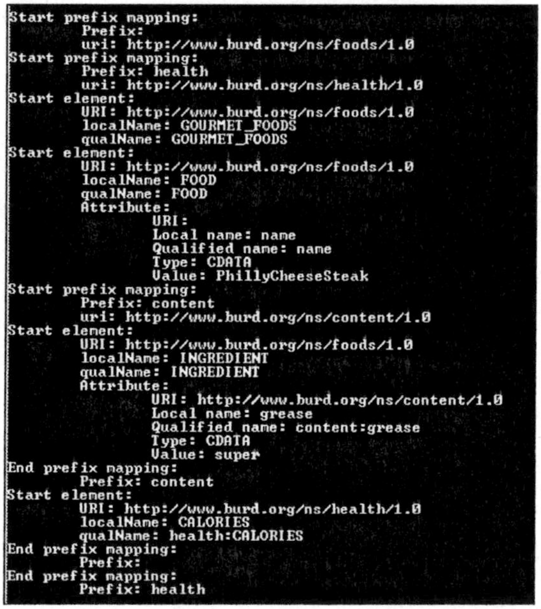

Figure 5-4:
Gourmet
foods with
namespace
awareness.

```
Start prefix mapping:
        Prefix:
        uri: http://www.burd.org/ns/foods/1.0
Start prefix mapping:
        Prefix: health
        uri: http://www.burd.org/ns/health/1.0
Start element:
        URI: http://www.burd.org/ns/foods/1.0
        localName: GOURMET_FOODS
        qualName: GOURMET_FOODS
Start element:
        URI: http://www.burd.org/ns/foods/1.0
        localName: FOOD
        qualName: FOOD
        Attribute:
                URI:
                Local name: name
                Qualified name: name
                Type: CDATA
                Value: PhillyCheeseSteak
Start prefix mapping:
        Prefix: content
        uri: http://www.burd.org/ns/content/1.0
Start element:
        URI: http://www.burd.org/ns/foods/1.0
        localName: INGREDIENT
        qualName: INGREDIENT
        Attribute:
                URI: http://www.burd.org/ns/content/1.0
                Local name: grease
                Qualified name: content:grease
                Type: CDATA
                Value: super
End prefix mapping:
        Prefix: content
Start element:
        URI: http://www.burd.org/ns/health/1.0
        localName: CALORIES
        qualName: health:CALORIES
End prefix mapping:
        Prefix:
End prefix mapping:
        Prefix: health
```

Compare the GOURMET_FOODS situation with the output for the CALORIES element. In Listing 5-5, the word CALORIES gets prefaced with the namespace health. So, in Figure 5-4, element's local name is CALORIES, and the qualified name is health:CALORIES.

Handling Processing Instructions

An XML processing instruction is a note. It's a note from the XML document to some processor. For instance, with an XML processing instruction you can say "When displaying this document, please use the AnnoyingBlink stylesheet." Here's a processing instruction to do that kind of thing:

```
<?xml-stylesheet type="text/xsl" href="AnnoyingBlink.xsl"?>
```

Other processing instructions send all kinds of messages. In fact, a processing instruction can say almost anything you want it to say (as long as you have software that understands the message).

SAX has a nice callback for responding to processing instructions. To show off this callback, I've created an XML document and some Java code. This stuff is shown in Listings 5-8 and 5-9.

Listing 5-8:   Some Processing Instructions

```
<?xml version="1.0" standalone="no"?>
<?xml-stylesheet type="text/xsl" href="AnnoyingBlink.xsl"?>
<!-- Birthday.xml -->

<Birthday>
   <?debug FirstLine.log ?>
   <Line>Happy Birthday!</Line>

   <?debug SecondLine.log ?>
   <Line>Wow! You're really that old?</Line>
</Birthday>
```

Listing 5-9:   Handling Processing Instructions

```
import org.xml.sax.helpers.DefaultHandler;
import java.io.FileOutputStream;
import java.io.FileNotFoundException;
import java.io.PrintStream;

class MyContentHandler extends DefaultHandler
{
    PrintStream log = null;


    public void processingInstruction (String target,
                                        String data)
```

(continued)

Listing 5-9 *(continued)*

```
    {
        System.out.println("Processing instruction");
        System.out.println("\tTarget: " + target);
        System.out.println("\tData   : " + data);

        if (target.equals("debug"))
            try
            {
                FileOutputStream f =
                    new FileOutputStream(data);
                log = new PrintStream(f);
            }
            catch (FileNotFoundException e)
            {
                e.printStackTrace();
                System.exit(1);
            }
    }


    public void characters
        (char[] charArray, int start, int length)
    {
        String charString =
            (new String(charArray, start, length)).trim();
        if (charString != null && log != null)
            log.print (charString);

    }

}
```

To call the code in Listing 5-9, you need the usual kind of main method. The code in Listing 5-6 will do just fine (although that code's call to setNamespaceAware isn't needed in this example).

The output

The screen output from Listings 5-8 and 5-9 is in Figure 5-5. In addition to this screen output, the program creates two disk files — one named FirstLine.log, and another named SecondLine.log. The file FirstLine.log contains the words

```
Happy Birthday!
```

The file SecondLine.log contains the words

```
Wow! You're really that old?
```

(Editor's note: You'll have to excuse the author. As a Baby Boomer, he's feeling self-conscious about his age. We editors try not to think about it.)

Figure 5-5:
The screen
output from
a run of the
code in
Listing 5-9.

```
Processing instruction
        Target: xml-stylesheet
        Data  : type="text/xsl" href="AnnoyingBlink.xsl"
Processing instruction
        Target: debug
        Data  : FirstLine.log
Processing instruction
        Target: debug
        Data  : SecondLine.log
```

Method calls

The example, in Listing 5-9, hinges on the method named processingInstruction. When the parser encounters almost any processing instruction, the parser makes a callback to this method.

The document in Listing 5-8 has four processing instructions (?xml, ?xml-stylesheet, and two ?debug instructions), but only three of the instructions trigger callbacks. The first instruction (the ?xml instruction) never triggers a callback, because the ?xml instruction is of interest to the parser only. Each of the three remaining instructions triggers a callback. (See Figure 5-5.)

Each processing instruction comes in two parts.

✔ **The first part, immediately after the opening question mark, is called the *target*.**

For instance, Listing 5-8 has a processing instruction with target xml-stylesheet. To hit this target is to tell a processor what style-sheet belongs here. (For more on stylesheets, see Chapter 12.)

✔ **The second part (everything after the target), is called the *data*.**

That same instruction in Listing 5-8, has data

```
type="text/xsl" href="AnnoyingBlink.xsl"
```

These two parts get passed to the processingInstruction method as parameters (named target and data, of course).

Listing 5-9 has System.out.println statements that display the target and data on the screen (and you can see the results in Figure 5-5). But Listing 5-9 does more if a processing instruction's target happens to be the word debug. In that situation, the method calls new FileOutputStream(data). The call takes whatever string is in the processing instruction's data part, and uses that string to create a new file.

Once your program calls the new FileOutputStream("FirstLine.log") constructor, any bytes in any FirstLine.log file are gone. If a file with that name didn't already exist, then the computer creates a new file. If a file with that name already existed, the computer blows away the old file and creates a brand new file.

Inside the processing instruction method, the new file gets associated with the variable name log. Later, when the parser encounters an element and the characters method gets called, the characters method uses the log file for output.

Listing 5-8 has two debug processing instructions, and the instructions are intermingled with a couple of Line elements. By the time the parser reaches the first Line element, the value of the log variable is "FirstLine.log", so the characters method writes to the FirstLine.log disk file. Then, when the parser reaches the second Line element, the value of the log variable has changed to "SecondLine.log", so the characters method writes to the SecondLine.log disk file. It's pretty clever, heh?

Chapter 6

SAX Programming Techniques

***

In This Chapter

▷ Using stacks in your code

▷ Falling back on lexical parsing

▷ A big case study! Playing music with Java and XML

***

*H*ello again. As the orchestra members take their seats, we welcome you to another edition of *Afternoon Music* here on KXML-FM. This afternoon's selection comes to you from the annals of American blues: "XML Baby," arranged for MIDI interface and solo SAX by conductor and raconteur Barry Burd. Written in 1920 by blues legend Lumpy Scludero, the tune "XML Baby" has been a favorite among singers and songwriters for several decades. The tune was featured in the recent film *XMN*, with the professor's crazy mutants. It was also used as the main theme for the cyber-thriller TV series, *The XML Files*. I see Dr. Burd at the podium, raising his virtual baton — so it's time to relax, sit back, boot up, and enjoy "XML Baby" . . .

Stacks for SAX

We interrupt this broadcast to bring you an important message: *Some things are awkward to do when you're using SAX*. Take, for instance, the XML document in Listing 6-1. The document represents a pile of papers on my office desk. On Monday, I get a note from the boss. On Tuesday, I get junk mail from a bank and from a long-distance telephone company. On Wednesday, I get a letter from a client.

Listing 6-1:   A Pile of Paper Mail

```
<?xml version="1.0" encoding="UTF-8"?>
<!--ClutteredDesk.xml-->

<Mail day="Monday">
   <Mail day="Tuesday">
      <Mail day="Wednesday">
```

(continued)

Listing 6-1 *(continued)*

```
        <Item>Client: Let's close that deal.</Item>
    </Mail>
    <Item>Bank: Get a home equity loan today!</Item>
    <Item>Telephone: Switch carriers today!</Item>
  </Mail>
  <Item>Boss: Do this ASAP.</Item>
</Mail>
```

The paper mail piles up for a few days. Then, late on Wednesday afternoon, I decide to go through my mail. First, I deal with whatever's on the top of the pile. In Listing 6-1, the top of the pile contains Wednesday's letter from my client. After dealing with the client's letter, I consider whatever remains on the top of the pile. Now the top of the pile has Tuesday's junk mail — the mail from the bank and the telephone company. Once I've tossed the junk mail into the trashcan, I deal with the only item remaining on the pile. That remaining item is Monday's letter from my boss. "Please attend to this matter by Tuesday," the letter says. Oops!

Hey, what's your problem?

When I process the document in Listing 6-1, an interesting question arises. The question is, how do I handle the text within elements? When I'm displaying the words `Boss: Do this ASAP`, how can I display the day that this piece of mail arrived on my desk?

Let's pose the same issue in a slightly different way. What's the difference between a SAX parser and an elephant? Give up? Well, a SAX parser always forgets. A SAX parser just scans a document from top to bottom. When the parser fires a new event, the parser remembers almost nothing about any previously fired events. So, in Listing 6-1, when the parser sees `Boss: Do this ASAP`, the parser doesn't remember that this text is inside the `day="Monday"` element. If you want to create the output in Figure 6-1, how can you do it?

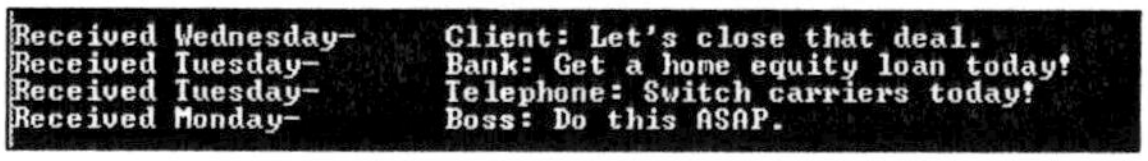

Figure 6-1:
Displaying mail with a date stamp.

```
Received Wednesday-     Client: Let's close that deal.
Received Tuesday-       Bank: Get a home equity loan today!
Received Tuesday-       Telephone: Switch carriers today!
Received Monday-        Boss: Do this ASAP.
```

Alternative solutions

In a SAX content handler, neither the `endElement` method nor the `characters` method has an `Attribute` parameter. (For that matter, the `characters` method has no parameters at all — no qualName, no localName, nothing like that.) So, in Listing 6-1, if you want to display the day attribute's value, you have two alternatives:

✔ **You can display the** day **attribute when the Mail tag's** startElement **method gets called.**

If you do this, then you'll be visiting the document's attributes in the wrong order. You'll display the day when a piece of mail arrives, but you won't display the text for a piece of mail until that piece of mail is opened. You'll get some misleading output, like the output in Figure 6-2.

✔ **You can store each attribute's value somewhere so that, when the** characters **method runs, the method knows the relevant attribute's value.**

This is the right way to go — but it's not simply a matter of putting a value into a String variable. Sure, when you reach the Mail start tag, you can store the day attribute's value in a String variable. But then later, when you reach the next Mail start tag, you may clobber the word *Monday* to store the word *Tuesday* in that same String variable. So the problem is, as you exit from Tuesday's Mail element, how do you recover the fact that you were previously inside Monday's Mail element?

Figure 6-2:
A failed attempt to display mail with a date stamp.

```
Received Monday
Received Tuesday
Received Wednesday
Client: Let's close that deal.
Bank: Get a home equity loan today!
Telephone: Switch carriers today!
Boss: Do this ASAP.
```

The answer is to use a *stack* — an area of memory set up to serve as a "warehouse" for items a program may need later. Stacks are a venerable feature of computing — but the concept behind them is simple: You add things to a stack, add other things without destroying what's already there, and later you remove things from the stack. Whenever you remove things from the stack, they come out in an order opposite of the order in which you added them.

There's a pretty simple way to remember how the stack works: *You always remove the item that went into the stack most recently.* The last thing to go into the stack is the first thing to come out of the stack.

Using a stack

Look up the class java.util.Stack in Java's API documentation. Notice all the *p* methods — the methods push, peek, and pop.

✔ The push method adds a new object to the top of the stack.

✔ The peek method tells you what object is currently at the top of the stack.

✔ The pop method takes whatever element is at the top of the stack, and removes that element from the stack.

Now, the crucial thing to notice is that an XML document's elements work like a stack. When you're done processing Wednesday's mail, you're ready to process Tuesday's mail. In Listing 6-1, when you're ending the Wednesday element, you find yourself back inside the Tuesday element. So, to keep track of your elements, create a stack:

1. In the Mail element's startElement method, push the day attribute's value onto the stack.

2. In the characters method (or wherever else you need to know the current attribute's value), take a peek at the stack.

3. In the Mail element's endElement method, pop the day attribute's value off the stack.

The code to illustrate this technique is shown in Listing 6-2. You've already seen some of the stuff that goes along with this listing. With the content handler in Listing 6-2, and the XML document in Listing 6-1, you get the output shown in Figure 6-1. For the code to call MyContentHandler, you can use Listing 4-2 (or almost any other SAX calling code in Chapters 4 and 5, for that matter).

Listing 6-2:   Using a Stack

```
import org.xml.sax.helpers.DefaultHandler;
import org.xml.sax.Attributes;
import java.util.Stack;

class MyContentHandler extends DefaultHandler
{
    Stack stack = new Stack();

    public void startElement(String uri,
                             String localName,
                             String qualName,
                             Attributes attribs)
    {
        if (qualName.equals("Mail"))
            stack.push(attribs.getValue("day"));
    }


    public void characters
```

```
              (char[] charArray, int start, int length)
    {
        String charString =
            (new String(charArray, start, length).trim());

        if (charString != null && !charString.equals(""))
        {
            System.out.print("Received ");
            System.out.print(stack.peek());
            System.out.print("-\t");
            System.out.println(charString);
        }
    }



    public void endElement(String uri,
                           String localName,
                           String qualName)
    {
        if (qualName.equals("Mail"))
            stack.pop();
    }
```

Why a stack works so nicely

Figure 6-3 shows you what happens when you start running the code in
Listing 6-2. For the document in Listing 6-1, the parser calls the startElement
method (with its call to the push method) three times in a row.

✔ After the first call to push, the stack contains only the "Monday" string.

✔ After the second call to push, the stack contains the strings "Monday"
   and "Tuesday". Because "Tuesday" is the most recent string to have
   been pushed, the string "Tuesday" is at the top of the stack.

✔ After the third call to push, the stack contains three strings. The most
   recently pushed string is the "Wednesday" string, so the "Wednesday"
   string is at the top of the stack.

When the code in Listing 6-2 processes end tags, the endElement method
calls the stack's pop method. At that point, things come off the stack in
reverse order. For a graphic illustration, see Figure 6-4.

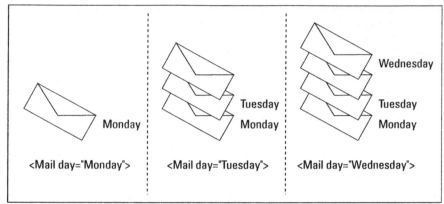

Figure 6-3:
Pushing
items onto
the stack.

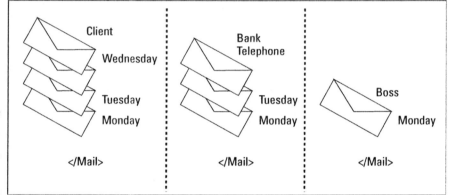

Figure 6-4:
Popping
items off of
the stack.

Words, Words, Words

My first example in Chapter 3 was a MyThreeSins document. When I started
writing the chapter, the document was a bit different. The original document
had no Sin tags — only a root tag and some line breaks. The document
looked something like the one in Listing 6-3.

Listing 6-3:   Adopting a New Sin

```
<?xml version="1.0" encoding="UTF-8"?>
<MyFourSins>
    Micromanaging
    Robbing a bank
    Having a Chip on your shoulder
    Earning too much money
</MyFourSins>
```

The document in Listing 6-3 is certainly well formed. To the human eye, the document conveys its intended message — but the lack of a `Sin` tag makes the document more difficult to process. Listing 6-3 has all the desired data, but the data isn't conveniently categorized.

Once I realized my mistake, I corrected it. But in this chapter, I'm thinking, "How many times have I had to deal with other peoples' mistakes?" People create misshapen XML documents all the time — and when you write code to handle other peoples' data, often you have to play the hand dealt to you.

So, even though it's not strictly a SAX programming technique, I'd like to include a few words about *lexical parsing*. The word *lexical* means *having to do with words*. When you're reduced to doing lexical parsing, you're dealing with things smaller than XML elements and smaller than XML tags. You're taking the text inside an element, and processing the text word by word. As an XML aficionado, lexical parsing is probably not your favorite activity. But XML documents are text-based, so lexical parsing comes up time after time, document after document.

This section is devoted to my favorite lexical parsing technique — the use of a string tokenizer. First, a look at what can go wrong; then, a way to fix it.

Don't do this

Listing 6-4 contains a bad content handler — bad because the programmer makes an incorrect assumption. The programmer assumes that the SAX `characters` method gets called once for each line of character text. For a look at the bad output, see Figure 6-5.

Listing 6-4: A Bad Content Handler

```
import org.xml.sax.helpers.DefaultHandler;

class MyContentHandler extends DefaultHandler
{
    public void characters
        (char[] charArray, int start, int length)
    {
        String charString =
            new String(charArray, start, length);

        System.out.println("Sin: " + charString);
    }
}
```

In Figure 6-5, the content handler's characters method is called just once. Whoever wrote the code didn't realize that four lines of text would look like one big lump to the SAX parser.

```
Sin:
    Micromanaging
    Robbing a bank
    Having a Chip on your shoulder
    Earning too much money
```

Do this

To remedy the mistake made in Listing 6-4, you can write code that splits a block of text into parts. You can do this very elegantly with Java's string tokenizer. A better content handler, using the string tokenizer, is shown in Listing 6-5.

Listing 6-5:   Using the StringTokenizer Class

```java
import org.xml.sax.helpers.DefaultHandler;
import java.util.StringTokenizer;


class MyContentHandler extends DefaultHandler
{
    public void characters
        (char[] charArray, int start, int length)
    {
        String charString =
            new String(charArray, start, length);

        StringTokenizer tokenizer =
            new StringTokenizer(charString, "\n");

        while (tokenizer.hasMoreTokens())
        {
            String token = tokenizer.nextToken().trim();
            if (token != null && !token.equals(""))
                System.out.println("Sin: " + token);
        }

    }
}
```

The work of the content handler in Listing 6-5 is shown in Figure 6-6. The handler properly separates the four text lines in the document of Listing 6-3. The reason for this separation is that the handler uses a StringTokenizer. The tokenizer's constructor designates the chopping point for each portion of the text. (This chopping point can be anything, but in Listing 6-5, the chopping point is the carriage return.)

Figure 6-6:
Four sins,
displayed
correctly.

```
Sin: Micromanaging
Sin: Robbing a bank
Sin: Having a Chip on your shoulder
Sin: Earning too much money
```

After the `charString` has been chopped into four tokens, the code in
Listing 6-5 makes successive calls to the `nextToken` method. Each call to
`nextToken` returns a line of text. (In Listing 6-3, each line of text is a separate
sin.) Each line gets displayed with the word `Sin:` in front of it, which is exactly
what we wanted from the beginning. At long last, all is right with the world.

In practice, you can never count on the SAX `characters` method to get a
chunk of text of any particular size. A parser that's scanning the document in
Listing 6-3 may make one call, four calls, or any strange number of calls to the
SAX `characters` method. To write an industrial-strength SAX program, you
must take all these possibilities into account.

Case Study: MIDI Music Synthesis

When you learn a new technology, it's nice to start with a simple `Hello`
program. But, once you're past the `Hello` program, you want to see the
technology applied to some reasonable problem. A real problem always
forces some new issues to surface, and it's good to see how those issues
can be tackled.

With this in mind, we now return to our regularly scheduled program —
Afternoon Music on KXML-FM. To start off the show, I've created a simple
markup language called Barry's Music Markup Language. (Calling it Barry's
MML distinguishes this language from the real, industrial strength MusicXML,
which is described at www.musicxml.org.)

I've even created a sample XML document. For this afternoon's selection,
I've chosen the song "XML Baby" by blues artist Lumpy Scladero.

> *My screen's a freezin' up baby, but my heart's XML-ting for you.*
>
> *My screen's a freezin' up baby, but my heart's XML-ting for you.*
>
> *You're my XLover baby, but I just can't get over you.*

Yes, I have sheet music. It's in Figure 6-7.

A document that describes the beginning of "XML Baby" is shown in Listing 6-6.

Figure 6-7:
From the
Lumpy
Scladero
Foundation's
archives.

Listing 6-6: XML Baby!

```xml
<?xml version="1.0" standalone="no"?>
<!DOCTYPE song SYSTEM "song.dtd">

<song tempo="&Andante;">
   <measure beatlength="&eighth;">
      <beat/><beat/><beat/><beat/><beat/>

      <beat><!-- My -->
         <note pitch="&Eflat;" duration="&eighth;"/>
      </beat>

      <beat><!-- screen's -->
         <note pitch="&Eflat;" duration="&eighth;"/>
      </beat>

      <beat><!-- a -->
         <note pitch="&C;" duration="&eighth;"/>
      </beat>
   </measure>

   <measure beatlength="&eighth;">
      <beat><!-- free- -->
         <note pitch="&Eflat;" velocity="&forte;"
                            duration="&eighth;"/>
         <note pitch="&C;" octave="-1"
               velocity="&piano;" duration="&quarter;"/>
         <note pitch="&G;" octave="-1"
               velocity="&piano;" duration="&quarter;"/>
      </beat>
      <beat><!-- zin' -->
         <note pitch="&Eflat;" duration="&eighth;"/>
      </beat>

      <beat><!-- up -->
         <note pitch="&Eflat;" duration="&eighth;"/>
         <note pitch="&A;" velocity="&piano;"/>
      </beat>
```

```
      <beat><!-- ba- -->
         <note pitch="&Eflat;" duration="&eighth;"/>
      </beat>

      <beat>
         <note pitch="&Bflat;" velocity="&piano;"/>
      </beat>
      <beat><!-- by -->
         <note pitch="&C;" duration="&half;"/>
      </beat>

      <beat>
         <note pitch="&A;" velocity="&piano;"/>
      </beat>
      <beat/>
   </measure>

   <measure beatlength="&sixteenth;">
      <beat>
         <note pitch="&C;" octave="-1" velocity="&piano;"/>
         <note pitch="&G;" octave="-1" velocity="&piano;"/>
      </beat>
      <beat/>
      <beat><!-- but -->
         <note pitch="&F;" duration="&sixteenth;"/>
      </beat>
      <beat><!-- my -->
         <note pitch="&F;" duration="&sixteenth;"/>
      </beat>

      <beat><!-- heart's -->
         <note pitch="&F;" velocity="&forte;"
                          duration="&eighth;"/>
         <note pitch="&A;" velocity="&piano;"/>
      </beat>
      <beat/>
      <beat><!-- X -->
         <note pitch="&G;" duration="&sixteenth;"/>
      </beat>
      <beat><!-- M -->
         <note pitch="&F;" duration="&sixteenth;"/>
      </beat>

      <beat><!-- L- -->
         <note pitch="&Eflat;" velocity="&forte;"
                               duration="&eighth;"/>
         <note pitch="&Bflat;" velocity="&piano;"/>
      </beat>
      <beat/>
      <beat><!-- ting -->
         <note pitch="&C;" duration="&eighth;"/>
      </beat>
```

(continued)

Listing 6-6 *(continued)*

```
        <beat/>

        <beat><!-- for -->
            <note pitch="&Bflat;" duration="&eighth;"/>
        </beat>
        <beat/>
        <beat><!-- you. -->
            <note pitch="&C;" duration="&half;"/>
        </beat>
        <beat/>
    </measure>

</song>
```

Barry's music markup language

Compared with real sheet music, the rules for my music markup language are pretty dim-witted. Even so, you need some knowledge of musical notation to understand my markup language's rules. If you're musically illiterate, you can skip this whole sidebar and jump right to Listing 6-8.

Anyway, here are some highlights of Barry's music markup language:

✔ **Each document has one song element.**

Each song has a `tempo` attribute. The default tempo is `"&Moderato;"` which stands for 2000 milliseconds per whole note.

✔ **Each song has some measure elements.**

✔ **Each measure has some beat elements.**

What I call a beat isn't quite the same as what most musicians would call a beat. In my terminology, a *beat* is just a uniform slice of time within a measure. I can describe one measure with eight beats, and then describe the next measure (in less detail) with only four beats. It depends on how many notes I need to squeeze into a measure.

So each measure start tag has its own `beatlength` attribute. The default

beatlength is `"0.25"` or `"&quarter;"` which stands for one quarter note.

✔ **Each beat has some note elements.**

A note has its own `pitch`, `octave`, `velocity`, `duration`, and `dotted` attributes. Some of these attributes have defaults.

In the Java code, the `pitch` and `octave` attributes get combined to make one piano-key pitch. I number the notes on a piano, so that Middle C is in octave 0, C below middle C is in octave -1, and so on. Octaves start on the A notes. So A below Middle C is in octave 0, and A above middle C is in octave 1.

The `duration` and `dotted` attributes, along with the song's `tempo` attribute, get multiplied together to make one note's duration.

The note's `velocity` attribute (a number from 0 to 127) represents the volume with which the note is played. (The term *velocity* comes from the MIDI music world.)

Of course, you can recover many of these details from a DTD. The DTD for my simple music markup language is in Listing 6-7.

Listing 6-7: Defining My Music Markup Language

```xml
<?xml version="1.0" encoding="UTF-8"?>
<!-- Song.dtd -->

<!ENTITY Largo "4000">
<!ENTITY Andante "3000">
<!ENTITY Moderato "2000">
<!ENTITY Allegro "1000">

<!ELEMENT song (measure*)>
<!ATTLIST song tempo CDATA "&Moderato;">

<!ENTITY sixteenth "0.0625">
<!ENTITY eighth "0.125">
<!ENTITY quarter "0.25">
<!ENTITY half "0.5">
<!ENTITY whole "1.0">

<!ELEMENT measure (beat*)>
<!ATTLIST measure beatlength CDATA "&quarter;">

<!ELEMENT beat (note*)>

<!ELEMENT note EMPTY>
<!ATTLIST note
    pitch CDATA #REQUIRED
    octave CDATA "0"
    velocity CDATA #IMPLIED
    duration CDATA "&quarter;"
    dotted CDATA "false"
>

<!ENTITY A "57">
<!ENTITY Asharp "58">
<!ENTITY Bflat "58">
<!ENTITY B "59">
<!ENTITY C "60">
<!ENTITY Csharp "61">
<!ENTITY Dflat "61">
<!ENTITY D "62">
<!ENTITY Dsharp "63">
<!ENTITY Eflat "63">
<!ENTITY E "64">
<!ENTITY F "65">
<!ENTITY Fsharp "66">
<!ENTITY Fflat "66">
<!ENTITY G "67">
<!ENTITY Gsharp "68">
<!ENTITY Aflat "68">

<!ENTITY piano "45">
<!ENTITY forte "120">
```

Java sound

As with almost any XML document, the document in Listing 6-6 is useless without a computer program to interpret it. That's why I've written a SAX program to read documents and play songs.

My SAX program uses the Java Sound API to play tones. This API is part of the standard core Java implementation. If you've never worked with the Java Sound API, then you're in for a treat. The API uses *MIDI (Musical Instrument Digital Interface)* notation to play tones on a computer's sound card. To keep things simple, my program uses only two features of the Java Sound API:

✔ **The program creates a MIDI channel.**

This MIDI channel is the bare necessity for playing tones.

✔ **The program plays notes.**

A MIDI channel has methods named noteOn and noteOff. My program puts a delay between the calling of these two methods. That's what sustains each note for a short period of time.

A program to interpret the XML document

I'm very proud of myself. In this section's Java code, I've managed to separate the XML stuff from the music stuff. I've done it by dividing the code into five classes. Classes CallSAX and MyContentHander deal almost exclusively with XML. The other three classes — Song, Measure, and Note — do all the music work. So, if you're not a musician, you can skip right past the three music classes. (Why not? I skipped some music classes in high school . . .) Just read the names of the method calls in classes Song, Measure, and Note. Then nod your head knowingly, and continue onward.

With that in mind, let's look at this section's content-handler class. That class is in Listing 6-8.

As usual, you call the content handler by running a main method (the one in Listing 4-2 will do just fine).

Listing 6-8: A Content Handler That Plays Music

```
import org.xml.sax.helpers.DefaultHandler;
import org.xml.sax.Attributes;

class MyContentHandler extends DefaultHandler
{
    Song song;
```

```
Measure measure;

public void startDocument()
{
   song = new Song();
}


public void startElement(String uri,
                         String localName,
                         String qualName,
                         Attributes attribs)
{
   if (qualName.equals("song"))
      song.setTempo(attribs.getValue("tempo"));
   if (qualName.equals("measure"))
      measure = new Measure
         (song, attribs.getValue("beatlength"));
   if (qualName.equals("note"))
   {
      Note note = new Note(song);

      note.setPitch (attribs.getValue("pitch"));
      note.setOctave (attribs.getValue("octave"));
      note.setVelocity (attribs.getValue("velocity"));
      note.setDuration (attribs.getValue("duration"));
      note.setDotted (attribs.getValue("dotted"));

      Thread noteThread = new Thread(note);
      noteThread.start();
   }
}


public void endElement(String uri,
                       String localName,
                       String qualName)
{
   if (qualName.equals("beat"))
   {
      try
      {
         Thread.sleep(measure.getBeatlength());
      }
      catch (InterruptedException e)
      {
         e.printStackTrace();
      }
   }
```

(continued)

Listing 6-8 *(continued)*

```
    }

    public void endDocument()
    {
        System.exit(0);
    }

}
```

Running the code

If you have a sound card and a tolerance for bad musicianship, you can try out my music-playing code on your own. Just follow these simple steps:

1. **Copy this section's listings from the book's Web site to your hard drive.**

2. **Compile the** `.java` **files.**

3. **Run the** `CallSAX` **class's** `main` **method.**

   If you're working from your system's command prompt, just type

```
java CallSAX JavaJive.xml
```

When you do this you'll hear your computer play a ding-dong version of the "XML Baby" tune. (For all the complexity of my Music Markup Language, you'll wonder why the music sounds so crude. That's just the nature of music making. Pounding notes on a simulated MIDI keyboard is easy. Making notes sound truly musical is more difficult.)

Normally, when I introduce a new program, I provide a figure to illustrate the program's output. With a program that plays a song, a figure wouldn't do justice to the real output. So I asked my publisher if we could put one of those sound-generating chips on the next page of this book. That would turn the next page into a little music-playing greeting card. When you flip to the next page, you hear a tune!

Oh, well. Maybe it wasn't such a good idea.

When you run the `PlaySong` program, any one of three things can happen. Either you hear the song (great!), or you see an error message on your screen (not so great), or you see no error message and hear nothing (very un-great). If you get nothing (no error message and no sound), then check your computer's sound settings. On a Windows computer, go to your system tray and right-click the little speaker icon. Then choose Open Volume Controls and start playing around a bit. Remember, when you're in the Volume Control panel, you can click Options➪Properties to switch between Recording and Playback.

Understanding the content handler

Let's examine some of the ideas in Listing 6-8.

When the parser starts its parsing, the startDocument method gets called. This startDocument method creates a new Song object. I'll dissect the Song class's code a bit later in this section.

The startElement method

In Listing 6-8, all if statements in the startElement method do roughly the same thing. Each if statement takes attributes from the XML document's tag, and uses those attributes to set the properties of an object. This point in the code is the juncture between XML-handling code and music-handling code. The XML-handling code worries about document attributes, and the music-handling classes encapsulate things like tempo, octave, and pitch.

Spawning threads

At the end of the note element's if statement, the code starts up a new Java thread. (Threads are important in Java, even when you're not using Java to play music.) In Listing 6-8, I spawn threads to play several notes at once.

Why startElement methods can get ugly

A parser moves on beyond the start of a document. When the parser encounters a start tag, the startElement method gets called.

Now, since this section of *Java & XML For Dummies* is a case study, I feel free to reveal my innermost thoughts about startElement methods. To be truthful, I feel guilty when I write a startElement method like the one in Listing 6-8. My startElement method has several if statements. Sometimes, when I write a startElement method, I create a separate if statement for each possible element name. That kind of code feels like one big kludge. I read articles by programming gurus in which they discourage this kind of code. I see

my fellow programmers jump through hoops to avoid the mushrooming of if statements. Isn't there a better way to pick and choose among the names of the document's elements?

Well, there are slicker ways, but slicker doesn't necessarily mean better. I've tried slicker ways, and all they do is make my code more complicated. That, in turn makes me feel even guiltier. So in most of the startElement methods that I write, I follow the old programmer's rule. Simple and naive is better than fancy and obtuse.

Do I use too many if statements in my startElement methods? No, bring on those if statements.

You see, in Listing 6-6, each note element is inside a beat element. Two or more notes inside the same beat element should get played at (almost) the same instant. (See Figure 6-8.)

```
<beat><!-- free -->
   <note pitch="&Eflat;" ... duration="&eighth;"/>
   <note pitch="&C;"     ... duration="&quarter;"/>
   <note pitch="&G;"     ... duration="&quarter;"/>
</beat>
<beat><!-- zin' -->
   <note pitch="&Eflat;" duration="&eighth;"/>
</beat>


<beat>                   </beat>   <beat>                   </beat>

<note ... duration="&eighth;"/>     <note ... duration="&eighth;"/>

<note pitch="&C;" ... duration="&quarter;"/>

<note pitch="&G;" ... duration="&quarter;"/>


0                       750                      1500
milliseconds
```

Figure 6-8: The timing of a few notes.

To play several notes at once, the computer has to do a juggling act. Think about the "free-zin'" beats of the "XML Baby" song.

```
<beat><!-- free -->
   <note pitch="&Eflat;" velocity="&forte;"
                         duration="&eighth;"/>
   <note pitch="&C;" octave="-1"
         velocity="&piano;" duration="&quarter;"/>
   <note pitch="&G;" octave="-1"
         velocity="&piano;" duration="&quarter;"/>
</beat>
<beat><!-- zin' -->
   <note pitch="&Eflat;" duration="&eighth;"/>
</beat>
```

✔ The computer starts playing an E flat. Seven hundred fifty milliseconds later, the computer will stop playing this E flat.

✔ The computer starts playing a C below Middle C. Fifteen hundred milliseconds later, the computer will stop playing this C.

✔ The computer starts playing a G below Middle C. Fifteen hundred milliseconds later, the computer will stop playing this G.

✔ Seven hundred fifty milliseconds into the measure, the first E flat has stopped playing, but the C and G are still playing. At that instant, the computer starts playing the second beat's E flat.

If all four of these actions take place in the same thread of Java code, then you'll hear four separate notes, one after another. After the first note has started, the one and only thread is kept busy counting up the milliseconds. Only after the first note's counting is finished can the second note's playing begin.

So, instead of having just one thread, we spawn a separate thread for each note. Each note's thread counts milliseconds on its own darn time. While a note's thread is counting milliseconds, the startElement method back in the original thread can begin processing the next note in the beat.

If you have trouble visualizing this action, just turn Figure 6-8 into a shore-line with boats. Picture yourself traveling along the shore, doing what the startElement method in Listing 6-8 does. When you get to the statements

```
Thread noteThread = new Thread(note);
noteThread.start();
```

you quickly build a boat (a new thread) and set the boat asail. The new boat does the following:

```
Start E flat;
Count 750 milliseconds;
Stop E flat.
```

In the meantime, you go about your other business back on the shore. Your other business includes making more boats. Each boat does its own thing while you perform your shore duties. When, finally, everyone has reached the right edge of Figure 6-9, the whole team of people, boats, and landlubbers has managed to play four notes, with some of them playing simultaneously.

With this description of threads, boats, and other things, you may be wondering why I didn't solve the simultaneous-note problem some other way. You may have some other solution to the problem — say, using threads in a different way, or using some mechanism other than threads. Rest assured that you're probably not on the wrong track. There are many ways to solve a problem like this, and the code in Listing 6-8 shows you just one way to do it.

When you create a Java thread, you write a method named run. To get the thread going, you don't call the run method. Instead, you call the thread's start method. That's why, in Listing 6-8, you see the statement noteThread.start().

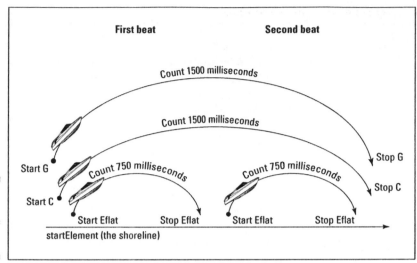

First beat **Second beat**

Count 1500 milliseconds

Count 1500 milliseconds

Start G

Stop G

Count 750 milliseconds   Count 750 milliseconds

Stop C

Start C

Start Eflat   Stop Eflat   Start Eflat   Stop Eflat

startElement (the shoreline)

Figure 6-9:
Boats in
place of
notes.

The endDocument method

The song-playing problem gives you an interesting excuse to use the SAX `endDocument` method. When all the code in Listing 6-8 runs its course, some of the threads that you've created are still dangling in midair. If you do nothing about it, then the Java Virtual Machine just sits there, waiting for nothing in particular to happen. Depending on how you got the program to start running, you may not see your command prompt again, even after the song has finished playing. To remedy this unsightly situation, I write my own `endDocument` method.

When the parser reaches the end of the document, the callback to the `endDocument` method executes `System.exit(0)`. This command tells the Java Virtual Machine to halt its execution. When the virtual machine's execution stops, your get your command prompt back.

The music classes

We're examining all the code that plays music on your computer's sound card. With the content handler in Listing 6-8 out of the way, the only thing left to do is to look at the music-specific classes. There are three such classes, each more boring than the one before it. (Sometimes, after a long look at some intense code, a little boredom is very refreshing.) The classes are shown in Listings 6-9, 6-10, and 6-11.

Listing 6-9: The Song Class

```
import javax.sound.midi.MidiChannel;
import javax.sound.midi.Synthesizer;
import javax.sound.midi.MidiSystem;
import javax.sound.midi.MidiUnavailableException;

public class Song
{
   private MidiChannel channel;
   private int tempo;
   private final int altoSax = 65;


   public Song ()
   {
      MidiChannel[] channels = null;

      try
      {
         Synthesizer synth = MidiSystem.getSynthesizer();
         synth.open();
         channels = synth.getChannels();
      }
      catch (MidiUnavailableException e)
      {
         e.printStackTrace();
      }

      channel = channels[0];
      channel.programChange(altoSax);
   }


   public MidiChannel getMidiChannel()
   {
      return channel;
   }


   public void setTempo(String tempo)
   {
      this.tempo = Integer.parseInt(tempo);
   }


   public int getTempo()
   {
      return tempo;
   }
}
```

The Song class (Listing 6-9) defines what it means to have a tempo, and to have a usable MIDI channel. My music markup language is so simple that an entire song has to have just one tempo. As for the MIDI channel, you need that in order to send tones to your computer's sound card.

The MIDI channel in Listing 6-9 is meant to sound like an alto SAXophone. (I couldn't resist the pun.) To be truthful, when I run the program, the music sounds more like a generic electronic squawk than a saxophone. Anyway, you're a Java/XML expert, not a MIDI sound expert, right? (But of course.) You can just copy this code and paste it into your own application.

To hear tones with better definition, you can experiment with other musical instruments. Change the number 65 in Listing 6-9 to some other numbers. Try 1 for a bright piano sound.

Listing 6-10: The Measure Class

```
public class Measure
{
    private int beatlength;

    public Measure(Song song, String beatlength)
    {
        this.beatlength =
            (int)( song.getTempo() *
                    Double.parseDouble(beatlength) );
    }

    public int getBeatlength ()
    {
        return beatlength;
    }
}
```

The Measure class is shown in Listing 6-10. For a particular measure, I make the beatlength be the duration of the measure's shortest note.

- ✔ If I have a measure with an eighth note in it, I make the measure's beatlength be &eighth;. I put eight beat elements in that measure, even if some of the beat elements are empty. (Those empty beat elements just preserve the measure's timing.) See Listing 6-6.

- ✔ For a measure containing only quarter notes, I make the beatlength be &quarter;. In that case, I put four beat elements into the measure. (Again, see Listing 6-6.)

Listing 6-11:   The Note Class

```
public class Note implements Runnable
{
   private Song song;
   private int pitch;
   private int velocity=70;
   private int duration;


   public Note(Song song)
   {
      this.song = song;
   }


   public void setPitch(String pitch)
   {
      this.pitch = Integer.parseInt(pitch);
   }


   public void setOctave(String octave)
   {
      pitch += 12*Integer.parseInt(octave);
   }


   public void setVelocity(String velocity)
   {
      if (velocity != null)
         this.velocity = Integer.parseInt(velocity);
   }


   public void setDuration(String duration)
   {
      this.duration =
              (int)( Double.parseDouble(duration) *
                     song.getTempo() );
   }


   public void setDotted(String dotted)
   {
      if (Boolean.getBoolean(dotted))
         duration = (int)(1.5 * duration);
   }


   public void run()
```

(continued)

Listing 6-11 *(continued)*

```
    {
        song.getMidiChannel().noteOn(pitch, velocity);
        try
        {
            Thread.sleep(duration);
        }
        catch (InterruptedException e)
        {
            e.printStackTrace();
        }
        song.getMidiChannel().noteOff(pitch);
    }
}
```

The Note class (Listing 6-11) buries all the details about playing a single note. For instance, the Note class knows how to handle dotted notes, and knows to multiply the duration by the tempo. Because the Note class has a run method, every note object can be run as an individual thread. The run method turns a note on, then does nothing for the right number of milliseconds, and (finally) turns the note off.

Congratulations! You are now one of the secret society of savants who can play music from an XML document.

Chapter 7

Scanning Data from the Inside Out (Using DOM)

In This Chapter

▶ Understanding the Document Object Model

▶ Using the DOM node types

▶ Writing basic DOM code

There are two kinds of people in this world — linear thinkers and holistic thinkers. A linear thinker starts each project at the beginning, and works cautiously toward the end; a holistic thinker blasts straight into the middle of every project.

> ✔ Put two people beside a swimming pool in 65-degree weather. The linear thinker starts with a big toe and proceeds with the immersion, body part by body part. The holistic thinker just takes a dive.
>
> ✔ Seat two ill-mannered people at the dinner table. The linear thinker arranges peas on a knife. The holistic thinker goes in face first.
>
> ✔ Start a big Java programming project at work. The linear thinker says "Let's form a committee." The holistic thinker says "@#!% your stinking committee."

Each approach has its advantages — and its limitations. XML code, no less than the human beings that create it, is amenable to a linear (SAX) or a holistic (DOM) approach. This chapter explains how — and what those differences are good for.

Introducing DOM: The Document Object Model

Let's look at two ways to think about an XML document. An XML document has at least two incarnations.

✔ On the one hand, the document is a list. It's just one word after another. One tag ends and another tag begins. That's one way to think about the document. It's the way a linear thinker approaches an XML document.

✔ What's underneath all this linear text? In fact, an XML document really represents a tree. The document is an element within an element within yet another element.

So how do you climb those trees? Well, one way (the holistic way) is to grab all the gusto you can get. Start by working with the whole tree. Later on, narrow your focus to the tree's parts. But narrow your focus in a way that respects the tree's structure. Deal with one branch at a time, with all of its sub-branches and sub-sub-branches. Treat each branch as if it were a tree in its own right.

This dichotomy between linear thinking and holistic thinking separates (respectively) SAX from DOM. SAX (the stuff in Chapters 3 through 6) treats an XML document linearly. But with DOM (the *Document Object Model*), you jump in and look at the whole document. A bit later, you zoom in on the root element, and then focus more closely on an element within the root element. In some situations, jumping in is exactly what you need to do.

DOM nodes

With DOM, you think of an XML document as having several *nodes*. Examples of nodes include elements, attributes, comments, and the characters between a pair of start and end tags. An entire XML document is itself a node. All in all, an XML document can have twelve different types of nodes. (There's a list of node types later in this chapter.)

The nodes of a tree

Taken together, all the DOM nodes in an XML document form a tree. Take, for instance, the document in Listing 7-1. This document's DOM tree looks like the tree shown in Figure 7-1.

Listing 7-1:   The Anchovy Lovers Club

```
<?xml version="1.0" encoding="UTF-8"?>
<!--AnchovyLoversClub.xml-->

<AnchovyLoversClub>
    <Member firstname="Herbert">
        <Standing>
            Founder, President, Secretary, Publicity Manager
        </Standing>
    </Member>
</AnchovyLoversClub>
```

The tree has eleven nodes. To count them, start by counting the tree's branches (conveniently displayed in Figure 7-1). Then count the Member firstname = "Herbert" branch a second time. (This branch has two DOM nodes on it. The element named Member is a node, and the element's attribute firstname="Herbert" is a node.)

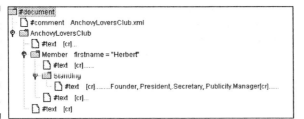

Figure 7-1:
A tree
representing
the
document in
Listing 7-1.

A treatise on trees

There are a few things you'll discover by staring at the tree in Figure 7-1.

✔ **Some nodes are children of other nodes.**

For instance, the Member node is a *child* of the AnchovyLoversClub node. That's because, in Listing 7-1, the Member element is nested inside the AncoverLoversClub element.

In a similar way, the Standing node is a child of the Member node. This family analogy goes on and on. The Member node is the *parent* of the Standing node, and the AncoverLoversClub is the parent of the Member node.

✔ **The entire document is a node.**

This is an important point, and it's really easy to forget. In Listing 7-1, the document's root element is AnchovyLoversClub. But in Figure 7-1, the name AnchovyLoversClub isn't at the top of the tree. Instead, the word #document is at the top of the tree.

A DOM tree's topmost node represents an entire XML document. I've seen error after error caused by programmers thinking that the document's root element starts the tree. (It doesn't. And when I say "programmers," I mean me.)

✔ **Comments and pieces of text are nodes.**

In Figure 7-1, the comment <!—AnchovyLoversClub.xml—> is a child node of the document node. That's because, in Listing 7-1, the comment is part of the document. The comment isn't nested inside any of the document's elements.

Once again, we play genealogy. We say that the #document node has two children — a comment node and an AnchovyLoversClub node. These two nodes — the comment and the AnchovyLoversClub — are called *siblings.*

Also in Figure 7-1, the text Founder, President, Secretary, Publicity Manager is part of a node. In Listing 7-1, the text Founder, President, Secretary, Publicity Manager is inside the Standing element. So, in Figure 7-1, this text node is a child of the Standing node.

✔ **Even ignorable text is part of a node.**

According to Figure 7-1, the AnchovyLoversClub node has three direct child nodes — two nodes labeled #text, and another node labeled Member. That's because, as far as DOM is concerned, the AnchovyLoversClub node has three things in it.

```
<AnchovyLoversClub>
    carriage return and three blanks
    Member element
    carriage return
</AnchovyLoversClub>
```

The situation is illustrated in Figure 7-2.

The three children of the Member node — two pieces of whitespace and one Standing element — are all siblings.

Now, notice the dots and the [cr] in Figures 7-1 and 7-2. In the tree diagram, I use a dot to represent a blank space, and I use [cr] to represent a carriage return. With DOM, all the ignorable whitespace between the AnchovyLoversClub start tag and the Member start tag forms a node. Starting with the angle bracket that terminates the AnchovyLoversClub start tag, you go to the next line, and then you have three blank spaces before the angle bracket that opens the Member start tag. All that stuff is a DOM node.

Figure 7-2:
Two text
nodes in
Listing 7-1.

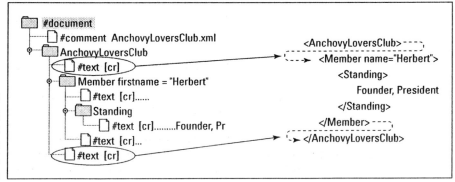

✔ **End tags aren't nodes.**

If you digested the SAX material in Chapters 3 through 6, you may be thinking in terms of starting the Member element, and later ending the Member element. In DOM, you don't think this way. Instead, you visit the Member element just once. Within that visit, you visit the Standing element and some text. DOM has no method corresponding to the SAX endElement method.

SAX versus DOM (a battle of bits)

At this point in our story, it's standard practice to compare the two APIs — SAX and DOM. SAX was the topic of Chapters 3 through 6, and DOM is the topic of Chapters 7 through 9. Well, SAX and DOM are quite different animals. Here's a slogan you can use:

SAX does; DOM is.

When you work with SAX, you get a parser that calls methods. But DOM doesn't call methods. Instead, DOM creates a new object. This new object is an image of an XML document's data. The image exists inside the computer's memory.

Two versions of the data

It helps to think about two versions of an XML document's data.

✔ There's a "paper" version of the data — but usually this "paper" isn't really hard copy. It's a file on a hard drive. I call this a "paper" copy because you can see the copy if you want. You can examine the characters in the file (the angle brackets, the tags, and all the other text) by opening the file in your favorite editor.

✔ When you run a DOM program, you get an in-memory DOM version of the data. This DOM version has all the information that a "paper" version would have, but the DOM version has no inherent textual representation. The DOM version is a tree, with element nodes, attribute nodes, and all the other kinds of nodes. Sure, you may have a graphical visualization for the DOM tree, like the visualization in Figure 7-1. But that visualization isn't the real data. Instead, the data is stored in some structure inside the computer's memory. The data consists of all these DOM nodes, along with all their parent-child and other structural relationships.

Now, when you're working with DOM, you must remember that these two versions of the data (the paper version and the in-memory version) are on equal footing. The invisible, in-memory DOM nodes form a complete, accurate representation of the data. There's nothing sacred about the paper version. You can work with either the paper version or the DOM version; in practice, you often work with both.

Compare this in-memory DOM story with the SAX situation. On the face of things, SAX presents a fairly concrete picture of an XML document's content. You have startElement, endElement, and other such things. It reminds you of the tags in the .xml file. But, in reality, SAX doesn't create an in-memory version of an XML document's data.

Unlike DOM, the SAX API pays little attention to the data's tree structure. SAX takes everything one tag at a time, tossing out each tag when it sees a new tag that's worth examining. SAX says "Ah hah! I've found a start tag!" or "Yikes! Here are some characters!" But SAX doesn't say "I'm inside the AnchovyLoversClub element, and I'm encountering a child Member element." When SAX is done making a callback, SAX leaves no in-memory traces of the document — nor of the document's structure.

A tale of two committees

Here's another way to think about SAX versus DOM.

- ✔ SAX is like an interpreter at a United Nations Security Council meeting. SAX hears a sentence, tells you what it heard, then hears another sentence and tells you what it heard. SAX takes a tag, makes a callback, takes another tag and makes another callback. SAX makes no permanent copy of the data that flies by.

- ✔ DOM is like a translator, sitting quietly in a library cubicle. A foreign language translator takes *Java and XML For Dummies* and makes *Java et XML Pour Les Nuls*. In a way, DOM does the same thing.

  DOM examines a document, and uses the document to create a brand new representation of the data. Like the original document, the new DOM representation is a faithful representation of the data. But the DOM representation is different. The DOM representation uses a different language. In particular, the DOM representation uses structure rather than text.

In a SAX program (like the program in Listings 3-2 and 3-3), you get started by calling a parse method. That parse method responds to XML tags by doing active things — in particular, making callbacks. If, at the end of the program, there's a new copy of the XML data, then it's because of what the callback methods in the content handler did, and not because of what the SAX parser itself did.

In a DOM program, you still call a parse method, but this parse method returns an object of type Document. Like the foreign language translator, a DOM parser does its work, creates a second incarnation of the data, and then hands this incarnation over to someone who uses it.

How to Get Up and Running (A Basic Example)

Our first DOM program displays some nodes from an XML document. The program doesn't display all the nodes, because the program's node-hopping procedure is quite crude. We'll refine the node-hopping procedure later in this chapter. In the meantime, peruse the code in Listings 7-2 and 7-3.

Listing 7-2:   Calling DOM into Action

```java
import javax.xml.parsers.DocumentBuilderFactory;
import javax.xml.parsers.DocumentBuilder;
import javax.xml.parsers.ParserConfigurationException;
import org.xml.sax.SAXException;
import java.io.IOException;
import java.io.File;
import org.w3c.dom.Document;


public class CallDOM
{
    public static void main(String args[])
        throws ParserConfigurationException,
               SAXException,
               IOException
    {
        DocumentBuilderFactory factory =
            DocumentBuilderFactory.newInstance();
        DocumentBuilder builder =
            factory.newDocumentBuilder();
        Document doc;


        if (args.length == 1)
        {
            doc = builder.parse
                (new File(args[0]).toURL().toString());
            new MyTreeTraverser (doc);
        }
        else
            System.out.println
                ("Usage: java CallDOM file-name.xml");


    }

}
```

Listing 7-3: Displaying a Few Nodes

```
import org.w3c.dom.Node;
import org.w3c.dom.NamedNodeMap;


class MyTreeTraverser
{

  MyTreeTraverser (Node node)
    {
       System.out.println(node.getNodeName());


       node = node.getFirstChild();
       System.out.println(node.getNodeName());

       node = node.getNextSibling();
       System.out.println(node.getNodeName());

       node = node.getFirstChild();
       System.out.println(node.getNodeName());

       node = node.getNextSibling();
       System.out.println(node.getNodeName());
    }

}
```

Run the code in Listings 7-2 and 7-3 against the AnchovyLoversClub document in Listing 7-1. The output you get is shown in Figure 7-3.

Figure 7-3:
Visiting
a few
nodes in a
DOM tree.

```
#document
#comment
AnchovyLoversClub
#text
Member
```

Calling DOM

The program that starts the ball rolling (the code in Listing 7-2) is no big deal. If you read about the corresponding SAX code, you'll see very few differences. (See the explanation of Listing 3-2 in Chapter 3.) The only important difference is how the parser operates:

✔ In the SAX code of Listing 3-2, the last thing you did was to call the parser. From there on, the parser took over, and made all the appropriate callbacks.

✔ In the new DOM code of Listing 7-2, you still call a parser. But this DOM parser returns an object to you. (In the code of Listing 7-2, the variable doc points to that returned object.)

The DOM parser makes no callbacks. Instead, you take the doc object returned to you by the parser, and you plug that object into a call to some other method. In Listing 7-2, you do this by calling

```
new MyTreeTraverser (doc);
```

The name MyTreeTraverser is something that I made up. It's a class that drills deep down into the doc object, and displays the doc object's parts.

In Chapter 3, I mentioned that I'd be using SAX calling code (the code in Listing 3-2) over and over again. Well, the same is true of the DOM-calling code in Listing 7-2. I use, reuse, and re-reuse the same CallDOM class in Chapters 7, 8, and 9. So just read about CallDOM once in this section, and then flash it back into your mind for almost every other DOM program.

Processing the DOM result

The code in Listing 7-3 is crude indeed. To make the code look a little better, I could have created a little for loop. But the for loop wouldn't have made the code any better. Instead, the loop would have obscured the code's basic crudeness.

Anyway, Listing 7-3 has its bad points and its good points. The two bad points are

✔ The code is shamefully repetitious.

✔ The code doesn't visit every node in the document's tree.

But there's a bright side. The two good points are

✔ The code shows you how to hop from one DOM node to another.

✔ The code motivates us to come up with a better overall node-hopping strategy.

So notice what happens in Listing 7-3 and in Figure 7-3. The MyTreeTraverser constructor makes successive calls to methods getFirstChild and getNextSibling. For each call, the constructor moves on to a different node in the DOM tree.

The topmost node (the node handed to the constructor by the call in Listing 7-2) is the node named #document. This #document node represents the entire XML document shown in Listing 7-1.

After displaying the name of this #document node, the MyTreeTraverser constructor calls method getFirstChild. This call makes the node variable point to the comment in Listing 7-1. Now look at Figure 7-1 and notice that the comment isn't an only child. The comment has one sibling — namely, the AnchovyLoversClub element. So, after calling getNextSibling, the code in Listing 7-3 displays the name AnchovyLoversClub.

The action continues in this way until we've drilled down to the Member element. At that point we stop and say, "Thank you, Barry. This use of getFirstChild and getNextSibling is very enlightening. But there must be a smoother way to travel from one node to the next."

And indeed there is. I show you a better way in the very next section.

Swinging from Node to Node on a Tree

Our next DOM program displays all the nodes in an XML document. In order to do this, we need a special trick. The trick is called *recursion*.

The document we're going to display is the AnchovyLoversClub document, back in Listing 7-1. To do the displaying, we'll reuse the CallDOM class from Listing 7-2. In addition, we'll create a brand new MyTreeTraverser class (shown in Listing 7-4.)

Listing 7-4:   Traversing the DOM Tree

```
import org.w3c.dom.Node;
import org.w3c.dom.NamedNodeMap;


class MyTreeTraverser
{
    Node node;


    MyTreeTraverser (Node node)
    {
        this.node = node;

        displayName();
        displayValue();
        if (node.getNodeType() == Node.ELEMENT_NODE)
```

```
            displayAttributes();

      System.out.println();

      displayChildren();
   }


   void displayName()
   {
      System.out.print("Name: ");
      System.out.println(node.getNodeName());
   }


   void displayValue()
   {
      String nodeValue = node.getNodeValue();
      if (nodeValue != null)
         nodeValue = nodeValue.trim();

      System.out.print("Value: ");
      System.out.println(nodeValue);
   }


   void displayAttributes()
   {
      NamedNodeMap attribs = node.getAttributes();

      for (int i = 0; i < attribs.getLength(); i++)
      {
         System.out.println();
         System.out.print("Attribute: ");
         System.out.print(attribs.item(i).getNodeName());
         System.out.print(" = ");
         System.out.println(attribs.item(i).getNodeValue());
      }
   }


   void displayChildren()
   {
      Node child = node.getFirstChild();
      while (child != null)
      {
         new MyTreeTraverser (child);
         child = child.getNextSibling();
      }
   }
}
```

The output of a run of Listings 7-2 and 7-4 is shown in Figure 7-4.

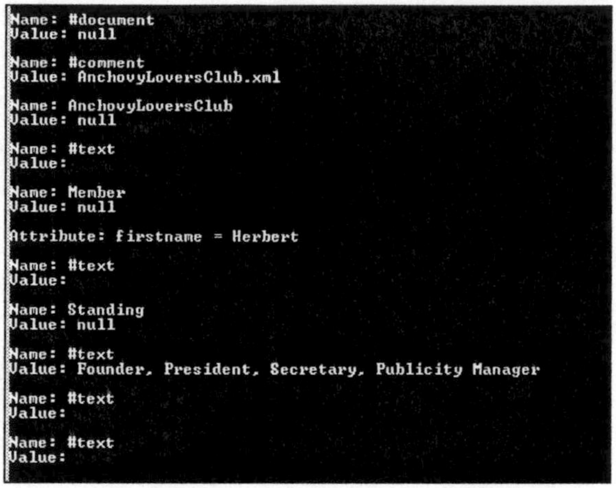

```
Name: #document
Value: null

Name: #comment
Value: AnchovyLoversClub.xml

Name: AnchovyLoversClub
Value: null

Name: #text
Value:

Name: Member
Value: null

Attribute: firstname = Herbert

Name: #text
Value:

Name: Standing
Value: null

Name: #text
Value: Founder, President, Secretary, Publicity Manager

Name: #text
Value:

Name: #text
Value:
```

Figure 7-4:
The output
of the code
in Listings
7-2 and 7-4.

Understanding the MyTreeTraverser class

The main method in Listing 7-2 calls the MyTreeTraverser constructor. When this happens, the constructor does four things: It displays the node's name, the node's value, the node's attributes, and the node's children. The constructor performs these wonderful tasks by making method calls.

The first two calls are relatively simple. One call uses the DOM node's getNodeValue method, and the second call uses the node's getNodeName method. What counts as a name (as opposed to a value) differs from one node to another. Look, for instance, at Figure 7-4:

✔ There's a node with name Standing, and no value. All element nodes work this way.

✔ There's a node with name #text, and value Founder, President, Secretary, Publicity Manager. All text nodes work this way.

Introducing DOM node types

In XML, only elements have attributes. No other DOM nodes (like the document node, or any of the text nodes) have attributes. So, before your program launches into attribute-handling code, you should check to make sure you're dealing with an element.

In the `MyTreeTraverser` constructor (Listing 7-4), you perform the check by calling the `getNodeType` method.

```
if (node.getNodeType() == Node.ELEMENT_NODE)
   displayAttributes();
```

Java's `org.w3c.dom.Node` interface has twelve constants — one for each type of DOM node. In Listing 7-4, I test the node's type to see if the node has value `Node.ELEMENT_NODE`. Other node type constants include `Node.COMMENT_NODE`, `Node.ATTRIBUTE_NODE`, and `Node.TEXT_NODE`. (A rundown on all the DOM node types comes later in this chapter.)

Getting Attributes

To get an element's attributes, you make yourself a `NamedNodeMap`. (See Listing 7-4.) Then you step through the map, item-by-item, calling `getNodeName` and `getNodeValue` for each attribute.

Notice the use of the word "node" in the names `NamedNodeMap`, `getNodeName`, and `getNodeValue`. Each attribute of an element is really a separate DOM node.

Only element nodes have attributes but, of course, some elements have no attributes. In the DOM API, there's an easy way to find out if any node (element or not) has any attributes. Just call the node's `hasAttributes` method.

Children

The most interesting part of the `MyTreeTraverser` class is the action inside the `displayChildren` method. To understand the action, think about the way you'd go about climbing a real tree. Imagine that you need to visit every single branch of the tree.

```
Start at the tree trunk.
Climb up until the trunk divides into branches.
For each branch:
   Start at the bottom of the branch.
   Climb up until the branch divides into smaller branches.
   For each smaller branch:
      Start at the bottom of the smaller branch.
      Climb up until you reach even smaller branches.
      For each even smaller branch:

         ...
      And so on.
```

The point is, you climb a tree by going up a certain distance, and then climbing smaller sub-trees. So the instructions for climbing a branch are the same as those for climbing the whole tree. To see this more clearly, imagine the following (bizarre) scenario:

> *You have amnesia, and you find yourself holding onto a tree trunk. Instead of looking down, you start shimmying up the trunk. When you get to some branching, you choose one of the branches, and continue to climb. This is a very thick branch so, while you're climbing it,...*

> *You suddenly develop another case of amnesia. You don't look down so, since the branch is so thick, you think you're holding onto a whole tree trunk. You start shimmying up the trunk. When you get to some branching, . . .*

Well the basic idea is, processing each piece of a tree is just like processing any other piece. To process a branch, you just start the processing all over again. That's why the code to process a tree branch should just call another copy of itself whenever a new branch is about to start. This notion of having code call a copy of itself is known as *recursion*.

Recursion in action

Look again at the code in Listing 7-2. You call the MyTreeTraverser constructor, and you hand the constructor a DOM node. (In Listing 7-2, this DOM node is the entire DOM document.) So now you have a MyTreeTraverser object that processes a particular node.

But what happens in Listing 7-4 when the MyTreeTraverser object processes that node? Well, the object displays the node's name, the node's value, and possibly the node's attributes. Then, the object calls displayChildren, which in turn calls getFirstChild (and later, getNextSibling).

With each call to getFirstChild or getNextSibling, the MyTreeTraverser object grabs one node's child. Of course, a node's child is yet another node. So, to process the node's child, the MyTreeTraverser object calls the MyTreeTraverser constructor. In other words, one MyTreeTraverser object calls a constructor that creates another MyTreeTraverser object. (Look at the bold text in Listing 7-4.)

That brand new MyTreeTraverser object processes a child node. Like all good children, the child node's code will eventually reach the displayChildren method, which will, in turn, construct more MyTreeTraverser objects. This whole business (a MyTreeTraverser object's creating another MyTreeTraverser object) is illustrated in Figure 7-5.

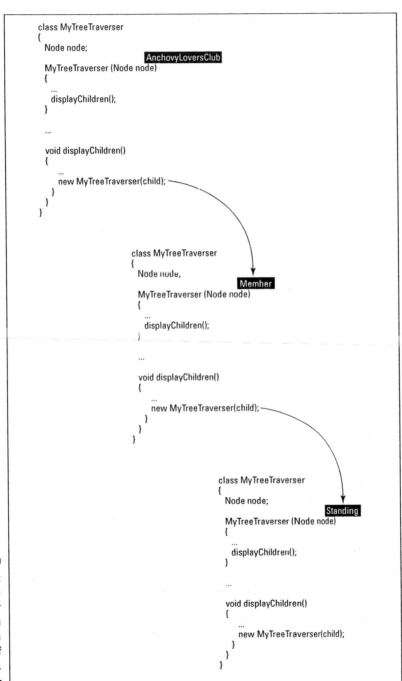

Figure 7-5:
A MyTree
Traverser
object can
spawn a
copy of
itself.

DOM Node Types

The code in Listing 7-4, calls a method named `getNodeType` and uses a constant named `Node.ELEMENT_NODE`. In DOM, every node has a type. There's the `ELEMENT_NODE` type, the `ATTRIBUTE_NODE` type, and other node types. In fact, DOM has twelve different types of nodes.

When you call the `getNodeType` method (as in Listing 7-4), the method returns a number from 1 to 12. Happily enough, the Java API has 12 `Node.blah_blah_blah_NODE` constants, and the constants have values 1 to 12. So you seldom need to refer to a node's type by number. Instead, you refer to each node's type by one of the constant names.

Table 7-1 has a list of node type constant names in the Java API.

Table 7-1	**DOM Node Types**		
Constant	*Numeric Value*	*nodeName*	*nodeValue*
`ELEMENT_NODE`	1	Tag name	Null
`ATTRIBUTE_NODE`	2	Name of the attribute	Value of the attribute
`TEXT_NODE`	3	"#text"	Content of the text node
`CDATA_SECTION_NODE`	4	"#cdata-section"	Content of CDATA the Section
`ENTITY_REFERENCE_NODE`	5	Name of the referenced entity	Null
`ENTITY_NODE`	6	Entity name	Null
`PROCESSING_INSTRUCTION_NODE`	7	Target	Entire content excluding the target
`COMMENT_NODE`	8	"#comment"	Content of the comment
`DOCUMENT_NODE`	9	"#document"	Null

Constant	Numeric Value	nodeName	nodeValue
DOCUMENT_TYPE_NODE	10	Document type name	Null
DOCUMENT_FRAGMENT_NODE	11	"#document-fragment"	Null
NOTATION_NODE	12	Notation name	Null

Strictly speaking, Java's node type constants are not int values. Each node type constant is a value of type short, and a call to the getNodeType method returns a value of type short.

There's more information on DOM node types on the org.w3c.dom.Node page of the official Java 1.4 API documentation.

Node type constants, such as Node.ELEMENT_NODE, aren't just for convenience. The use of a constant helps avoid errors, and helps keep your code from becoming obsolete. Never put a type number (a number from 1 to 12) in your code. (Well, don't do it unless someone twists your arm and leaves you no other choice.)

Understanding the node types

The DOM API has 12 node type constants. So what do all these node type constants mean? Some of them, like Node.ELEMENT_NODE, are easy to figure out. But others like, Node.DOCUMENT_FRAGMENT_NODE, may be a bit more obscure. To illustrate the node type constants, I've created a sample XML document. The document, with nodes labeled, appears in Figures 7-6 and 7-7. For a cleaner view of the document (without all the node label clutter), see Listing 7-5.

Listing 7-5:   What Your Cat Thinks About

```
<?xml version="1.0" encoding="UTF-8"?>

<!DOCTYPE CatThoughts
[
    <!ELEMENT CatThoughts (Image, Thought+)>
```

(continued)

Listing 7-5 *(continued)*

```
    <!ATTLIST CatThoughts frequency CDATA #REQUIRED>

    <!NOTATION JPEG SYSTEM "image/jpeg">
    <!ENTITY CuteCat SYSTEM "weelie.jpg" NDATA JPEG>
    <!ELEMENT Image EMPTY>
    <!ATTLIST Image source ENTITY #REQUIRED>

    <!ELEMENT Thought (#PCDATA)>
    <!ENTITY meow "Feed me">
]>

<?xml-stylesheet type="text/xsl" href="ThoughtFormat.xsl"?>
<!-- CatThoughts.xml -->

<CatThoughts frequency="high">
    <Image source="CuteCat" />
    <Thought>Eating</Thought>
    <Thought>Grooming</Thought>
    <Thought>Hunting</Thought>
    <Thought>Napping</Thought>
    <Thought>&meow;</Thought>
    <Thought><![CDATA[<nothing>]]></Thought>
</CatThoughts>
```

Figure 7-6:
Some nodes
in an XML
document.

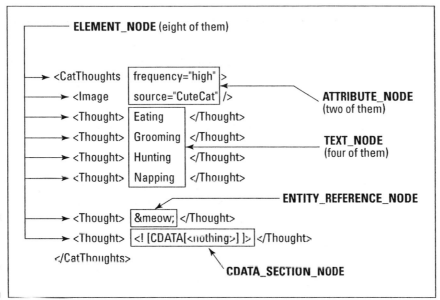

Figure 7-7:
More nodes
in an XML
document.

Of course, I can't throw a document and diagrams at you without making
some observations. So, here are my observations about the stuff in Figures 7-6
and 7-7:

✔ **The line** `<?xml version="1.0" encoding="UTF-8"?>` **isn't a node.**

The DOM philosophy considers this line to be of interest only to the
parser. (This line isn't useful to your Java application — the program
that calls the parser.)

This attitude isn't unique to DOM. Look back at the chapter on SAX.
(Look at the discussion surrounding Listing 5-9.) In that chapter, you see
the same philosophy in action.

✔ **The entire** `DOCTYPE` **declaration has a type of its own.**

The node of type `DOCUMENT_TYPE_NODE` has no children. However, this
node can have entities and notations within it. (The entities and notations
may be inside the `DOCTYPE` declaration. Even so, they're not considered to
be children of the `DOCTYPE` declaration.)

✔ **Nodes of type** `ENTITY_NODE` **and** `NOTATION_NODE` **appear only in
the DTD.**

If you supply a `DOCTYPE` declaration with entities or notations in it, then
the DOM parser will find these nodes. The parser will find these nodes
even if the DTD is in a separate file, and even if the parser isn't set to be
validating.

✔ **The type** ENTITY_REFERENCE_NODE **shows up less often than you'd think.**

Much of the time, an entity reference gets replaced before DOM sees it. For instance, with the document in Listing 7-5, DOM doesn't normally see a node &meow; of type ENTITY_REFERENCE_NODE. Instead, DOM sees a node "Feed me" of type TEXT_NODE.

So why do I label the word &meow; in Figure 7-7 to be of type ENTITY_ REFERENCE_NODE? Well, I can keep the parser from replacing &meow; with "Feed me". To do this, I add the statement

```
factory.setExpandEntityReferences(false);
```

to the code in Listing 7-2. With this line in my code, DOM sees two nodes when it encounters the &meow; line in Listing 7-5. First, DOM sees &meow; and calls it a node of type ENTITY_REFERENCE_NODE. Then DOM sees the substituted text "Feed me", and calls it a node of type TEXT_NODE.

I'll have more to say about the type ENTITY_REFERENCE_NODE in the discussion that goes with Listing 7-6.

✔ **The entire document is a node.**

This idea isn't illustrated in Figures 7-6 and 7-7. I figured yet another label would clutter up the diagrams. Anyway, the document itself is a node of type DOCUMENT_NODE.

✔ **When a document is under construction, a piece of that document can be a** DOCUMENT_FRAGMENT_NODE.

In Chapter 8, there's an example of a DOM program that constructs an XML document from scratch. While you're in the process of constructing a document, you may find yourself holding an incomplete document chunk. The question is, what are you going to call this chunk? It's more than an element, and less than a whole document. Well, as with anything else in DOM, you call this chunk a Node. And what type of Node is it? It's a DOCUMENT_FRAGMENT_NODE.

Unlike the other types of nodes, a DOCUMENT_FRAGMENT_NODE isn't something that the parser would find in an existing XML document. That's why I don't label anything as a DOCUMENT_FRAGMENT_NODE in Figures 7-6 and 7-7. In order to see a DOCUMENT_FRAGMENT_NODE, you have to take a snapshot of a document being created.

Displaying the node types

To make sure I haven't been lying to you about document node types, I wrote a program to report on the nodes in Listing 7-5. I think it's helpful to see how all these nodes can be reached. The program is in Listing 7-6, and the program's output is in Figure 7-8.

Listing 7-6: **Displaying a Document's Nodes**

```
import org.w3c.dom.Node;
import org.w3c.dom.NamedNodeMap;
import org.w3c.dom.DocumentType;

class MyTreeTraverser
{

  MyTreeTraverser (Node node)
  {
    System.out.println (getNodeInfo(node));

    NamedNodeMap attribs = node.getAttributes();
    visitAll(attribs);


    if (node.getNodeType() == Node.DOCUMENT_TYPE_NODE)
    {
      NamedNodeMap entities =
                    ((DocumentType)node).getEntities();
      visitAll(entities);

      NamedNodeMap notations =
                    ((DocumentType)node).getNotations();
      visitAll(notations);
    }


    Node child = node.getFirstChild();
    while (child != null)
    {
      new MyTreeTraverser(child);
      child = child.getNextSibling();
    }
  }


  final static String [] nodeTypes =
                    {"none",
                     "ELEMENT_NODE",
                     "ATTRIBUTE_NODE",
                     "TEXT_NODE",
                     "CDATA_SECTION_NODE",
                     "ENTITY_REFERENCE_NODE",
                     "ENTITY_NODE",
                     "PROCESSING_INSTRUCTION_NODE",
                     "COMMENT_NODE",
                     "DOCUMENT_NODE",
                     "DOCUMENT_TYPE_NODE",
                     "DOCUMENT_FRAGMENT_NODE",
```

(continued)

Listing 7-6 *(continued)*

```java
                                "NOTATION_NODE"};


   String getNodeInfo(Node node)
   {
      String nodeInfo = nodeTypes[node.getNodeType()];
      nodeInfo += ", ";
      nodeInfo += node.getNodeName();
      nodeInfo += ", ";

      String nodeValue = node.getNodeValue();
      if (nodeValue != null)
      {
         nodeValue = nodeValue.replaceAll("\n", "[cr]");
         nodeValue = nodeValue.replaceAll(" ", ".");
      }
      nodeInfo += nodeValue;

      return nodeInfo;
   }


   void visitAll (NamedNodeMap nodeMap)
   {
      if (nodeMap != null)
         for (int i = 0; i<nodeMap.getLength(); i++)
         {
            Node node = nodeMap.item(i);
            System.out.println (getNodeInfo(node));
         }
   }
}
```

Figure 7-8:
Listing the
nodes in the
Cat
Thoughts
document.

```
DOCUMENT_NODE, #document, null
DOCUMENT_TYPE_NODE, CatThoughts, null
ENTITY_NODE, CuteCat, null
ENTITY_NODE, meow, null
NOTATION_NODE, JPEG, null
PROCESSING_INSTRUCTION_NODE, xml-stylesheet, type="text/xsl".href="ThoughtFormat.xsl"
COMMENT_NODE, #comment, .CatThoughts.xml.
ELEMENT_NODE, CatThoughts, null
ATTRIBUTE_NODE, frequency, high
TEXT_NODE, #text, [cr]...
ELEMENT_NODE, Image, null
ATTRIBUTE_NODE, source, CuteCat
TEXT_NODE, #text, [cr]...
ELEMENT_NODE, Thought, null
TEXT_NODE, #text, Eating
TEXT_NODE, #text, [cr]...
ELEMENT_NODE, Thought, null
TEXT_NODE, #text, Grooming
TEXT_NODE, #text, [cr]...
ELEMENT_NODE, Thought, null
TEXT_NODE, #text, Hunting
TEXT_NODE, #text, [cr]...
ELEMENT_NODE, Thought, null
TEXT_NODE, #text, Napping
TEXT_NODE, #text, [cr]...
ELEMENT_NODE, Thought, null
ENTITY_REFERENCE_NODE, meow, null
TEXT_NODE, #text, Feed.me
TEXT_NODE, #text, [cr]...
ELEMENT_NODE, Thought, null
CDATA_SECTION_NODE, #cdata-section, <nothing>
TEXT_NODE, #text, .[cr]
```

Each line in Figure 7-8 represents a node from the document of Listing 7-5. Each node's line contains three pieces of information. Those three pieces (separated from one another by commas) are the node's type, the node's name, and the node's value. As usual, I've replaced carriage returns with [cr] marks, and I've replaced blank spaces with dots.

In Figure 7-8, notice how many nodes have no value (the null value). To find out why, look again at Table 7-1. According to Table 7-1, only five of the twelve types of nodes have non-null values.

Finding an entity reference node

Now that you have some real output to examine, you can check an earlier claim of mine. When DOM encounters the line with the entity reference &meow; in it, DOM sees two nodes. DOM sees the ENTITY_REFERENCE_NODE named &meow; and the TEXT_NODE with value "Feed me". This happens only if you add the line

```
factory.setExpandEntityReferences(false);
```

to the code that calls the MyTreeTraverser constructor. (Add it to a method like the main method in Listing 7-2.) If you don't add this line, then DOM sees only the "Feed me" TEXT_NODE.

When you create your DOM calling code, put the call to setExpandEntity References before the call to factory.newDocumentBuilder. If you call setExpandEntityReferences after calling newDocumentBuilder, then the call to setExpandEntityReferences will have no noticeable effect. By the time you've called setExpandEntityReferences, you'll have already created the wrong kind of DocumentBuilder.

Recursion: a recurring theme

Notice a similarity between the code in Listings 7-4 and 7-6. Both listings are structured like this:

```
class MyTreeTraverser
{
    Node node;

    MyTreeTraverser (Node node)
    {
        ...
            new MyTreeTraverser(child);
    }
}
```

In both listings, we have a MyTreeTraverser object that calls its own constructor (thus creating yet another MyTreeTraverser object). Both listings use recursion to visit all the nodes in the DOM tree. This isn't surprising (well, not to me, anyway). When you represent an XML document with DOM, you get a tree — and programs that deal with tree structures almost always use recursion.

When to Use the DOM API

I don't know about you, but personally I hate making decisions. Often, I prefer someone else's wrong decision over my own right decision. It doesn't matter how things turn out, as long as I don't feel guilty about the process. Do the ends justify the means? No, maybe they don't. But, for me, the means never justify the ends.

Anyway, after reading such an inspiring paragraph, you'd probably like to know when you should decide to use DOM. The gist of it is, DOM gobbles up an entire XML document all at once. This has both advantages and drawbacks.

✔ **Avoid DOM when you expect your XML document to be very large.**

When you use DOM, the computer creates an in-memory copy of an entire document's tree structure. For the piddling little documents in all the *Java & XML For Dummies* listings, this in-memory storage never amounts to much. But, for a real-life document, the amount of storage can be quite weighty.

Imagine the burden on a system when DOM processes a large document (let's say, 100,000 lines or more). Remember that DOM doesn't store the document's text. Instead, DOM stores a tree structure. DOM plops this structure into RAM and, no matter how much RAM you have, you always run short and need more.

Aside from the storage requirements, jumping back and forth within a large tree structure is time-consuming. DOM is a big octopus, juggling all branches of the tree structure all at once.

In comparison, SAX picks up a tag, deals with the tag, then trashes the tag and moves on. Nothing gets stored over the long term in memory, and no part of the document gets processed along with any other part. In general, SAX programs run more efficiently than DOM programs.

✔ **Use DOM when your document makes heavy use of element nesting.**

Some kinds of problems just scream out for DOM. Imagine that you're dealing with genealogical information. They don't call it a "family tree" for no reason at all. A family has parents, children, and siblings. Hey, where did we hear that terminology before? (Hint: See the start of this DOM chapter.)

The SAX API pays no attention to trees, or to the nesting of one XML element inside another. That's why working with nested structures in SAX is such a pain. In SAX, you're constantly reinventing the wheel by pushing things onto a homemade stack. (See Chapter 6 for details.)

In contrast, DOM makes a stack for you. Sure, you have to write recursive code, and writing recursive code isn't always a picnic. But the whole DOM API presupposes the notion of parent nodes, child nodes, and sibling nodes. When you're dealing with data that's naturally tree-shaped, this parent-child-sibling stuff can be a huge advantage.

✔ **Use DOM when you need a global view of the data.**

What does it take to sort the data in an XML document? Sorting means rearranging data so that the data is in order — numerical order, alphabetical order, or whatever order. Well, when you sort data, you usually jump back and forth between distant places within the data. You move an item from here to a place all the way over to there. You compare this value near the beginning with that value near the end. Sometimes, you jump headfirst into the midst of the data.

The point is, sorting data tends not to be linear. You normally don't start at the beginning and work your way step by step to the end. You don't traverse the data the way SAX does it. Instead, you do what DOM does. You gulp up all the data at once, and then process different pieces in several places. (Coincidentally, there happens to be a very cute sorting method that relies on the storage of data in tree form.)

So, that's the story. SAX takes a microscopic view of the data, and this microscopic view works poorly when you need the big picture. If you're dealing with all the data, all at once, and you're not particularly worried about efficiency or performance, then use DOM instead of SAX.

✔ **Use DOM when you need fine-tuned control.**

This holds true for both SAX and DOM. Neither SAX nor DOM are like the specialized business-to-business APIs. With SAX and DOM, you don't get fast-track coding of the commonly used, high-level tasks.

But both SAX and DOM are good low-level tools. With SAX and DOM, you twiddle with a document's minute, inner details. You do exactly what you want to an XML document, and you do all this on your own terms.

Chapter 8

Useful Tools in the DOM API

* *

In This Chapter

▶ Validating with DOM

▶ Using namespaces

▶ Creating an XML document with DOM code

* *

*L*ike a certain obsessive chapter before it, this chapter fusses about details — here's a method, here's an object, use this interface, don't use that class.

Since I wrote that earlier chapter (well, okay, it's Chapter 5), I've been wondering if there's a connection among the different kinds of details in life. For instance, I'm a packrat. I keep lots of things. Does that say anything about my orientation toward details?

By my reasoning, a person who doesn't keep things should be a non-detail-oriented person. That person has just one guiding principle — throw stuff out; whatever it is, if you need it later, you can get another. I, on the other hand, should be detail-oriented. (No, *don't* throw away that old oil drain pan! You never know when drain pans will be in short supply. Besides, that one is special — it has an annoying leak that sets it apart from all others — a detail worth treasuring. . . .)

In Chapter 5, I said I wasn't a detail person; maybe I should revise that opinion.

A Bag Full of Tricks

Like so much else in life, the DOM API comes in two parts — the big picture and the picky detail stuff. In the big picture, we have parsers, nodes and recursive tree traversal. In the details, we have error checking, namespaces, and some other interesting tricks.

Many DOM tricks are similar (or identical) to the corresponding SAX tricks. So instead of revealing tricks one example at a time, I'll show you a whole bunch of tricks in one program. The program takes an XML document and displays its contents. Well, okay, it *does* work much like the code in Listing 7-4 — but the code in this section takes some enlightening twists and turns.

The document and some needed classes

For our sample XML document, we'll use the Honeymooners.xml file in Listing 8-1. The file's DTD is in Listing 8-2.

Listing 8-1:   Alice, You're da' Greatest!

```
<?xml version="1.0" encoding="UTF-8"?>
<!DOCTYPE tv:Honeymooners SYSTEM "tv.dtd">
<!-- Honeymooners.xml -->

<?debug Errors.log ?>

<tv:Honeymooners xmlns:tv="http://www.burd.org/ns/tv/1.0">
    <tv:Family surname="Kramden"/>
    <tv:Family surname="Norton"/>
</tv:Honeymooners>
```

Listing 8-2:   The TV DTD

```
<?xml version="1.0" encoding="UTF-8"?>
<!-- tv.dtd -->

<!ELEMENT tv:Honeymooners (tv:Family+)>
<!ATTLIST tv:Honeymooners xmlns:tv CDATA #REQUIRED>

<!ELEMENT tv:Family EMPTY>
<!ATTLIST tv:Family surname CDATA #REQUIRED>
```

The program to create a parser isn't very different from some earlier programs of its kind. The big enhancements are validation, namespace awareness, and the use of an error handler. This more sophisticated code is in Listing 8-3. The enhancements are set in bold.

Listing 8-3:   Running DOM with Finesse

```
import javax.xml.parsers.DocumentBuilderFactory;
import javax.xml.parsers.DocumentBuilder;
import javax.xml.parsers.ParserConfigurationException;
import org.xml.sax.SAXException;
import java.io.IOException;
```

```
import java.io.File;
import org.w3c.dom.Document;

public class CallDOM
{
    public static void main(String args[])
        throws ParserConfigurationException,
               SAXException,
               IOException
    {
        DocumentBuilderFactory factory =
            DocumentBuilderFactory.newInstance();
        factory.setValidating(true);
        factory.setNamespaceAware(true);

        DocumentBuilder builder =
            factory.newDocumentBuilder();
        builder.setErrorHandler(new MyErrorHandler());

        Document doc;

        if (args.length == 1)
        {
            doc = builder.parse
                (new File(args[0]).toURL().toString());
            new MyTreeTraverser (doc);
        }
        else
            System.out.println
                ("Usage: java CallDOM file-name.xml");
    }
}
```

So now, with the CallDOM class out of the way, we need two more classes —
a MyTreeTraverser class and an error-handler class. The error-handler class
is simpler, so I'll show that one to you first. It's in Listing 8-4.

Listing 8-4: An Error Handler

```
import org.xml.sax.helpers.DefaultHandler;
import org.xml.sax.SAXParseException;

class MyErrorHandler extends DefaultHandler
{
    public void warning(SAXParseException e)
    {
```

(continued)

Listing 8-4 *(continued)*

```
        System.out.println("Warning:");
        showSpecifics(e);
        System.out.println();
    }

    public void error(SAXParseException e)
    {
        System.out.println("Error:");
        showSpecifics(e);
        System.out.println();
    }

    public void fatalError(SAXParseException e)
    {
        System.out.println("Fatal error:");
        showSpecifics(e);
        System.out.println();
    }

    public void showSpecifics(SAXParseException e)
    {
        System.out.println(e.getMessage());
        System.out.println("   Line " + e.getLineNumber());
        System.out.println("   Column " + e.getColumnNumber());
        System.out.println("   Document " + e.getSystemId());
    }
}
```

Is there anything about Listing 8-4 that surprises you? If not, then take a careful look. Listing 8-4 is a ripoff of the SAX code in Listing 4-4. (Gee, maybe I'll hear from my lawyer. It'll be the world's first recursive lawsuit.) Listing 8-4 even uses SAXParseException, like the code in Listing 4-4. So what's up?

Well, having DOM fall back on SAX isn't new. Way back in Listing 7-2, we had a DOM program importing org.xml.sax.SAXException. So this new code, Listing 8-4, just goes all the way. The code unabashedly handles SAX exceptions, and does everything (and only the things) that Listing 4-4 does. That's just the way it works.

The heart of the DOM code

Let's move on to our feature presentation. The code to display information about Honeymooners.xml is in Listing 8-5, and the code's output is in Figure 8-1.

Listing 8-5:   Traversing the DOM Tree

```
import org.w3c.dom.Node;
import org.w3c.dom.NamedNodeMap;


class MyTreeTraverser
{
   Node node;

   MyTreeTraverser (Node node)
   {
      this.node = node;

      displayName();
      displayNamespaceStuff();
      displayValue();
      if (node.getNodeType() == Node.ELEMENT_NODE)
         displayAttributes();

      System.out.println();

      displayChildren();
   }


   void displayName()
   {
      System.out.print("Name: ");
      System.out.println(node.getNodeName());
   }


   void displayNamespaceStuff()
   {
      String namespaceURI = node.getNamespaceURI();
      if (namespaceURI != null)
      {
         System.out.print("Namespace URI: ");
         System.out.println(namespaceURI);

         System.out.print("Prefix: ");
         System.out.println(node.getPrefix());

         System.out.print("Local name: ");
         System.out.println(node.getLocalName());
      }
   }


   void displayValue()
```

(continued)

Listing 8-5 *(continued)*

```
   {
      String nodeValue = node.getNodeValue();
      if (nodeValue != null)
         nodeValue = nodeValue.trim();

      System.out.print("Value: ");
      System.out.println(nodeValue);
   }


   void displayAttributes()
   {
      NamedNodeMap attribs = node.getAttributes();

      for (int i = 0; i < attribs.getLength(); i++)
      {
         System.out.println();
         System.out.print("Attribute: ");
         System.out.print(attribs.item(i).getNodeName());
         System.out.print(" = ");
         System.out.println(attribs.item(i).getNodeValue());
      }
   }


   void displayChildren()
   {
      Node child = node.getFirstChild();
      while (child != null)
      {
         new MyTreeTraverser(child);
         child = child.getNextSibling();
      }
   }
}
```

Because the parser in Listing 8-3 is namespace-aware, the calls to
`getNamespaceURI`, `getPrefix`, and `getLocalName` produce useful results.
These results are a lot like the values of the `uri`, prefix, and `localName`
parameters in Listing 5-7. So, if you're in doubt about the meanings of the
results in Figure 8-1, take a gander back at the discussion of Listing 5-7.

While creating Listings 8-1 and 8-2, I decided not to build in a well-formedness
or validation error. If either the document or its DTD were flawed in some
way, then the problem would show up in the output of Figure 8-1.

```
Name: #document
Value: null

Name: tv:Honeymooners
Value: null

Name: #comment
Value: Honeymooners.xml

Name: debug
Value: Errors.log

Name: tv:Honeymooners
Namespace URI: http://www.burd.org/ns/tv/1.0
Prefix: tv
Local name: Honeymooners
Value: null

Attribute: xmlns:tv = http://www.burd.org/ns/tv/1.0

Name: #text
Value:

Name: tv:Family
Namespace URI: http://www.burd.org/ns/tv/1.0
Prefix: tv
Local name: Family
Value: null

Attribute: surname = Kramden

Name: #text
Value:

Name: tv:Family
Namespace URI: http://www.burd.org/ns/tv/1.0
Prefix: tv
Local name: Family
Value: null

Attribute: surname = Norton

Name: #text
Value:
```

Figure 8-1:
Listing the
DOM nodes
in an XML
document.

Using DOM to Make a Document

Until this point in the book, we've analyzed XML documents — in effect,
breaking existing XML documents into tags, elements, nodes, and other
simpler components. But this section works in the opposite direction,
taking chunks of stuff and mushing them together to make a brand new XML
document.

It's no accident that we waited this long to create XML documents. If we were
still working with SAX alone, the task would be nearly impossible. After all, a
SAX program produces no in-memory copy of a document (a point beaten to
death in Chapter 7). Without some copy to work from, it's nearly impossible
to create an XML file.

Building a document from scratch

To build an XML file using the DOM classes in Java, you just run the code in
Listing 8-6. When you run this code, use command-line parameters as follows:

```
java CreateDoc Moose-cara Cowlogne "Hoof Polish"
```

And why do you need command-line parameters? Well, when I wrote the `CreateDoc` program (Listing 8-6), I was aiming for easy reading, rather than good Java programming style. I used Java features that would show how simple it is to create an XML document with DOM. I ignored much of the conventional wisdom about production-quality code. In this example, I think I made the right choice. Judge for yourself by examining Listing 8-6.

Listing 8-6:   Creating an XML Document

```
import org.w3c.dom.Document;
import org.w3c.dom.Element;
import org.w3c.dom.Node;
import org.w3c.dom.ProcessingInstruction;
import org.w3c.dom.Comment;
import org.w3c.dom.Attr;

import javax.xml.parsers.DocumentBuilderFactory;
import javax.xml.parsers.DocumentBuilder;
import javax.xml.parsers.ParserConfigurationException;

import javax.xml.transform.TransformerFactory;
import javax.xml.transform.Transformer;
import javax.xml.transform.OutputKeys;
import
    javax.xml.transform.TransformerConfigurationException;
import javax.xml.transform.TransformerException;

import javax.xml.transform.dom.DOMSource;
import javax.xml.transform.stream.StreamResult;

import java.io.File;

class CreateDoc
{
    static Document doc;
    static Element rootElt;

    public static void main(String args[])
        throws ParserConfigurationException,
               TransformerConfigurationException,
               TransformerException
    {

        makeDOMdoc();
        addProcessingInstruction();
        addComment();
        makeRootElt();
        addAttribute();
        addElements(args);
        outputFile();
```

```
}

static void makeDOMdoc()
   throws ParserConfigurationException
{
   DocumentBuilderFactory factory =
      DocumentBuilderFactory.newInstance();
   DocumentBuilder builder =
      factory.newDocumentBuilder();
   doc = builder.newDocument();
}


static void addProcessingInstruction()
{
   ProcessingInstruction pi =
      doc.createProcessingInstruction
         ("xml-stylesheet",
          "type=\"text/xsl\" href=\"ThoughtFormat.xsl\"");
   doc.appendChild(pi);
}


static void addComment()
{
   Comment comment =
      doc.createComment("Author: H.Ritter");
   doc.appendChild(comment);
}


static void makeRootElt()
{
   rootElt = doc.createElement("BovineBeautyProducts");
   doc.appendChild(rootElt);
}


static void addAttribute()
{
   Attr attrib = doc.createAttribute("customerResponse");
   attrib.setValue("Moo");
   rootElt.setAttributeNode(attrib);
}


static void addElements(String[] args)
{
   for (int i=0; i<args.length; i++)
   {
      Node eltNode = doc.createElement("Item");
```

(continued)

Listing 8-6 *(continued)*

```
            rootElt.appendChild(eltNode);
            Node textNode = doc.createTextNode(args[i]);
            eltNode.appendChild(textNode);
        }
    }


    static void outputFile()
        throws TransformerConfigurationException,
               TransformerException
    {
        File file = new File("BovineBeautyProducts.xml");

        TransformerFactory transformerFactory =
            TransformerFactory.newInstance();
        Transformer transformer =
            transformerFactory.newTransformer();
        transformer.setOutputProperty
                             (OutputKeys.INDENT, "yes");

        DOMSource source = new DOMSource(doc);
        StreamResult result = new StreamResult(file);

        transformer.transform(source, result);
    }
}
```

Your brand new XML document

When you run the code in Listing 8-6, you see no output on the command prompt screen. That's because there are no System.out.print calls in Listing 8-6. Instead of creating command-prompt output, the program creates a new XML file — a file that you can examine with your favorite text editor. The file, which makes its debut in Listing 8-7, goes by the name BovineBeautyProducts.xml.

Listing 8-7: The File BovineBeautyProducts.xml

```
<?xml version="1.0" encoding="UTF-8"?>
<?xml-stylesheet type="text/xsl" href="ThoughtFormat.xsl"?>

<!--Author: H.Ritter-->
<BovineBeautyProducts customerResponse="Moo">
<Item>Moose-cara</Item>
<Item>Cowlogne</Item>
<Item>Hoof Polish</Item>
</BovineBeautyProducts>
```

At the Microsoft Windows command prompt, you can view the contents of the file `BovineBeautyProducts.xml` without a text editor. Just issue the command `type BovineBeautyProducts.xml`.

Steps in the creation of an XML document

I think about the process in Listing 8-6 as a seven-step creation of a new XML document — one step for each of the statements in the `CreateDoc` class's main method. Here are some tidbits about each step:

- **Making a DOM document:** In my method `makeDOMdoc`, I define a `Document` variable. Defining this variable is nothing new. (I defined such a variable in each of my `CallDOM` classes.) What's new is that, in Listing 8-6, I get a `Document` instance by calling `builder.newDocument`. In previous examples (such as Listing 8-3), I got my `Document` instance my calling `builder.parse`. (That is, I got the instance by parsing an existing `.xml` file.)

- **Adding nodes:** In five of the methods in Listing 8-6 (starting with `addProcessingInstruction`, and going all the way down to `addElement`), I add more nodes to the DOM document tree.

  Each kind of node (processing instruction, attribute, element, or whatever) has its own method for being created, and each has its own method for being added to the existing document structure. For instance, to create an attribute node, you call method `createAttribute`. Then, to hang an attribute on the document tree, you call method `setAttributeNode`.

  Note that every `create` method called in Listing 8-6 (`createComment`, `createElement`, and so on) belongs to the code's document object. (For instance, to make a new element node, you call `doc.createElement`.) Why is that fact noteworthy? Well, for one thing, it's counterintuitive; this use of the document object does not attach the newly created node to a place in the document.

  For an example, look at my `addComment` method. First, I use the `doc` object to create a comment. (That is, I call the `doc.createComment` method.) Then, I put the new comment into its place in the document by calling the `doc.appendChild` method.

You use an existing document to create a new node. But, until you've called the `appendChild` method or the `setAttributeNode` method, that new node doesn't have a place to hang in the document's tree.

Without going to some extra effort, you can't use one document to create a node, and then tack the node onto another document's tree. If you try to do so, you get an ugly looking `WRONG_DOCUMENT_ERR` message.

✔ **Creating an .xml file:** The final step in the creation of an .xml file is to do the stuff in my outputFile method (Listing 8-6). Most of the statements in that method are just boilerplate. You can copy them, almost word for word, to create your own .xml file.

Among all the statements in the outputFile method, the statement that tends to vary (from one program to another) is the statement that calls setOutputProperty. The setOutputProperty method changes the look of the resulting XML document. By setting various output properties, you can change the XML document's encoding, its DOCTYPE declaration, and other things that make one document different from another.

In Listing 8-6, I use call setOutputProperty to force the output to have nine lines instead of just three lines. (That's what happens when I set INDENT to "yes".) In a three-line version, everything from the comment onward would be bunched into one long, continuous line.

For a list of transformer properties that you can set, see the OutputKeys page in the Java API documentation.

Chapter 9

DOM Programming Techniques

* *

In This Chapter

▶ More examples using recursion

▶ Doing DOM without a stack

▶ A big case study! Displaying a document in tree form

* *

What an outrage! A reviewer who has read Chapters 7 and 8 believes that I've treated my readers unfairly — discussing *recursion* (a program calling itself — an important topic in DOM processing) without warning readers about the possible psychological dangers. Well, since this chapter uses recursion, I better remedy the situation.

The truth is, recursion relies on self-reference, and there's a long-standing history of insanity associated with the notion of self-reference. When you do recursion, you have (for example) an existing MyTreeTraverser object calling its own constructor. That's self-reference, and self-reference has been shown to be dangerous.

To clarify the nature of the danger, I present several pieces of evidence. Each piece of evidence is taken from official historical records.

▸ **Exhibit A:** From 1874 to 1897, mathematician Georg Cantor publishes a series of papers. In each of these papers, he uses self-reference. He proves that some infinite numbers are larger than others. He also debunks the notion of "everything," by showing that "everything" would have to contain more things than the number of things in it.

Between 1884 and 1891, Cantor suffers one nervous breakdown after another. (Here's my theory. It's his thinking about self-reference that drives Cantor crazy. But that's only a theory. . . .)

▸ **Exhibit B:** In 1901, Bertrand Russell uses self-reference to show that there's no such thing as the "set of all sets." If there is, then the set of all sets is not an element of itself. (Or, as Danny Wright used to say, the set of all knots is not a knot of itself.)

✔ **Exhibit C:** In 1931, Kurt Gödel considers the following sentence: "This is the 289,472,037th sentence, and no one can prove that the 289,472,037th sentence is true." Following up on this reasoning, Gödel demonstrates what every school child knows: Arithmetic is impossibly difficult to understand.

✔ **Exhibit D:** In 1936, Alan Turing studies computer programs that go into infinite loops. He considers writing a program to decide whether other programs will go into infinite loops. Such a program becomes impossibly confused when it tries to decide whether its own run (in which it's trying to make the decision) is performing an infinite loop.

Over time, Turing's discovery turns out to be very comforting. Imagine yourself sitting in front a computer that seems to have hung, but you don't press Ctrl+Alt+Del yet. Maybe, if you wait long enough, the computer will get over the hump and start processing again. You're unsure about that, and you feel really stupid — but Turing's discovery lets you off the hook! There's no way that you, or a certified computer geek, or anyone else, could tell for sure whether your computer *will* eventually revive itself. So go ahead with that three-finger salute. If it's the wrong choice, it's not your fault!

✔ **Exhibit E:** One morning, while opening the mirrored door of my bathroom cabinet, I wonder what would happen if I placed two mirrors directly opposite one another. I try it with the cabinet door, but the alignment isn't right. So I take a big mirror off of the living room wall, and hold it opposite my big bathroom mirror. The alignment is perfect, but there's still one problem. Between the two large mirrors, my head is in the way.

✔ **Exhibit F:** My son brings home an assignment from school. The assignment is to write a question that can't be answered. Wise guy that I am, I think for a while. After a ten-minute pause, I write, "Is 'no' the correct answer to the question that's written on this page?"

And there you have it — the hazards of self-reference that bedevil humans. Fortunately, computers have no inkling that a sticky bog of self-reference may lurk within recursive processes. They just do as they're told. That's where you, the programmer, can save the day with a DOM program — which turns recursion into a useful tool.

No Stacks Please, We're Skittish

As programs go, Listing 6-2 in Chapter 6 is an oldie but a goodie; it keeps track of the pile of mail on my office desk by using that grand old computer programmer's standby, the stack. When you use SAX, you need stacks — to help you remember what element you're working with. Those are the facts when you use SAX.

The goal in this section is to track that same pile of mail using a DOM program. Well, the news is that a DOM program can keep track of the mail without making you worry about a stack. You can think about this in either of two ways:

✔ **DOM doesn't separate the start tag from the end tag.**

When you play the SAX, the parser calls startElement method, then the parser does some other stuff, and then, a bit later, the parser calls the endElement method. Between the startElement method and the endElement method, you may do lots of other things. For instance, you may visit elements within elements.

So, by the time you reach an endElement method, you may have forgotten all about the element's attributes. To keep track of where you are, you have to leave breadcrumbs, and the best place to leave bread crumbs is inside a stack.

With DOM, there's no endElement method. (In fact, there's no startElement method, either.) You don't walk your way from tag to tag. Instead, you just visit a whole element. While you're visiting that element, you may take a side trip to visit the element's children. When you return from processing the children, you find yourself back inside the original element's code.

✔ **When you use recursion, as you do in a DOM program, the computer creates a stack for you behind the scenes.**

Look again at the document in Listing 7-1.

- In processing this document, a DOM program works for a while on the AnchovyLoversClub element. While working on AnchovyLoversClub, the program stumbles upon the Member element.

- The program puts the AnchovyLoversClub element on the back burner. (Yes, think about a frying pan with the words AnchovyLoversClub on it. In your mind, put the pan on the back burner.) With this AnchovyLoversClub temporarily out of the way, the program processes the Member element.

  Then, while working on the Member element, the program stumbles upon the Standing element.

- In order to work on the Standing element, the program puts the Member element on the back burner. Now envision this: the program puts the Member frying pan on top of the old AnchovyLoversClub pan.

- Later on, it comes time to take pans off of the back burner. Because the Member pan is still on top of the AnchovyLoversClub pan, the Member pan will come off of the back burner first.

  This *last in, first out* order is what you get when you visit DOM nodes and use recursion. It's also what happens when you do SAX parsing and form a stack.

A concrete example

With all this talk about not needing a stack, you're probably waiting to see a DOM program work its stackless magic. Well, wait no longer! The code in Listing 9-1 duplicates the work done by the stack in Listing 6-2. This new code works on the same XML document as the code in Chapter 6. (To save your index finger some work, I'm making a copy of the XML document in Listing 6-1. The copy is in Listing 9-2.) The new code's output, identical to the output in Chapter 6, is shown in Figure 9-1.

Listing 9-1: No Stacks, DOM It!

```java
import org.w3c.dom.Node;
import org.w3c.dom.NamedNodeMap;


class MyTreeTraverser
{
    private String day;

    MyTreeTraverser (Node node)
    {

        NamedNodeMap attribs = node.getAttributes();
        day = attribs.getNamedItem("day").getNodeValue();

        Node child = node.getFirstChild();
        while (child != null)
        {
            String childNodeName = child.getNodeName();
            if (childNodeName.equals("Mail"))
                new MyTreeTraverser(child);
            if (childNodeName.equals("Item"))
                handleItem(child);

            child = child.getNextSibling();
        }
    }


    void handleItem(Node child)
    {
        String text = child.getFirstChild().getNodeValue();
        if (text != null && !text.equals(""))
        {
            System.out.print("Received ");
            System.out.print(day);
            System.out.print("-\t");
            System.out.println(text);
        }
    }
}
```

Listing 9-2:   The Same Desk, Three Chapters Later

```
<?xml version="1.0" encoding="UTF-8"?>
<!--ClutteredDesk.xml-->

<Mail day="Monday">
   <Mail day="Tuesday">
      <Mail day="Wednesday">
         <Item>Client: Let's close that deal.</Item>
      </Mail>
      <Item>Bank: Get a home equity loan today!</Item>
      <Item>Telephone: Switch carriers today!</Item>
   </Mail>
   <Item>Boss: Do this ASAP.</Item>
</Mail>
```

Figure 9-1:
Displaying
mail with a
date stamp.

```
Received Wednesday-    Client: Let's close that deal.
Received Tuesday-      Bank: Get a home equity loan today!
Received Tuesday-      Telephone: Switch carriers today!
Received Monday-       Boss: Do this ASAP.
```

Starting with the root element

To get the code in Listing 9-1 running, you need a CallDOM class like the one
in Listing 7-2. In fact, if you steal the Listing 7-2 code, there's just one change
you need to make. Instead of calling

```
new MyTreeTraverser (doc);
```

you must call

```
new MyTreeTraverser (doc.getDocumentElement());
```

With this change, your first MyTreeTraverser object gets the document's
root element (the outermost Mail element), instead of getting the document
node itself. That's good because the first thing the MyTreeTraverser
constructor does is to look for a day attribute. In Listing 9-2, only the Mail
elements have day attributes.

I can't emphasize this enough: The top of a DOM tree is ordinarily *not* an XML
document's root element. Instead, the top of the DOM tree is an *entire* XML
document.

Because I can't overemphasize this point, I'll say the same thing in a slightly more technical way: In Listing 9-1, the call to the `parse` method returns a node of type `DOCUMENT_NODE`, not a node of type `ELEMENT_NODE`.

How recursion replaces a stack

Once your main program creates its first `MyTreeTraverser` object, then that `MyTreeTraverser` object creates a second object which, in turn, creates a third object. It's almost a snowball effect. To make this clearer (and a bit more boring), I will describe the work of Listing 9-1 in several steps. While you read, keep one eye on the bold print in Listing 9-1.

 ✔ **The** `MyTreeTraverser` **object gets a value for its** `day` **variable.**

In Listing 9-1, the day variable's value comes from the Mail tag's day attribute. Notice the cool use of the `getNamedItem` method. When you know the name of an attribute, you can use this method to scoop up the attribute's value.

The first time around, this day variable has the value `Monday`. (See the "1" bubble in Figure 9-2.)

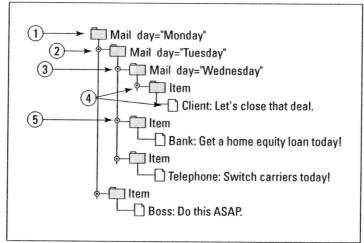

Figure 9-2:
The DOM tree for Cluttered Desk.xml.

 ✔ **The** `MyTreeTraverser` **object calls its own constructor, creating a second** `MyTreeTraverser` **object.**

When the second `MyTreeTraverser` calls

```
attribs.getNamedItem("day").getNodeValue();
```

the value returned by the call is Tuesday. This happens because the second MyTreeTraverser object is working with the second of the document's Mail elements. (See Figure 9-3, and follow along in Figure 9-2 by looking at the node with bubbled label "2".)

Now, here's the important part. If you take a snapshot of the action that I've described so far, you have two objects from the MyTreeTraverser class. The first object has day Monday, and the second object has day Tuesday. In the snapshot, both objects exist simultaneously. (Again, see Figure 9-3.)

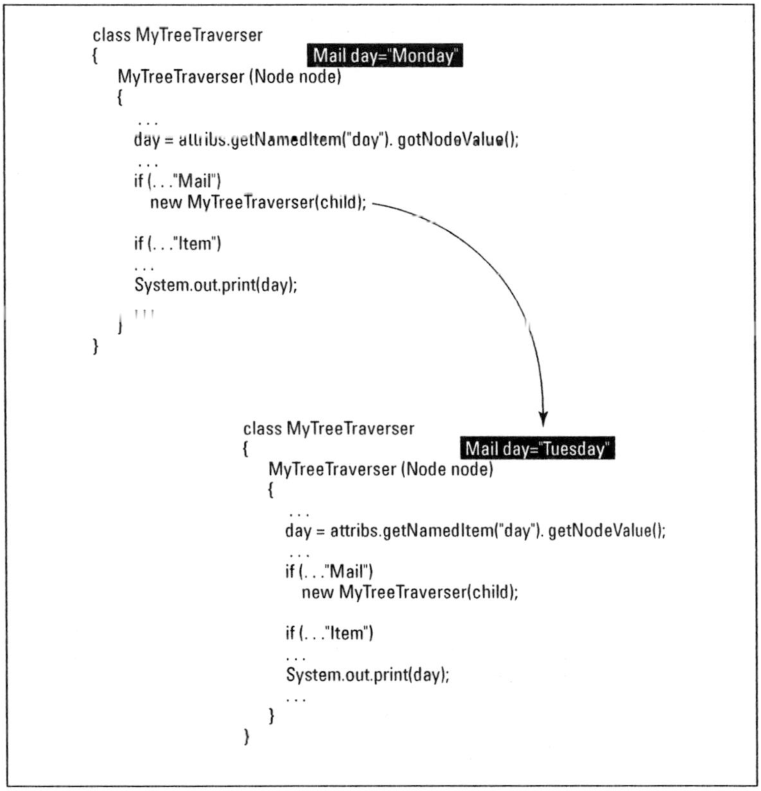

Figure 9-3:
Two MyTree
Traverser
objects.

✔ **The second** MyTreeTraverser **object creates a third**
MyTreeTraverser **object.**

The third object's day variable gets the value Wednesday. To verify this, see Figure 9-4, and see the node labeled "3" in Figure 9-2.

✔ **The third** MyTreeTraverser **object encounters an** Item **node.**

The discovery of an Item node triggers the printing of some informa-tion. This information includes the value of the day variable.

Now, the last time we set the day variable's value was when the third MyTreeTraverser object set day to Wednesday. That's how we get the Wednesday...Client output in Figure 9-1. (This stuff is labeled with the number "4" in Figure 9-2.)

```
class MyTreeTraverser
{                               Mail day="Monday"
    MyTreeTraverser (Node node)
    {
        . . .
        day = attribs.getNamedItem("day").getNodeValue();
        . . .
        if ( . . ."Mail")
            new MyTreeTraverser(child);

        if ( . . ."Item")
            . . .
            System.out.print(day);
        . . .
    }
}
                    class MyTreeTraverser
                    {                               Mail day="Tuesday"
                        MyTreeTraverser (Node node)
                        {
                            . . .
                            day = attribs.getNamedItem("day").getNodeValue();
                            . . .
                            if ( . . ."Mail")
                                new MyTreeTraverser(child);

                            if ( . . ."Item")
                                . . .
                                System.out.print(day);
                            . . .
                        }
                    }
                                class MyTreeTraverser
                                {                               Mail day="Wednesday"
                                    MyTreeTraverser (Node node)
                                    {
                                        . . .
                                        day = attribs.getNamedItem("day").getNodeValue();
                                        . . .
                                        if ( . . ."Mail")
                                            new MyTreeTraverser(child);

                                        if ( . . ."Item")
                                            . . .
                                            System.out.print(day);
                                        . . .
                                    }
                                }
```

Figure 9-4:
Three
MyTree
Traverser
objects.

✔ **After displaying the** `Wednesday...Client` **output, the third** `MyTreeTraverser` **object ends its run.**

The constructor runs out of statements to execute. The third `MyTreeTraverser` goes away (only to be chewed up by the next garbage collector that passes by). We're back to the two-object situation that we had in Figure 9-3. At this point, the `Monday` and `Tuesday` objects are still alive and well.

✔ **The code inside of Tuesday's** `MyTreeTraversal` **object takes over where it left off.**

Having found and dealt with one child, Tuesday's `MyTreeTraversal` object marches right on ahead to deal with another child.

Let me make this same point with slightly different wording. Having found and dealt with the `Mail` child (labeled "3" in Figure 9-2), Tuesday's `MyTreeTraversal` object marches right on ahead to deal with an `Item` child (labeled "5" in Figure 9-2).

At this point, we're executing the code in the bottom half of Figure 9-3. The value of the `day` variable is `Tuesday`, and the child's node name is `Item`. So the code jumps to the `handleItem` method, which displays the `Tuesday...Bank` message.

✔ **Things keep unraveling until only Monday's** `MyTreeTraversal` **object remains.**

When there's only one object left, the value of `day` is `Monday`, and the `Item` that gets displayed is the `Boss` item. So the output `Monday...Boss` gets displayed on the screen (as is shown in Figure 9-1) and the whole program ends its execution.

When you write programs like the one in Listing 9-1, please be patient with yourself. Some people find it difficult to understand how recursion works. Others read about recursion and say, "Oh, *that* sounds easy." But then they try writing recursive code on their own — and most of these people ask, "Why isn't it as easy as it looks?" Recursive code tends to be delicate. One misplaced statement and the whole thing crumbles into pieces. So be careful, take your time, and forgive yourself for making mistakes.

Making Good Use of the Technology (An Intriguing Example)

"Here," you say, "look at the data. I have all the information I need to prove my point. Just read through this lengthy XML document, and you'll see what I mean."

Yeah, right. You can't just toss a raw XML document in front of somebody's face. Instead, you need to display your data in human-readable form. Of course, what constitutes "human-readable form" depends on lots of things, including the nature of the data, and the humans who are reading it.

In this section, we display data in tree form. Tree displays are human-readable — otherwise you wouldn't see trees used in (for example) Windows Explorer, Linux KDE Konqueror, or Macintosh folders. So let's take an XML document, and display it as a tree.

Using swing with DOM

To create a tree, we'll need two things — some XML code and some Java Swing code. The Java Swing library has nice visual things like windows, buttons, and expandable tree displays. Our job is to make a Swing tree that mimics the structure of an XML document. Here's the basic idea: As your DOM program travels from a document's root to the document's innermost nodes, you add pieces to a Swing tree that you're building on the side.

Of course, the real details are a lot juicier:

✔ **The DOM program calls a constructor to make a new frame.**

What Java people call a "frame" is what most of the computing world calls a "window." This frame will hold your tree display.

✔ **The DOM program calls another constructor to make a new tree.**

The root of the tree will represent the root element in your XML document.

✔ **The DOM program assigns a label to the tree's root.**

In the Swing API, this "label" is called a *user object*. The idea is, you're adorning the tree with something that the ordinary user can see. In this section's example, we'll get our `root` user object by examining the `root` element in the XML document. (See Figure 9-5.)

✔ **Do similar things with each child of the document's `root` node.**

Here's where the well-worn recursion tactic comes into play. What happens to the child is a sequence of sub-steps:

• **We check to make sure that the child is worth displaying.**

We don't want to display comments or junky whitespace text. We choose not to display every nook and cranny in the DOM tree.

- **If the child is worth displaying, we make a brand new tree component.**

  We attach this component to the place on the tree where the child node should be. The new component becomes a leaf on the existing tree. (See Figure 9-6.)

  Later, when you add even more children, what is temporarily a leaf may become embedded in the middle of the tree, and no longer be a leaf. (See Figures 9-7 and 9-8.)

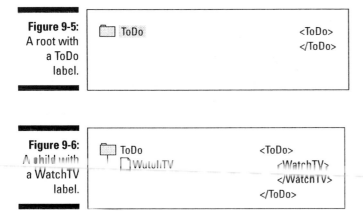

Figure 9-5: A root with a ToDo label.

```
  ToDo                          <ToDo>
                                </ToDo>
```

Figure 9-6: A child with a WatchTV label.

```
  ToDo                          <ToDo>
     WatchTV                       <WatchTV>
                                   </WatchTV>
                                </ToDo>
```

The whole deal is to string together a tree while you visit the nodes in the XML document. One thing that can make this task a bit confusing is the jumble of terminology. An XML document has DOM nodes, but a Java Swing tree has nodes also. To keep things clear, I have two different names for nodes in my Java code.

✔ For the DOM nodes from the XML document, I use variables with names like docNode, docRoot, and docChild.

✔ For the nodes on the Java Swing tree, I use variables with names like treeNode, treeRoot, and treeChild.

So, the whole point of the code is to create treeNode objects that mirror the structure of all the docNode objects. To do this, I visit docNode objects recursively, creating treeNode objects one-by-one along the way. (For some reason, I envision the action shown in Figure 9-9.)

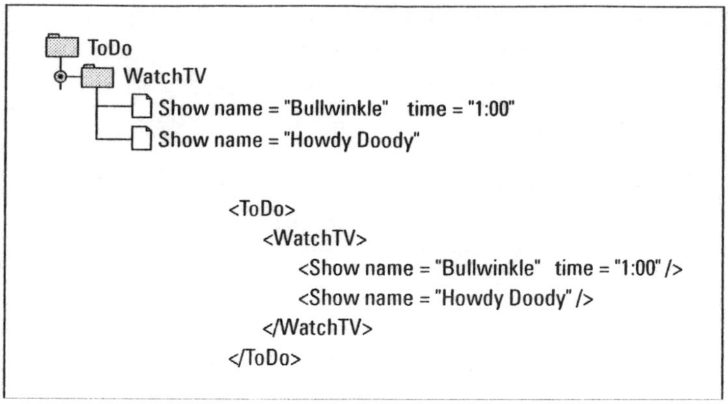

Figure 9-7:
Adding
children
to the
WatchTV
node.

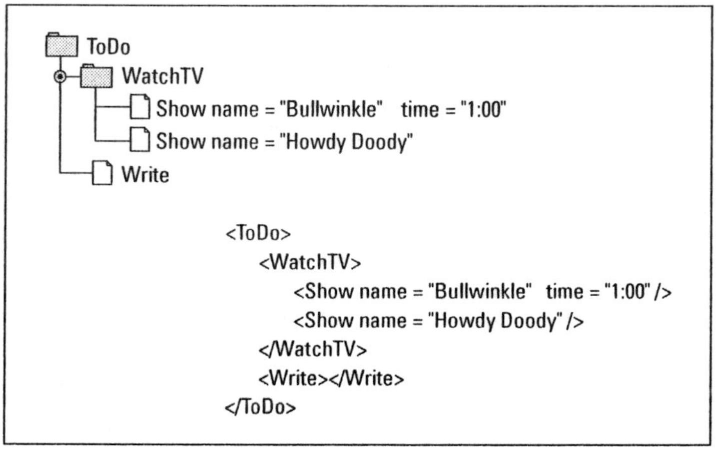

```
<ToDo>
    <WatchTV>
        <Show name = "Bullwinkle"   time = "1:00" />
        <Show name = "Howdy Doody" />
    </WatchTV>
</ToDo>
```

Figure 9-8:
Adding
a sibling
for the
WatchTV
node.

```
<ToDo>
    <WatchTV>
        <Show name = "Bullwinkle"   time = "1:00" />
        <Show name = "Howdy Doody" />
    </WatchTV>
    <Write></Write>
</ToDo>
```

Get a load of this code!

To start, we need an XML document. I just happen to have one in Listing 9-3.
The tree that we're trying to make from this document is shown in Figure 9-10.

Listing 9-3:   My To Do List

```
<ToDo>
    <WatchTV>
        <Show name="Bullwinkle" time="1:00" />
        <Show name="Howdy Doody" />
    </WatchTV>
    <Write>Java &amp; XML For Dummies</Write>
    <Eat><Food name="Chocolate" /></Eat>
```

```
    <WatchTV>
        <Show name="Ren and Stimpy" />
    </WatchTV>
</ToDo>
```

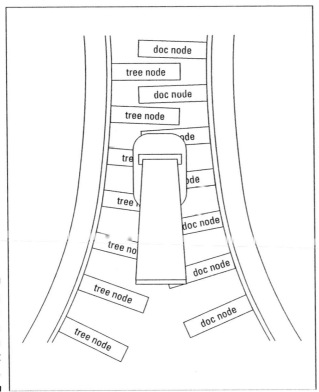

Figure 9-9:
Matching
up tree
nodes with
document
nodes.

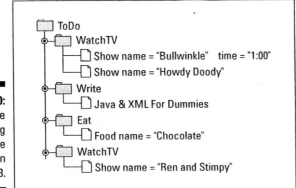

Figure 9-10:
A tree
illustrating
the
document in
Listing 9-3.

The tree in Figure 9-10 *is not a DOM tree.* A full DOM tree would start with a document node, and would include several additional text nodes. No, the goal in this section is to maximize human readability. The tree must represent the gist of Listing 9-3 in a single glance.

To include an ampersand within text in an XML document, you use the & entity reference. So, in Listing 9-3, my book becomes *Java & XML For Dummies.*

Creating a frame

For a CallDOM class, we can reuse the code from Listing 7-2. The only thing we need to change is the following statement:

```
new MyTreeTraverser (doc);
```

We'll change this line so that it creates a MyFrame object.

```
new MyFrame(doc);
```

And what, you ask, is a MyFrame object? The answer is in Listing 9-4.

Listing 9-4:   The MyFrame Class

```
import javax.swing.JFrame;
import javax.swing.JTree;
import org.w3c.dom.Document;
import org.w3c.dom.Node;
import java.awt.BorderLayout;


class MyFrame extends JFrame
{
    MyFrame (Document doc)
    {
        Node docRoot = doc.getDocumentElement();

        JTree tree = makeTree(docRoot);

        getContentPane().add(tree);
        setDefaultCloseOperation(JFrame.EXIT_ON_CLOSE);
        setSize(500,500);
        show();
    }


    JTree makeTree(Node docRoot)
    {
        MyTreeNode treeRoot = new MyTreeNode();
```

```
        new TreeExtender(treeRoot, docRoot);
        return new JTree(treeRoot);
    }
}
```

Using some Java Swing tools

Listing 9-4 uses some classes and methods from Java's windowing APIs. This book isn't supposed to be about windowing APIs, but I'll give you the lowdown on the classes and methods I use in Listing 9-4. Here it is

✔ **JFrame:** This is the Java Swing name for a window. When the XML tree program begins running, the first thing we do is to create a new JFrame object. After that, we can put a tree object onto the face of the JFrame.

✔ **add:** Use the add method to add something to the JFrame. In Listing 9-4, I add a tree to the JFrame. (I'll have more to say about the tree later.)

There's a quirk in the Java Swing API: You don't actually add things to the JFrame itself. Instead, you get the JFrame's content pane (whatever that is) and add things to the content pane. That's why I make a call to method getContentPane in Listing 9-4.

The add method in Listing 9-4 works fine for just one tree. But, to add more than one component to a JFrame, you'll need a more complicated form of the add method. If you use this plain old add method to plunk more than one component onto the frame, then you'll get some startling (and frustrating) results. For more information, see the Java documentation for the BorderLayout, and for the add(Component comp, Object constraints) method in Java's Container class.

✔ **setDefaultCloseOperation:** How do you close a window on your computer screen? If you use Microsoft Windows, or the Linux KDE, then you click a little *x* in the window's upper-right corner. If you use a Macintosh, you may click a square in the window's upper-left corner. Either way, your Java frame may never get the message. If you don't set the JFrame's default close operation, then the frame will just sit there as if you'd never clicked anything at all. (No, clicking a second time, much longer and harder than the first time, won't work.) To get the JFrame to close properly, set the default close operation to the constant value JFrame.EXIT_ON_CLOSE.

✔ **setSize:** Here's another possible pitfall. Forgetting to set the frame size causes the frame to appear as a small sliver somewhere on your computer screen. So, in Listing 9-4, the call to setSize makes the frame 500 pixels wide and 500 pixels high.

Once the frame is displayed, a user can change the frame's size by dragging the frame's edges with the mouse.

   ✔ **show:** This frame business has one trap after another. If you forget to call the show method, then your frame starts off being invisible. (Actually, that's not too strange. In a GUI environment, a window doesn't appear until the user does something to conjure it up.) In Listing 9-4, calling the show method makes your new frame appear on the screen.

   ✔ **JTree:** The Java Swing JTree class has all the methods and declarations for creating something that looks like a tree (with nodes, branches, and all that good stuff). When the JTree object is displayed, you can expand and collapse the tree's nodes with mouse clicks.

The silly MyTreeNode class

Listing 9-4 uses a class that I created myself. It's a cheap shot called MyTreeNode. The laughable code for the MyTreeNode class is in Listing 9-5.

Listing 9-5: The MyTreeNode Class

```
import javax.swing.tree.DefaultMutableTreeNode;

class MyTreeNode extends DefaultMutableTreeNode
{
    //Inherits everything, as is.
    //Provides shorter name in place of the
    //  unbearably cumbersome name "DefaultMutableTreeNode."
}
```

Here's why I defined class MyTreeNode: When you work with the JTree class, you're constantly adding new nodes to your tree. You get these nodes by creating instances of the DefaultMutableTreeNode class. But, every time you use the name DefaultMutableTreeNode, this 22-letter class name looks like a big blotch in your code.

To make my code more readable, I've created my own name, MyTreeNode. The new MyTreeNode class serves no purpose but to provide a short alias for the ugly DefaultMutableTreeNode class name.

A guided tour of the MyFrame class

Here's what the code in Listing 9-4 does:

✔ **The code makes a new JTree.**

   The crux of the action that makes the JTree lives inside the makeTree method. I'll describe the makeTree method in a moment.

✔ **The code adds the JTree to the frame.**

   The code does this by issuing the following call:

```
getContentPane().add(tree);
```

✔ **The code prepares the frame to be displayed, and then displays the frame.**

The code calls some `set` methods, and then calls the `show` method. Voilá! You have a frame.

And finally, here's what the `makeTree` method in Listing 9-4 does:

✔ The method makes the `treeRoot` variable point to a brand new node.

✔ The method calls `TreeExtender`, which does most of the work in the whole tree-making program. (I'll explain that work momentarily. For now, just put it on the back burner.)

✔ By calling the constructor `new JTree(treeRoot)`, the `makeTree` method creates a JTree whose `root` is the `treeRoot`.

For a conceptual look at the work done so far, see Figure 9-11.

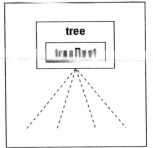

Figure 9-11:
A JTree with
a root node.

Up in the middle of Listing 9-4, the add method puts this JTree onto your frame, and then you're ready to display your wares.

The TreeExtender class

It's time to get down and get dirty! The `TreeExtender` class does the hard work of creating a tree node for every document node. This `TreeExtender` code is in Listing 9-6.

Listing 9-6: Adding Nodes to the Tree

```
import org.w3c.dom.Node;
import org.w3c.dom.NamedNodeMap;


class TreeExtender
{
    MyTreeNode treeNode;
```

(continued)

Listing 9-6 *(continued)*

```
    Node docNode;


    TreeExtender (MyTreeNode treeNode, Node docNode)
    {
        this.treeNode = treeNode;
        this.docNode = docNode;


        treeNode.setUserObject(getLabel());
        addChildren();
    }


    void addChildren()
    {
        Node docChild = docNode.getFirstChild();
        while (docChild != null)
        {
            if (shouldDisplay(docChild))
            {
                MyTreeNode treeChild = new MyTreeNode();
                treeNode.add(treeChild);
                new TreeExtender(treeChild, docChild);
            }
            docChild = docChild.getNextSibling();
        }
    }


    boolean shouldDisplay(Node docChild)
    {
        if (docChild.getNodeType() == Node.TEXT_NODE)
        {
            String nodeValue = docChild.getNodeValue();
            if (nodeValue != null &&
                !nodeValue.trim().equals(""))
                return true;
            else
                return false;
        }
        else
            return true;
    }


    String getLabel()
    {
```

```
      short nodeType = docNode.getNodeType();

      if (nodeType == Node.TEXT_NODE)
         return docNode.getNodeValue();
      else if (nodeType == Node.ELEMENT_NODE)
         return docNode.getNodeName() + stringOfAttribs();
      else
         return docNode.getNodeName();
   }


   String stringOfAttribs()
   {
      NamedNodeMap attribs = docNode.getAttributes();
      String label = "";

      for (int i = 0; i < attribs.getLength(); i++)
      {
         Node item = attribs.item(i);
         label += "      ";
         label += item.getNodeName();
         label += " = \"";
         label += item.getNodeValue();
         label += "\"";
      }

      return label;
   }

}
```

Here's how the `TreeExtender` in Listing 9-6 works:

✔ **The** `TreeExtender` **constructor puts a label on the new** `tree` **node.**

To do this, the constructor calls the node's `setUserObject` method.

```
   treeNode.setUserObject(getLabel());
```

A *user object* is whatever gets displayed beside a node on a tree. This user object is often a string of characters (a *label*). But sometimes the user object is a small image, or some other crazy thing.

In Listing 9-6, I paste a simple label beside each tree node. To find some words to put into the label, I call my own `getLabel` method. (The `getLabel` method is also in Listing 9-6.) This `getLabel` method, in concert with my `stringOfAttribs` method, composes a label based on the type of document node that's being represented. (Don't forget: Every tree node comes from *one* of the XML document's nodes!)

For a glimpse of the action so far, take a look at Figure 9-12.

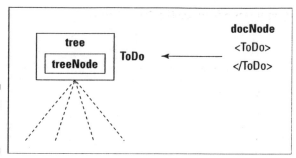

✔ **The** TreeExtender **constructor calls the** addChildren **method.**

This addChildren method has that same old loop — the loop that lurks inside every DOM program.

```
Node docChild = docNode.getFirstChild();
while (docChild != null)
{
    //Process the child node, like any
    //   other node in the document

    docChild = docChild.getNextSibling();
}
```

Look back at any incarnation of the MyTreeTraverser class. (For instance, see Listings 7-4, 7-6, 8-5, or 9-1.) You'll find very similar loops in each of these MyTreeTraverser classes. In Listing 9-6, the loop cycles through the document node's children, deciding whether each child is worthy of being displayed. (In my program, a node is worthy as long as it's not a text node, or it's a text node with some non-whitespace characters in it. In other tree programs, you'll have your own criteria for choosing the display-worthy nodes.)

✔ **For a display-worthy child, the** addChildren **method adds a new node to the tree.**

The method does this by calling

```
treeNode.add(treeChild);
```

This add method has nothing to do with the method that added a tree to a frame in Listing 9-4. In fact, this particular add method belongs to the DefaultMutableTreeNode (a.k.a. MyTreeNode) class. With this call to add, the node pointed to by treeChild gets attached underneath the node pointed to by treeNode. (See Figure 9-13.)

✔ **After a child has been added to the tree, the code creates a brand new
TreeExtender object.**

Here's our old friend recursion again. The new TreeExtender object will
treat this child the same way the current TreeExtender treated the
parent. In fact, for the new TreeExtender, all the node variable names
get renewed. (See Figure 9-14.)

- What's called the treeChild in the current TreeExtender gets
  called the treeNode in the new TreeExtender.

- What's called the docChild in the current TreeExtender gets
  called the docNode in the new TreeExtender.

✔ **History repeats itself.**

The new TreeExtender labels the new tree node, and starts adding
children to the new tree node. What was once the child now has a child
of its own. (See Figure 9-15.)

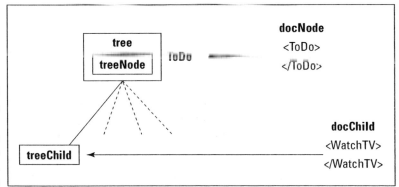

Figure 9-13:
A treeChild
node gets
added to the
JTree.

The cycle continues until everybody's test of docChild != null turns up
false. At that point the whole recursion chain unwinds. The addChildren
loop stops adding children, all the TreeExtender objects succumb to the
great Java garbage collector, and the JTree thus constructed gets plopped
onto the frame.

Look again at the result in Figure 9-10, and sigh with amazement.

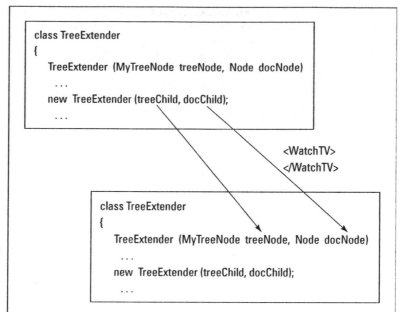

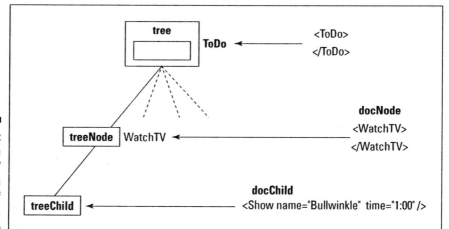

Chapter 10

Scanning Data the Elegant Way (Using JDOM)

* *

In This Chapter

▷ Why you should learn another API

▷ Analyzing an XML document with JDOM

▷ Creating an XML document with JDOM

* *

A recent study of the Institute for Rigorous Scientific Research revealed the three things that married couples fight about most often.

1. The husband is messy.

2. The husband leaves junk in the cluttered basement, always promises to clean the basement, but never gets around to it.

3. The husband, while writing his books, leaves papers all over the dining room table and never cleans up after himself.

(And you thought that messy cars, messy attics, and messy garages were the three biggest points of contention.) Anyway, the wife's typical claim is "You don't care enough about yourself to respect your own environment." To which the husband replies, "I care about myself so much that I don't need a pristine environment." At this point, the sparks start flying.

People look at this fellow's office and say, "Wow! What a mess — but I'll bet you know where everything is." He smiles and replies, "No, I can never find what I need in here." But this specimen of *Homo Authorus* has a dark secret: Although he couldn't care less about his physical surroundings, he's obsessive-compulsive about the state of his computer. One missing icon, one left-over temp file, one obsolete piece of software, and Homo Authorus goes berserk. He spends hours working on it until it's completely fixed.

Why is the tidiness of his computer so important to this guy (even though he downloads scads of shareware without running a virus checker)? No one knows for sure. Ask him, and he'll give you the following load of malarkey: "A neat house is nothing but cosmetics. A neat house isn't more functional than a messy house. But an organized *computer* makes everything run more smoothly."

Each person divides the world into two kinds of places — places for neatness, and places for chaos. For some people, the neat, orderly places are their physical surroundings. But for others, the orderly places are in the virtual caverns of computer programming. If your house of neatness is in the computer's processor, then this chapter is for you. This chapter is about JDOM — the neat, orderly API.

Elegant JDOM

If you've been following the book's story so far, you know that there are at least two APIs for XML processing. One is called SAX, and another is called DOM. While SAX fires one event after another, DOM plants a tree in your computer's memory. There may be other, vastly different approaches to XML parsing, but the people who created JDOM concentrated on tree building.

So, as you read this chapter, you won't see a drastically different approach to the handling of XML data. Instead, what you'll see is yet another tree structure. "And what's so great about that?" you ask. Well, as far as I can tell, JDOM is a response to DOM. While the official proponents say that the name "JDOM" isn't an acronym, I think of JDOM as a Java-optimized alternative to DOM.

Language independence

Both SAX and DOM are language-independent. This means you can write SAX and DOM programs in C++, and in other distasteful programming languages. All the DOM tricks (such as the use of nodes and the `NamedNodeMap`) aim to the common denominator between Java and C++. If some feature is available in Java, but not in C++, then DOM doesn't use that Java feature.

Whoa, there. Take a moment to compare a certain Java feature with the corresponding C++ feature. Java has an enormous collection of classes and methods called the Java API. In C++, the corresponding feature is called the Standard Template Library (STL). So far, Java and C++ match up nicely. But a problem arises. The C++ template library doesn't have the *same* classes and methods as the Java API. So, to keep everyone happy, SAX and DOM aren't built around either the Java API or the C++ STL. Neither SAX nor DOM take advantage of any language's pre-established library of classes and methods.

Go ahead. Use some other programming language. See if I care! You can find implementations of Xerces (with both SAX and DOM parsers) for the languages C++ and Perl. These implementations live at www.apache.org.

Of course, the people who created the Java API didn't go to all that work for nothing. They want you to use things like java.util.List and java.util.Map. The DOM API doesn't use these things because, no matter how many DOM programmers are stuck on Java (and, believe me, lots of them are), the DOM API isn't wedded to the Java programming language.

Moving toward language dependence

If you're wedded to Java (and to a spouse who's a neat freak), then you probably like using the tools in the Java API. At least, you like using these tools when they fit the problem at hand. For Instance, when you grab a bunch of XML element attributes, you'd like that "bunch" to be an object of type java.util.List. This is better — more useful — than receiving an org.xml.sax.Attributes object or an org.w3c.dom.NamedNodeMap object.

Why do you like using a Java List? Why is something from Java's standard API better than a specialized DOM class? There are several reasons.

- ✔ With the standard Java API, you can use all the cool methods that come with the Java API classes and interfaces.

- ✔ With standard Java, you can apply your existing Java skills to the processing of XML documents. If you manage employees, then they can apply their Java skills to the processing of XML documents (and that makes you look good).

- ✔ With standard Java classes, any future optimizations in the Java API get applied automatically to your XML processing code.

Unlike SAX and DOM, the JDOM API was written specifically for Java. When you use JDOM, you take advantage of all the pre-written Java API classes. Of course, when you use JDOM, you're committing yourself to using Java. (At least you're committing to Java for your XML processing.) That's the trade-off.

Using constructors in JDOM

Take a look at a typical SAX or DOM program. Look, for instance, at Listing 8-6. Somebody must be making money by selling methods whose names start with the word create! Everything in Listing 8-6 uses some indirect way of creating objects. Because org.w3c.dom.Element is an interface (and not a class), you can't make a straightforward call to an Element constructor. Instead, you have to call a `createElement` method. Because `org.w3c.dom.Document` is an interface, you can't make a call to a `Document` constructor. Instead, you have to call `builder.newDocument`.

Well, in JDOM, `org.jdom.Element` and `org.jdom.Document` are classes. Thus you make an element with a line like

```
Element elt = new Element("Item");
```

and you make a document with a line like this one:

```
Document doc = new Document(rootElt);
```

It's that simple. Like my wife's side of the bathroom cabinet, the whole JDOM API is neater, cleaner, and sleeker.

The JDOM tree

Another feature that distinguishes JDOM from DOM is what JDOM puts on its tree. With the DOM API, everything is a node. Look back at Table 7-1 and notice that the document is a node, elements are nodes, attributes are nodes, and even comments are nodes. So far, so good, because every part of the XML document *is the same kind of object.* (Node really? Yep, really.) To visit everything in a document, you just travel from one node to another. (It's like Tarzan swinging on vines.)

In JDOM, the tree consists of elements. Any other things (such as attributes and comments) aren't on main branches of the tree. The attributes, comments, and other such things hang as extra ornaments on the basic tree of elements.

Instead of the all-present `Node` interface, JDOM gives you an `Element` class, an `Attribute` class, a `Comment` class, and other useful classes. If you start at the tree's root, and then visit all the children, you get a big printout of all the elements in the XML document. This printout doesn't include things like the text between tags. To see the text between tags, you must make special side trips with methods like `getContent` and `getText`.

Doing without the omnipresent node

JDOM has no all-encompassing thing like the DOM `Node` interface. This aspect of JDOM is both a drawback and an advantage. When you're fishing around for stuff in a JDOM document, everything appears as a different kind of object. Instead of getting `Node`, `Node`, `Node`, you get a list of objects. You have to cast objects downward to classes like `Comment`, `ProcessingInstruction` and `Element`. (For a concrete demonstration of this, see Listing 10-7.)

On the upside, this view of the XML document as a tree of elements is very natural. If you think about it, an XML document is really some elements inside of other elements. The elements form the document's basic framework, and the other things (the comments, the attributes, and the other junk) are meant to hang off the framework like merry little helpers. The original DOM notion — that everything is a node of some kind, and that everything is a branch on one really big tree — is an artificial view of an XML document. Sure, this view can be useful, but the squeezing of everything onto one colossal tree framework can also be cumbersome.

Getting the JDOM API

Unlike SAX and DOM, the JDOM API doesn't come from Sun Microsystems. When you download Java 1.4 (or you do a separate download of JAXP), you'll get SAX and DOM, but not JDOM. For JDOM, you have to do a separate download. Just visit www.jdom.org and get the latest binary distribution.

The jdom.org Web site has three download pages. There's a "source" page for JDOM developers. There's a "binary" page with the latest stable version of the API. There's a "documentation" page with (you guessed it!) the API documentation. The documentation page also has articles and pointers to other interesting sites about JDOM. When you visit the binary page, and download the latest stable version, check to see if the stuff you've downloaded already has the API documentation stored inside of it. If so, you'll save yourself an extra download step. (You won't have to get the API documentation as a separate time-consuming download.)

After you've downloaded JDOM, installing it is easy.

- ✔ Unzip the file that you downloaded. This gives you a folder named jdom (or something like that).

- ✔ Put the unzipped jdom folder in a nice place on your hard drive. (The word "nice" means you should put the folder where you put similar folders. If you download to a temp directory, then don't leave jdom in the temp directory.)

- ✔ In your jdom folder, look for a file named jdom.jar. Add this jdom.jar file to your system's classpath.

The last of the three steps is very important. When you compile and run a Java program, you want the system to be able to find all the jdom.org classes. If jdom.jar isn't in your classpath, then you'll get one NoClassDefFoundError after another.

For hints on changing your system classpath, see Chapter 2. But please note: there's a chance that some classes in jdom.jar will have the same names as classes in the JAXP API. These jdom.jar names may come into conflict with JAXP names. To resolve any conflict, you may want to switch back and forth between two different classpath settings.

- ✔ For SAX and DOM, you'll have only a dot (representing the current working directory) in your system's classpath.
- ✔ For JDOM, you'll have both the dot and jdom.jar in your system's classpath.

You may even need to shove jdom.jar to the front, instead of the back, of your classpath.

 The way I change my classpath varies from one operating system to another. And the changes I make in my classpath depend on whether I'm using straight JAXP, or JDOM, or some other fancy API for XML. In any case, I leave notes to myself in each of my project directories. "This collection of classes uses the *such-and-such* API, and requires *so-and-so* (and not *this-or-that*) in the classpath." Sure, I could achieve the same effect with some sophisticated project-building tools. But in the absence of such tools, text files with notes to myself work fine for me.

How to Get Up and Running (A Basic Example)

I've heard plenty of software sales pitches. "Here are the top sixty features that make our software better than other software . . ." At the end of a sales pitch, I always say, "That's a nice list of features, but can you show me the software in action?" And the answer is, "The software is still in development." In other words, "Our software doesn't have any of those great features. We've just spent an hour telling you about our pipe dreams."

With that in mind, I'm going to short-circuit my sales pitch about JDOM (all the stuff I wrote up to this point in the chapter). I'll cut to the chase, and show you some real, running JDOM code.

Calling JDOM into action

Listing 10-1 has the code that starts things rolling.

Listing 10-1: Calling JDOM

```
import org.jdom.JDOMException;
import org.jdom.Document;
import org.jdom.input.SAXBuilder;
import java.io.File;
import java.io.IOException;

public class CallJDOM
{
   public static void main(String args[])
      throws JDOMException,
             IOException
   {
      Document doc;

      SAXBuilder builder = new SAXBuilder(false);

      if (args.length == 1)
      {
         doc = builder.build
            (new File(args[0]).toURL().toString());
         new MyEltTraverser (doc.getRootElement(), 0);
      }
      else
         System.out.println
            ("Usage: java CallDOM file-name.xml");
   }
}
```

Listing 10-1 contains my `CallJDOM` class — the class that doesn't change much from one example to another. And, sure enough, the code in Listing 10-1 isn't much different from its older cousins — the `CallSAX` and `CallDOM` classes in Listings 3-2 and 7-2.

Here are the things you should notice about the code in Listing 10-1:

✔ **Listing 10-1 borrows stuff from SAX.**

The listing starts by calling a `SAXBuilder` constructor. How about that? JDOM can use a SAX parser to scan an XML document!

In fact, you can plug any reasonable XML parser into a JDOM program. There's talk on the JDOM discussion lists about JDOM having its own `Builder` class but, as I write these words, the `Builder` class doesn't yet exist.

One way or another, you're not tied to a particular parser when you write a JDOM program. For instance, in Listing 10-1, you can substitute DOMBuilder in place of SAXBuilder. (The JDOM API has a class named org.jdom.input.DOMBuilder.) The only difference between SAXBuilder and DOMBuilder is that the DOMBuilder class has no build(String) method. To call the DOMBuilder parse method, you write

```
doc = builder.build(new File(args[0]).toURL());
```

You stuff a URL, not a string, into the build method's parameter list.

✔ **In Listing 10-1, the constructor for SAXBuilder takes a boolean parameter.**

The boolean value false means "no, don't do validation." If you use DOMBuilder instead of SAXBuilder, then you put this boolean value into the DOMBuilder constructor.

✔ **In Listing 10-1, I decided to start with the document's root element.**

In Listing 10-1, I feed doc.getRootElement() to the constructor for MyEltTraverser. I don't do this in every JDOM program, but I find it very convenient for many of my JDOM examples. Here's why:

In DOM, almost everything is a node of some kind. In particular, the whole DOM document is a node — and each element in the DOM document is a node. In Listing 7-3, I have a constructor

```
MyTreeTraverser (Node node)
```

When I call this constructor, I can feed it a document, an element, or any other kind of node.

But in JDOM, things are different. The only common superclass of org.jdom.Document and org.jdom.Element is the wimpy java.lang.Object class. So, in JDOM, when I create a MyTraverser constructor, the constructor's parameter can be a Document or an Element. I can't easily create a constructor that handles both Document objects and Element objects. (Even if I use a non-committal java.lang.Object parameter, I have a hard time writing code that applies to both documents and elements.)

In Listing 10-1, I call MyEltTraverser — a constructor that handles an element, but not a whole document. So to make things match, I call doc.getRootElement, feeding an element, not a document, to the MyEltTraverser constructor.

✔ **The constructor for** MyEltTraverser **takes a second parameter.**

In Listing 10-1, the value of this second parameter is 0. The second parameter is special to this section's example. (It's not a general feature of JDOM programs.) As you'll see in Listing 10-2, I'll use this second parameter to count levels of indentation.

An XML document

The goal of this section's example is to visit all the elements in an XML document. So, we need an XML document with elements that are worth visiting. I've placed such a document in Listing 10-2.

Listing 10-2: CosmoML

```
<?xml version="1.0" encoding="UTF-8"?><System
id="Solar System"><Planet id="Mercury" /><Planet id="Venus"
/><Planet id="Earth"><Moon id="Moon" /></Planet><Planet
id="Mars"><Moon id="Phobos" /><Moon id="Deimos" /></Planet>
<Planet id="Jupiter" /><Planet id="Saturn" /><Planet
id="Uranus" /><Planet id="Neptune" /><Planet id="Pluto" />
</System>
```

The line breaks in Listing 10-2 are in arbitrary places, making the document unfit for human reading. Even so, an XML parser has no trouble interpreting the document. This section's example will turn the hard-to-read document into a nicely formatted display. The display is shown in Figure 10-1.

Figure 10-1:
An astro-
nomical
tree.

Traversing the JDOM tree

The program to make the nice display of Figure 10-1 is shown in Listing 10-3. This program has two parts — a part that visits child elements, and a part that draws lines. For our purposes (as students of Java and XML), the part that draws lines isn't very interesting. But the part that visits children illustrates some important features of JDOM.

Listing 10-3:   Visiting the Elements

```
import org.jdom.Element;
import java.util.List;

class MyEltTraverser
{

    MyEltTraverser(Element element, int level)
    {
        Element child;
        List children;

        System.out.print(getLines(level));
        System.out.println(element.getAttributeValue("id"));


        children = element.getChildren();
        for (int i=0; i<children.size(); i++)
        {
            child = (Element)children.get(i);
            new MyEltTraverser(child, level+1);
        }

    }


    String getLines(int level)
    {
        String lines="";
        for (int i=0; i<level; i++)
            lines += "   |";
        lines += "\n";
        for (int i=0; i<level; i++)
            lines += "   |";
        lines += "__";
        return lines;
    }

}
```

In Listing 10-3, the constructor `MyEltTraverser` does two things:

✔ The `MyEltTraverser` constructor displays the name of a heavenly body.

✔ The `MyEltTraverse` constructor visits the heavenly body's children.

Visiting attributes

Displaying the body's name means calling the element's `getAttributeValue` method. This is quicker and more intuitive than the corresponding DOM trick. (To do the same thing with DOM, you call `node.getAttributes`, then you call the `NamedNodeMap` object's `getNamedItem` method, and finally, you call `node.getNodeValue`. For a review, see Listing 7-4.)

Getting the children

Visiting child elements means creating a small `for` loop. In Listing 10-3, the children variable is a standard Java `List`. That's good — you're using Java's tried-and-true classes and interfaces. Of course, there's a downside. Java's `List` is a collection of plain old objects. So, when you pluck an object from the `List`, you have to cast that object back into being a JDOM Element. You do this when you execute

```
child = (Element)children.get(i);
```

Here's a more rigorous explanation of the need for casting:

The `List` interface's get method returns a value of type `java.lang.Object`. But, in Listing 10-3, the child variable has to be of type `Element` (otherwise, you'll have trouble down the line calling the child's `getAttributeValue` method). So, to stuff a `List` item into the child variable, you have to do casting.

Making a recursive call

The loop in Listing 10-3 ends with a call to the `MyEltTraverser` constructor. In this call, the level variable gets 1 added to it. This is a standard recursive programming trick. One copy of *Whatever* calls another copy of *Whatever*, and passes a value that's 1 more than the value it already has. There's a picture in Figure 10-2.

In Listing 10-3, successive copies of `MyEltTraverser` have higher and higher values of the *level* variable. Each successive copy draws more and more lines when forming the tree in Figure 10-1.

```
class MyEltTraverser
{
                        ┌──────────────┐
                        │ SolarSystem  0 │
    MyEltTraverser (Element element, int level)
    {
       Element child;
       . . .
                        ┌──────────┐
                        │ Earth  1 │
       new MyEltTraverser (child, level+1);
       . . .
    }
}

        class MyEltTraverser
        {
                            ┌──────────────┐
                            │ Earth      1 │
            MyEltTraverser (Element element, int level)
            {
               Element child;
               . . .
                            ┌──────────┐
                            │ Moon    2 │
               new MyEltTraverser (child, level+1);
               . . .
            }
        }

                class MyEltTraverser
                {
                                    ┌──────────────┐
                                    │ Moon       2 │
                    MyEltTraverser (Element element, int level)
                    {
                       Element child;
                       . . .
                       new MyEltTraverser (child, level+1);
                       . . .
                    }
                }
```

Figure 10-2:
The value
of level
increases
by 1.

Covering All the Content with JDOM

If you've been reading every word of *Java & XML For Dummies*, then you know what just happened. In the previous section, I showed you a neat JDOM program. This program visited all the elements in an XML document. That's the good news.

Now here's the bad news. The previous section's program didn't visit all the *other* stuff in the XML document. If the document had any processing instructions, comments or text between tags, then the previous section's program just missed them.

To allay any criticism (and to keep you from calling me a complete slacker), my next program goes the whole nine yards. This section's program visits comments, processing instructions, disposable diapers, or whatever else is in the XML document. The start of the program is in Listing 10-4.

Listing 10-4:   Visiting a Document

```
import org.jdom.Document;
import org.jdom.DocType;
import java.util.List;

class MyDocVisiter
{
    MyDocVisiter(Document doc)
    {
        List content;
        DocType docType;

        if ((docType=doc.getDocType()) != null)
        {
            System.out.print("DOCTYPE: ");
            System.out.println(docType.getSystemID());
        }

        content = doc.getContent();
        new MyContentTraverser(content);
    }

}
```

To call the code in Listing 10-4, you can use a recycled version of the `CallJDOM` class in Listing 10-1. Just take out the call to `MyEltTraverser`, and replace it with

```
new MyDocVisiter (doc);
```

This new statement calls a different class's constructor. The statement also catches the entire XML document, not just the document's `root` element.

Getting the DOCTYPE

To get `DOCTYPE` information, the code in Listing 10-4 calls the document's `getDocType` method.

Take, for instance, the XML document in Listing 10-5. This document is a slight enhancement of the document in Listing 7-1. When you call `docType.getSystemID` on the document in Listing 10-5, you get the name `club.dtd`.

Listing 10-5: Yuck! More Anchovies!

```xml
<?xml version="1.0" encoding="UTF-8"?>
<!DOCTYPE AnchovyLoversClub SYSTEM "club.dtd">
<!-- AnchovyLoversClub.xml -->

<AnchovyLoversClub>
    <Member firstname="Herbert">
    <?Reminder "Unseat Herbert"?>
        <Standing>
            Founder, President, Secretary, Publicity Manager
        </Standing>
    </Member>
</AnchovyLoversClub>
```

Listing 10-5 points to a DTD named `club.dtd`. Way back in Listing 10-1, we decided that our parser wouldn't be validating. Even so, the parser complains if it can't find the file `club.dtd`. So, to keep the parser happy, we present Listing 10-6. This listing has a nice `club.dtd` file.

Listing 10-6: The Club DTD

```
<?xml version="1.0" encoding="UTF-8"?>
<!-- club.dtd -->

<!ELEMENT AnchovyLoversClub (Member)>
<!ELEMENT Member (Standing)>
<!ATTLIST Member firstname CDATA #REQUIRED>
<!ELEMENT Standing (#PCDATA)>
```

Passing the torch

In JDOM, almost everything is part of the document's *content*. So, in Listing 10-4, to get most of the stuff inside an XML document, you call the document's `getContent` method. Then you pass this content to another constructor that I wrote — a constructor named `MyContentTraverser`. The idea is, Listing 10-4 deals with a document, and everything downstream from Listing 10-4 deals with the document's content. The class `MyContentTraverser` (the class that deals with content) is in Listing 10-7.

Listing 10-7: Visiting a Document's Content

```java
import java.util.List;
import org.jdom.Element;
import org.jdom.Comment;
import org.jdom.ProcessingInstruction;
import org.jdom.Attribute;

class MyContentTraverser
```

```
{
    MyContentTraverser(List content)
    {
        Object obj;

        for (int i=0; i<content.size(); i++)
        {
            obj = content.get(i);

            if (obj instanceof Comment)
            {
                Comment comment = (Comment)obj;

                System.out.print("Comment: ");
                System.out.println
                    (Revealer.reveal(comment.getText()));
            }

            if (obj instanceof ProcessingInstruction)
            {
                ProcessingInstruction pi =
                    (ProcessingInstruction)obj;

                System.out.print("Processing Instruction: ");
                System.out.print(pi.getTarget());
                System.out.print(" ");
                System.out.println(pi.getData());
            }

            if (obj instanceof Element)
            {
                Element elt = (Element)obj;

                System.out.print("Element: ");
                System.out.println(elt.getName());

                System.out.print("Attributes: ");
                List attribs = elt.getAttributes();
                for (int j=0; j<attribs.size(); j++)
                {
                    Attribute attrib = (Attribute)attribs.get(j);

                    System.out.print(attrib.getName());
                    System.out.print(" = ");
                    System.out.println(attrib.getValue());
                }

                System.out.print("Text: ");
                System.out.println
```

(continued)

Listing 10-7 **Visiting a Document's Content** *(continued)*

```
                    (Revealer.reveal(elt.getText()));

            new MyContentTraverser(elt.getContent());
        }
    }
  }

}
```

As we roll on into the `MyContentTraverser` constructor, we notice the constructor's parameter. The parameter touches on a source of pride in the JDOM community. This thing we call content (the parameter for the `MyContentTraverser` constructor) is none other than an ordinary Java `List`. Because we've been writing Java programs for thirty or forty years now, we know all about stepping through Java `List` objects. We can create an iterator, use a simple `for` loop index, or do any number of other cool things. In Listing 10-7, I go the cheesy way, and use a `for` loop index. This loop takes us from one content object to another.

Dealing with a content object

You're inside of the `for` loop in Listing 10-7. You've got a particular content object — an item from the XML document. What happens next? Well, the code in Listing 10-7 branches into three `if` statements. The reason for this branching is that a JDOM document has three kinds of content — comments, processing instructions, and elements — each of which needs its own special handling.

At this point, we see the trade-off between JDOM and some other APIs. The JDOM API is elegant in many respects. But the program in Listing 10-7 is more complicated than the corresponding DOM program. If Listing 10-7 were a DOM program, then everything in sight would be a node. With JDOM, there are no nodes. Instead, JDOM has distinct `Comment`, `ProcessingInstruction`, and `Element` classes. (I call these classes "distinct" because they have no common parent. That is, they have no parent other than the bland `java.lang.Object` class.)

So in Listing 10-7, each of the three content types gets its own special treatment.

> ✔ **First, you use Java's rarely used `instanceof` operator.**
>
> With `instanceof`, you check to see what kind of object you're holding in your hand.

✔ **Next, you cast the object you're holding into either a** Comment, **a** ProcessingInstruction, **or an** Element.

If you forget to do the casting, then you can't use any methods peculiar to a Comment, a ProcessingInstruction, or an Element.

✔ **Finally, you use methods tailored to one of the three content types.**

If you have a Comment, then you call getText. If you have a ProcessingInstruction, then you call getTarget and getData. If you have an element, then you call all sorts of methods.

Dealing with a comment

When you call getText, you use my little Revealer class. The Revealer docs something that I did manually in earlier chapters: It turns newline characters into [cr] marks, and turns blank spaces into dots. The code for my Revealer is shown in Listing 10-8.

Listing 10-8:   Very Revealing!

```
class Revealer
{
    static String reveal(String string)
    {
        return
        string.replaceAll("\n", "[cr]").replaceAll(" ", ".");
    }
}
```

Dealing with an element

Back in Listing 10-7, you're checking the content to see if it's a comment, a processing instruction, or an element. If the content you've found is an element, then you can do some further digging.

✔ You can get a Java List containing the element's attributes. (You do this in Listing 10-7.)

✔ You can make a recursive call to the MyContentTraverser constructor, and feed the constructor the element's content. (You do this in Listing 10-7 too.)

When you make a recursive call to MyContentTraverser, the ball starts rolling. The new MyContentTraverser object hunts down Comments, ProcessingInstructions, and more elements in the XML document.

With the document in Listing 10-5, you get the output shown in Figure 10-3.

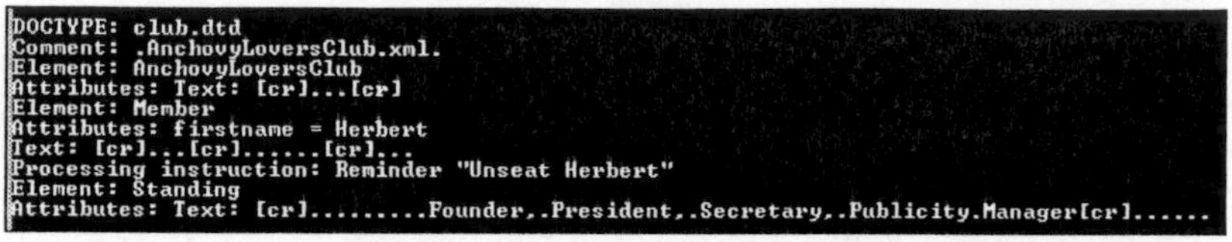

Figure 10-3:
Love them
anchovies!

```
DOCTYPE: club.dtd
Comment: .AnchovyLoversClub.xml.
Element: AnchovyLoversClub
Attributes: Text: [cr]...[cr]
Element: Member
Attributes: firstname = Herbert
Text: [cr]...[cr]......[cr]...
Processing instruction: Reminder "Unseat Herbert"
Element: Standing
Attributes: Text: [cr].........Founder,.President,.Secretary,.Publicity.Manager[cr]......
```

Using JDOM to Make a Document

Way back in Chapter 8, I showed you how to make a new XML document. The tool that I used was the DOM API. Well, there's a simpler, more elegant way to make an XML document. When you use the JDOM API, all the method calls are quicker, and more intuitive. So feast your eyes on the code in Listing 10-9. The code creates an XML file in a few nice, easy-to-understand steps.

Listing 10-9: Creating an XML File

```java
import org.jdom.Document;
import org.jdom.ProcessingInstruction;
import org.jdom.Comment;
import org.jdom.Element;
import org.jdom.output.XMLOutputter;

import java.io.File;
import java.io.FileOutputStream;
import java.io.FileNotFoundException;
import java.io.IOException;


class CreateJdoc
{
    static Document doc;
    static Element rootElt;

    public static void main(String args[])
    {
        makeRootElt();
        makeJDOMdoc();
        addProcessingInstruction();
        addComment();
        addAttribute();
        addElements(args);
        outputFile();
    }


    static void makeRootElt()
    {
        rootElt = new Element("BovineBeautyProducts");
```

```
   }

   static void makeJDOMdoc()
   {
      doc = new Document(rootElt);
   }


   static void addProcessingInstruction()
   {
      ProcessingInstruction pi = new ProcessingInstruction
         ("xml-stylesheet",
            "type=\"text/xsl\" href=\"Cows.xsl\"");
      doc.addContent(pi);
   }


   static void addComment()
   {
      Comment comment = new Comment("Author: H.Ritter");
      doc.addContent(comment);
   }


   static void addElements(String args[])
   {
      Element elt;

      for (int i=0; i<args.length; i++)
      {
         elt = new Element("Item");
         rootElt.addContent(elt);
         elt.addContent(args[i]);
      }
   }


   static void addAttribute()
   {
      rootElt.setAttribute("customerResponse", "Moo");
   }


   static void outputFile()
   {
      try
      {
         File file = new File("BovineBeautyProducts.xml");
         FileOutputStream result =
```

(continued)

Listing 10-9   Creating an XML File *(continued)*

```
            new FileOutputStream(file);

        XMLOutputter outputter = new XMLOutputter();
        outputter.setNewlines(true);
        outputter.setIndent("    ");

        outputter.output(doc, result);
    }
    catch (IOException e)
    {
        e.printStackTrace();
    }
  }

}
```

Running the JDOM code

To run the code in Listing 10-9, you have to do two things.

✔ Make sure that the file jdom.jar is in your classpath.

✔ Run CreateJdoc with some command line arguments.

The command

```
java CreateJdoc Moose-cara Cowlogne "Hoof Polish"
```

will work nicely. When you use this command, you get the
BovineBeautyProducts.xml file shown in Listing 10-10.

Listing 10-10:   BovineBeautyProducts.xml

```
<?xml version="1.0" encoding="UTF-8"?>
<BovineBeautyProducts customerResponse="Moo">
    <Item>Moose-cara</Item>
    <Item>Cowlogne</Item>
    <Item>Hoof Polish</Item>
</BovineBeautyProducts>
<?xml-stylesheet type="text/xsl" href="Cows.xsl"?>
<!--Author: H.Ritter-->
```

Admiring the JDOM code

When I wrote my `CreateJdoc` program, I modeled the program after the code in Listing 8-6. I divided `CreateJdoc` (Listing 10-9) into a sequence of method calls. When it's called, a typical method turns right around and calls a constructor. Then the method calls `addContent`, like this:

```
Comment comment = new Comment("Author: H.Ritter");
doc.addContent(comment);
```

This code is much simpler than the corresponding DOM code in Listing 8-6. The big improvement comes from two features of the JDOM API.

✔ In JDOM, you use ordinary constructors (not `create` methods) to make a document, an element, an attribute, and other such things.

✔ Because you're not using `create` methods, the making of an element or an attribute (or whatever) doesn't hinge on the use of a particular document.

Back in Listing 8-6, you called the document's `createElement` method. Then, in a separate instruction, you hung the new element onto the document. If you tried to hang the new element onto a different document, then the DOM API became upset with you.

With JDOM, you create an element without involving a particular document. So, once you have an element, you place the element on any document that you choose.

You can't place the same element onto two documents at once. If you try, then JDOM will holler at you. Of course, you can place two different elements, each with the same name, same attributes (same everything), onto two different documents at once.

When to Use the JDOM API

The people who like SAX say "Use the SAX API." Meanwhile, in another corner, the DOM lovers say, "Don't use SAX. Use DOM." And the proponents of JDOM scream, "Don't use SAX or DOM. Use JDOM instead." So what do you do? Well, what you do depends on your situation. Here are some guidelines:

✔ **Use JDOM if clean, elegant code makes you happy.**

Whenever you write a program, you're splitting your time between two tasks. You're developing logic in your head and, at the same time, you're translating that logic into code.

The first task — developing logic — is definitely worth doing. (Without logic, most technical tasks are impossible.) But the second task — translating logic into code — is a necessary evil. When you translate logic into code, there's a big dialog going on your head. "Let's see, I want to do this, but how do I express it? What primitive tools do I use to accomplish my overall goal?" The whole endeavor can be really tedious.

So what can you do to fight that tedium? How can you ease your way from having good logic to having great code? Well, you can use an API that naturally reflects your thinking process. If you think (for example), "I want to create a new document," then your API should have a Document constructor. When the API is shaped the way you form your logic, then you don't waste effort translating from logic to code.

That's the major strength of JDOM. The JDOM API uses constructs that are clear, natural, and easy to use.

✔ **Use JDOM to create brand new XML documents.**

Compare the programs in Listings 7-4 and 10-7. Both programs dig through an existing XML document, and display the document's pieces. The first of these programs is a DOM program, and the second is a JDOM program. Which program is simpler? Which is more straightforward?

Well, both programs are about 60 lines long. The DOM program (the program in Listing 7-4) uses nodes all over the place. The JDOM program (Listing 10-7) uses casting in place of nodes. Which program is better? It's not really clear.

But remember: XML is a language for data exchange. This means that one program produces an XML document, and another program consumes the XML document. So the business in Listings 7-4 and 10-7 — the business of consuming and analyzing an XML document — is only one side of the story. To do a fair comparison, you must consider both sides — the producing and the consuming of XML documents.

Listing 8-6 has a DOM program that produces an XML document. The program is okay, but it's not nearly as nice as the corresponding JDOM program. The JDOM program, in Listing 10-9, is much simpler, much cleaner, and much more straightforward than its cousin in the DOM world.

So that's an advantage of JDOM. If you do half of all the XML work, and your half is the document producing half, then you should strongly consider using JDOM.

✔ **Use JDOM as a lightweight alternative to DOM.**

The developers of JDOM are aiming for leanness and efficiency. So programs written in JDOM tend to be smaller and less bulky than programs written in DOM. Many programs that use JDOM tend to run faster than their DOM counterparts.

✔ **Use JDOM if your organization is committed to Java.**

Neither SAX nor DOM are optimized for Java. So, if you start writing SAX code in Java, you can turn around later and pull the old switcheroo. You can migrate from SAX in Java to SAX in C++ without breaking all your logic. The same is true with DOM.

But JDOM uses tools in the standard Java API. If you choose JDOM, then you're announcing "I use Java, I plan to keep on using Java, and I want my code to be the best Java that it can be."

That's the story. Java and JDOM go hand in hand together. JDOM leverages Java's strengths. SAX and DOM do not.

Chapter 11

Using JDOM to the Max

*W*hat would Sigmund Freud say? When I dream, I can jump out of character. Here's an example:

I'm in a fancy restaurant with Bill Gates. We step up and greet the maitre d'.

"Table for two?" asks the maitre d'.

"Yes," I say. "And, please put both of our meals on my tab."

Bill Gates, hearing my remark about the tab, says "Thank you." And, at this point, Murphy's Law for Dreams kicks in. (The law says, *If you're dreaming, and something embarrassing can happen, then it will.*) I reach for my wallet, and find nothing inside it. I have no money, no credit cards, nothing I can use to pay for the meal. So here's the situation: Mr. Gates is impressed that I'm treating for dinner, and I have no way to pay. I'm completely broke. What can I do?

Well, the solution is simple. "I hope you know," I say to Gates. "I won't really have to pay for our meals." And Gates gives me a "why" kind of look. So I explain. "A big meal fills my stomach. And I'm sleeping on my belly right now. So, after I eat, I'll have to roll over. And rolling over always wakes me up."

"Hmm!" says Gates.

"This dream will be done. I'll be gone and you won't exist anymore. Now, what do you think about that?"

Bill Gates thinks for a minute, and then says, "Okay. I believe you. Let's eat while we still have the chance."

I have dreams like that all the time. In my dream, I look at someone and say, "If you think that you're real, and you believe that you're not part of my dream, then prove it to me. Try not to read my thoughts."

One time I got tired of dreaming, and yelled, "This party is over. All you imaginary characters leave the room right now." And they said, "Oh, all right. We'll leave now, but we'll be back tomorrow night."

Now, here's the really strange part. I think that computers can do the same thing. Like an actor in a play, and like me in my dreams, a computer program can sometimes jump out of character. A program can say "Oops! I did something wrong. I'm waking up." An instruction, interpreted loosely, can say "Hey, I'm part of a computer program!" And a Java program can look at some text, decide that the text is part of a computer program, and then execute the instructions described in the text.

Well, maybe I'm stretching too far. Maybe computers don't jump out of character. But, then again, I could be right on target. Read this chapter and decide for yourself.

What We Need to Do

It's time for another case study, and the case study in this chapter is a real doozie. I spent the wee hours of one night learning about Java Reflection in order to bring you this cool case study.

The case study tackles an interesting problem — a problem that gets ignored by many authors of computer programming books. The problem is, how do you read the name of a class or method, and turn that name into a usable Java class or method?

In many programming situations, you have no need for such a trick. But XML is special. An XML document is a bunch of text, so the computer reads this text and deals with all the text's characters. Now, occasionally, some of those characters have to be turned into actions. For instance, hiding quietly inside an XML document may be the name of a Java method. Your goal is to take the name, find the corresponding method, and then call that method.

For a human being, this process (turning a name into a callable method) is almost invisible. "Self," I say, "write some code that calls the `println` method." So I type the word `println`, and I'm off and running. But for a computer, going from a name to a method isn't nearly as easy. The computer takes the letters *p-r-i-n-t-l-n*, and turns them into a reference to some instructions. That's a big step, and it seems even bigger when (as in this chapter's example) you control the way the computer takes the step.

Of course, once you learn the stuff, the steps don't seem so big anymore. In fact, I should tell you three nice things about the material in this chapter:

- ✔ The package I'm using, `java.lang.reflect`, is fun to learn about, and fun to use.

- ✔ The material in this chapter is useful, even if you don't get to use it very often. (When you need `java.lang.reflect`, it's sort of like a parachute — there's no acceptable substitute.)

- ✔ This chapter's XML document is quite interesting. The document describes a window on a computer screen in a very sensible, straight- forward way.

So let's go. C'mon, read the next section.

Describing a Java Frame

If you've ever done any GUI programming (programming involving windows in a Graphical User Interface), then you know how tedious that programming can be. Even if you're using a drag-and-drop environment, you often have to dig down into the Java code, and the Java code can be murky and unintuitive. I wish there was a sleek, easily readable way to describe the contents of a GUI window.

Poof! Presto! A genie suddenly appears. "There is a sleek way to describe a window's contents," says the genie. "All you need is Barry's Java Frame Markup Language. Get some today! There's a sample document in Listing 11-1, and a picture of the resulting frame in Figure 11-1."

Listing 11-1:   Barry's Java Frame ML

```xml
<?xml version="1.0"?>
<!-- JFrame.xml -->

<JFrame>
    <JPanel Region="North" Layout="java.awt.BorderLayout">
        <JPanel Region="West">
            <JButton Text="Copy"/>
            <JButton Text="Cut"/>
            <JButton Text="Paste"/>
        </JPanel>
        <JPanel Region="East">
            <JButton Text="Help"/>
        </JPanel>
    </JPanel>
    <JPanel Region="Center" Layout="java.awt.GridLayout">
        <JTextArea Rows="10" Columns="40"
```

(continued)

Listing 11-1 Barry's Java Frame ML *(continued)*

```
            Text="Java and XML For Dummies"/>
    </JPanel>
    <JPanel Region="South">
        <JLabel Text="Status:"/>
    </JPanel>
</JFrame>
```

Figure 11-1:
The window
described in
Listing 11-1.

The element names in Listing 11-1 aren't arbitrary in any way. Each element gets its name from one of the `javax.swing` classes. There's some information on Swing back in Chapter 9, and this chapter has a little more about Swing to help you follow the example. (Even so, this chapter won't turn you into a Java Swing expert. Most Java Swing details are best left to a book on GUI Java programming.)

You don't need to do anything special to get the Java Swing tools. The package `javax.swing` comes standard with Java 1.2 (and later versions).

Some Swing classes

Here's a list of some classes in the `javax.swing` package:

- **JFrame:** A Java `JFrame` is just a window on a computer screen. Chapter 9 has lots of information about the Java `JFrame` class.

- **JComponent:** A `JComponent` is a widget that you put somewhere on a Java `JFrame`. Each class that follows this one in this list is actually a *subclass* (in one way or another) of the `JComponent` class.

- **JPanel:** A `JPanel` is a *Tabula rasa* (that's Latin for "blank slate," and no, I don't know the Latin for "blank stare"). The things you put onto a `JPanel` include all kinds of `JComponent` objects. You can put `JButton` objects, `JTextArea` objects, `JLabel` objects and, yes, other `JPanel` objects, onto a single `JPanel` object.

In the Swing API, JPanel objects get very heavy use. When you're work-ing with a JFrame, you never put components directly onto the frame. Instead, you put components onto a JPanel, and put the JPanel onto the JFrame. That's why, in Listing 11-1, the JFrame root element has three immediate JPanel child elements.

✔ **JButton:** A JButton is one of those things that you "press" by clicking a mouse. Each JButton has its own text. The button's text is the collec-tion of characters that appear on the face of the button.

A few paragraphs back, I mentioned that the element names in Listing 11-1 come from the names of Java Swing classes. Well, the attribute names in Listing 11-1 aren't arbitrary either. Most of the attribute names come from properties of Java Swing objects.

  • The JButton element in Listing 11-1 has a Text attribute.

  • Each JButton object in a Java program has a setText method.

Read on and you'll see. This is no coincidence.

✔ **JTextArea:** A JTextArea is a big white space that displays characters. A user can type characters into (and delete characters from) the text area.

Once again, you can compare the attributes in Listing 11-1 with the methods available to JTextArea objects. In Listing 11-1, the JTextArea element has attributes Rows, Columns, and Text. And, in the Java Swing API, each JTextArea object has methods setRows, setColumns, and setText.

✔ **JLabel:** A JLabel is a harmless-looking set of characters planted some-where on a panel.

The JLabel element in Listing 11-1 has a Text attribute and, sure enough, each JLabel object in a Java program has a setText method.

Java layouts

To understand the stuff in Listing 11-1, there's another aspect of Java's win-dowing tools that you should explore. Back in 1995, the folks who created Java decided that Java's windowing tools should be based on layouts. And what is a layout? A *layout* is a description of a logical arrangement of compo-nents. The word "logical" is important, because a layout doesn't normally describe exact locations.

For instance, in Figure 11-1, there's a Copy button in the upper right-hand corner of the frame. Meanwhile, in Listing 11-1, there's no indication that the Copy button starts 11 pixels from the left edge, and 29 pixels from the top, of the Java Jframe. Instead, Listing 11-1 describes panels within panels.

✔ There's a panel inside the northern region of the JFrame. (Let's call it the "north panel.")

✔ There's a panel inside the western region of the north panel. (Let's call this second panel the "west panel.")

✔ The Copy button is inside the west panel. So the Copy button is in the northwest corner of the frame.

In Figure 11-1, the Help button is tucked up against the rightmost edge of the frame. This is also because of the panel arrangements described in Listing 11-1.

✔ The north panel is inside the northern region of the frame.

✔ There's a panel (which I'll call the "east panel") in the eastern region of the north panel.

✔ The Help button is inside the east panel. So the Help button is in the northeast corner of the frame.

This business about regions comes from the java.awt.BorderLayout class. A frame or panel with BorderLayout is divided into five regions, as I show in Figure 11-2. You can put one component in each of the five regions. So, in Figure 11-3, the frame has three panels — a panel in the North region, a panel in the Center region, and a panel in the South region.

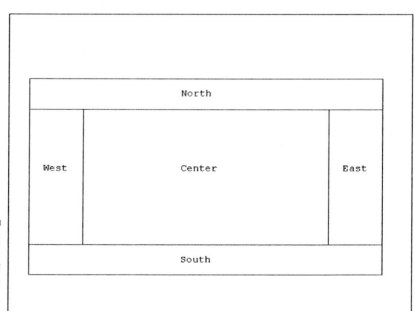

Figure 11-2:
The five regions of a border layout.

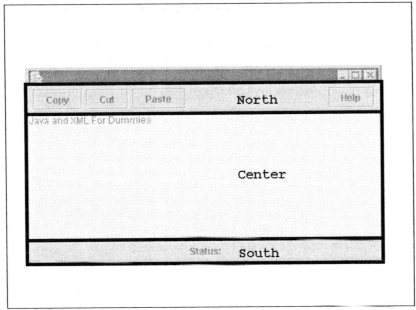

Figure 11-3:
Three
panels have
been added
to the frame.

In Figure 11-4, the panel in the North region has two panels inside it. There's
one panel in the East region, and another panel in the West region.

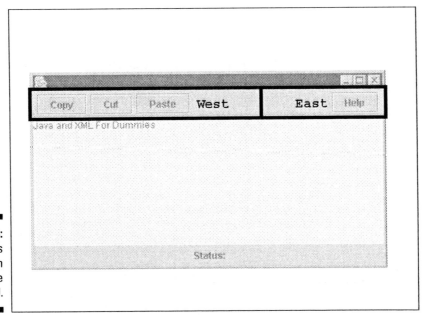

Figure 11-4:
Two panels
have been
added to the
north panel.

Hard-coding a frame into a Java program

There's much more to the Java layout story than what I'm telling you in this book. The usual deal is, you write a long, unfriendly-looking Java program to construct a frame piece by piece. To show you what I mean, I've written a full-blown Java program to create the frame shown in Figure 11-1. The program is in Listing 11-2.

Listing 11-2: Building a Frame from Scratch

```java
import javax.swing.JFrame;
import javax.swing.JPanel;
import javax.swing.JButton;
import javax.swing.JTextArea;
import javax.swing.JLabel;

import java.awt.LayoutManager;
import java.awt.BorderLayout;
import java.awt.GridLayout;


class GoAhead_MakeMyJ
{
    public static void main(String args[])
    {
        new MyJFrame();
    }
}


class MyJFrame extends JFrame
{
    MyJFrame()
    {
        JPanel pane = (JPanel)getContentPane();

        JPanel northPanel = new JPanel();
        pane.add(northPanel, "North");
        northPanel.setLayout(new BorderLayout());

            JPanel westPanel = new JPanel();
            northPanel.add(westPanel, "West");

                JButton copyButton = new JButton();
                westPanel.add(copyButton);
                copyButton.setText("Copy");

                JButton cutButton = new JButton();
                westPanel.add(cutButton);
                cutButton.setText("Cut");

                JButton pasteButton = new JButton();
```

```
            westPanel.add(pasteButton);
            pasteButton.setText("Paste");

        JPanel eastPanel = new JPanel();
        northPanel.add(eastPanel, "East");

            JButton helpButton = new JButton();
            eastPanel.add(helpButton);
            helpButton.setText("Help");

    JPanel centerPanel = new JPanel();
    pane.add(centerPanel, "Center");
    centerPanel.setLayout(new GridLayout());

        JTextArea textarea = new JTextArea();
        centerPanel.add(textarea);
        textarea.setRows(10);
        textarea.setColumns(40);
        textarea.setText("Java and XML For Dummies");

    JPanel southPanel = new JPanel();
    pane.add(southPanel, "South");

        JLabel label = new JLabel();
        southPanel.add(label);
        label.setText("Status:");

    setDefaultCloseOperation(JFrame.EXIT_ON_CLOSE);
    pack();
    show();
  }
}
```

When I wrote the code in Listing 11-2, I took liberties with standard Java
indentation rules. I did this to help you see which lines of code would match
up with which lines in Listing 11-1. (I like it! I think the non-standard indentation tells you a lot about the nesting of panels and components!) But please
take note: Listings 11-1 and 11-2 are completely independent of one another.
Listing 11-1 is one description of a Java JFrame, and listing 11-2 is a different
description of the same JFrame.

The program in Listing 11-2 doesn't read the document in Listing 11-1. Instead,
the program in Listing 11-2 has a frame hard-coded into its statements. In a
sense, Listings 11-1 and 11-2 are alternate descriptions of the same frame. So,
if you have to pick one way or the other to represent the frame in Figure 11-1,
which way will you choose?

Well, for the sheer simplicity of the representation, there's no contest. The
XML document (Listing 11-1) is much easier to read than the Java code in
Listing 11-2. That's why I'm an advocate for XML.

Of course, when you're representing important data, simplicity isn't your only concern. While the Java code in Listing 11-2 comes with years of Sun Microsystems development, the XML document in Listing 11-1 is Barry's one-shot, proof-of-concept effort. When you see the code behind Listing 11-1 (the code that turns an XML document into a visible frame), you'll see the code's limitations and disclaimers. As simple as it is, Barry's Java Frame Markup Language isn't ready for prime time. Still, the Java Frame Markup Language is a good idea — an idea that illustrates some interesting XML processing concepts.

So read on. The next section shows you the code lurking behind the scenes — the code that reads an XML document, and uses the document to display a nice-looking JFrame.

Reading and Interpreting the XML Document

If I've done it once, I've done it a hundred times. Listing 11-3 has that old standby — a main method to start the rest of the Java code running.

Listing 11-3:   Yawn! Another JDOM Calling Class

```
import org.jdom.JDOMException;
import org.jdom.Document;
import org.jdom.input.SAXBuilder;
import java.io.File;

/* Copout: Lots of exceptions checked with the lame
            'throws Exception' clause. Exceptions that
            can be thrown by this code include:
            ClassNotFoundException, InstantiationException,
            NoSuchMethodException, IllegalAccessException,
            InvocationTargetException.
*/

public class CallJDOM
{
    public static void main(String args[]) throws Exception
    {
        Document doc;

        SAXBuilder builder = new SAXBuilder(false);

        if (args.length == 1)
        {
            doc = builder.build
                (new File(args[0]).toURL().toString());
```

```
        new FrameMaker (doc);
    }
  else
      System.out.println
          ("Usage: java CallDOM file-name.xml");
  }
}
```

How boring can it get? Listing 11-3 reminds me of Listing 10-1, which reminds me of Listing 7-2. And Listing 7-2 reminds me of Listing 4-2, which bears a striking resemblance to the code in Listing 3-2. After so many classes that look so much alike, the only interesting thing about Listing 11-3 is what it noticeably fails to do. The code fails to do a respectable job with exception handling.

As I've done with so many examples in this book, the code in this chapter sacrifices robustness for readability. This chapter's case study uses Java reflection, and one use of the reflection API can throw so many exceptions! By the time you're done catching them all, you have a very robust, but extremely cluttered, piece of code. So, to help you focus on the logic (not the softball game with gloves, bats, and exceptions), I've bunched all the exception handling code into a few, chintzy throws clauses.

The code that makes a frame

At this point, I have no choice but to let you in on a little secret. The secret is that the code in this chapter represents a compromise. You see, I have two conflicting goals:

✔ I want code that's as generic as possible — code that can take any XML file, with any Java swing components as its element names, and render the file on a GUI screen.

It's one thing to assume that you have elements named JPanel, JButton, and JTextArea, as you do in Listing 11-1. But what if you throw in a JMenu, a JScrollBar, or a JToolTip? These are all names of classes in the Java Swing API. A good program handles any of these class names, and handles new class names that are developed in future versions of Swing.

✔ I want code that's readable. After all, this is a book about Java and XML programming, not a project to send a rocket to Mars.

My first compromise for readability comes in Listing 11-4. In that listing, I assume that we're starting with a JFrame. Sure, there are other swing components that could form an outer boundary on my screen, but the JFrame is quite generic and very widely used. So Listing 11-4, builds a JFrame. The listing also starts the drilling process — the process of drilling for more elements inside the XML document.

Listing 11-4:   Making the Frame

```
import org.jdom.Document;
import org.jdom.Element;

import javax.swing.JFrame;
import javax.swing.JPanel;

import java.util.List;


class FrameMaker
{

    FrameMaker (Document doc) throws Exception
    {
        JFrame frame = new JFrame();
        JPanel pane = (JPanel)frame.getContentPane();

        List children = doc.getRootElement().getChildren();

        for (int i=0; i<children.size(); i++)
            new ComponentMaker((Element)children.get(i), pane);

        frame.setDefaultCloseOperation(JFrame.EXIT_ON_CLOSE);
        frame.pack();
        frame.show();
    }

}
```

After the explanation of the code in Listing 9-4, there's not much new about frames in Listing 11-4. One new feature is the use of the JFrame pack method. When you call pack, the computer resizes the frame. Take whatever components you've added to the frame. After packing, the frame's new size is just big enough to hold those components comfortably.

The code that makes a component

Besides calling a few swing methods, Listing 11-4 just looks at an XML document, grabs the children of the root element, and then starts marching right along. This "marching right along" means paying visit after visit to the ComponentMaker constructor. The ComponentMaker looks at elements like JButton, and creates a button to be displayed on the computer screen. The code for ComponentMaker is in Listing 11-5.

Listing 11-5:   Making a Component

```
import org.jdom.Element;
import org.jdom.Attribute;

import javax.swing.JComponent;
import javax.swing.JPanel;

import java.util.List;


class ComponentMaker
{

    ComponentMaker (Element elt, JPanel panel)
        throws Exception
    {
        Class eltClass =
            Class.forName("javax.swing." + elt.getName());
        JComponent component =
            (JComponent)eltClass.newInstance();


        List attribs = elt.getAttributes();
        for (int i=0; i<attribs.size(); i++)
            new AttributeHandler (eltClass, component,
                                    attribs.get(i), panel);

        if (!panel.isAncestorOf(component))
            panel.add(component);


        List children = elt.getChildren();
        for (int i=0; i<children.size(); i++)
            new ComponentMaker
                ((Element)children.get(i), (JPanel)component);
    }

}
```

In is broadest outline, the code in Listing 11-5 does four things:

 ✔ The code creates a `swing` component from the name of an element.
 ✔ The code creates an `AttributeHandler` (something I made up) to deal
   with the attributes of the element.
 ✔ If the component hasn't already been added to a panel, then the code
   plops the component onto a panel.
 ✔ The code calls itself recursively for each element in the XML document.

Let's look at each of these four tasks individually.

Creating a swing object

Here's where we start using Java reflection, and things begin to get spooky. In Listing 11-5, the call to `Class.forName` finds a Java class whose name is `javax.swing.JPanel` (or `javax.swing.Whatever`). Then the call to `eltClass.newInstance` creates a `swing` component. Later, we'll set this `swing` component's properties, and add the component to our frame.

In the meantime, we get our first glimpse of Java's reflection API. We start with a string of characters (the string `"JPanel"`, for instance). The string comes from the name of an element in the XML document (Listing 11-1). We use `forName` and `newInstance` to go from that string of characters to an actual object of type `JPanel`. It's a pretty neat trick.

Handling each attribute

In Listing 11-5, the next chunk of code deals with the attributes of an element. As usual, you get a Java `List` full of attributes, and then loop your way through the attributes one by one.

To be merciful, dear reader, I've buried all the sticky attribute-handling code inside my `AttributeHandler` class. We'll look at the `AttributeHandler` class soon.

Adding the component to a panel

A component that's not added to anything will never show up on your computer screen. The usual story is, you add a component (say, a button) to a panel, and then add the panel to the frame.

Now, there's a piece of the action that you don't see when you stare at Listing 11-5. While you're not looking, the `AttributeHandler` may be placing your component onto a panel. If this has already happened, then you don't want to call something like `panel.add(component)` again. So, before calling `panel.add(component)`, the code calls the `isAncestorOf` method. This call checks to see if the component has, or has not, been added to the panel.

Making recursive calls

You knew this was coming. In Listing 11-5, after doing everything that needs to be done with a particular element, we get a list of the element's children. Then, for each child in the list, we make a recursive call to the `ComponentMaker` constructor. That way, every element in the document of Listing 11-1 gets turned into a `swing` object.

The AttributeHandler class

In Listing 11-1, each attribute holds one of three things.

> ✔ **It holds the name of a Java layout manager class.**
>
> For instance, it holds `java.awt.BorderLayout`.
>
> ✔ **It holds the name of a region in a border layout.**
>
> For instance, it holds `"North"`, meaning that a component should be added to a border layout's northern region.
>
> ✔ **It holds the name and value of a component's property.**
>
> For instance, the attribute `Text="Copy"` says that the text on the face of a button should be the word `"Copy"`. The attribute `Rows="10"` says that the text area should have 10 rows.

The three kinds of attributes

At this point, you have a choice. You can follow along as I describe the `AttributeHandler` class, or you can skip this section entirely, and trust me. (When you "trust me," you're trusting that my `AttributeHandler` does the stuff that I listed in the previous three bullets.) The reason you may want to read this section is, the section does all that Java reflection stuff — the stuff that's so incredibly cool. The reason you may want to skip this section is, the section does very little with XML.

Well, you made it as far as this paragraph. Heck, you may as well keep reading. The previous three bullets correspond to three different kinds of method calls. Listing 11-2 has samples of all three kinds of calls.

> ✔ **You can set a panel's layout manager.**
>
> To give a layout manager to a panel, you call the `setLayout` method. For instance, in Listing 11-2, I call
>
> ```
> northPanel.setLayout(new BorderLayout());
> ```
>
> ✔ **You can add a component to a region in a panel.**
>
> Take a panel with a border layout (like the `northPanel` in Listing 11-2). To add a component to this panel, you call a panel's `add` method. For instance, in Listing 11-2, I call
>
> ```
> northPanel.add(westPanel, "West");
> ```
>
> This statement adds a particular component (namely, the `westPanel` component) to the western region of the `northPanel`'s border layout.

✔ **You can set the value of a component's property.**

In Java, a property is typically accompanied by a *setter* method. Let's say you have a variable named `copyButton`. To give the button's text property the value `"Copy"`, you call

```
copyButton.setText("Copy");
```

Let's say you have a variable named `textarea`. To give a text area's `rows` property the value 10, you call

```
textarea.setRows(10);
```

(Once again, these lines of code come from Listing 11-2.) The names of these setter methods are standardized. If you have a variable named `gooseneck`, and every such neck has a property named perimeter, then you can probably set the neck's perimeter by calling

```
gooseneck.setPerimeter(15);
```

Composing three kinds of method calls

In the previous bullets, I described three kinds of method calls. Now, with fancy use of Java reflection, I could deal with each kind of method call on the fly. I could write one big piece of code that composed each kind of method call based on an elaborate analysis of the Swing API. But, if I did this, then my `AttributeHandler` code would be horribly complicated.

So, in Listing 11-6, I cheat and check for the words `Layout` and `Region`. If I find either of these words, then I branch into a special case. If not, then I compose a `setter` method.

Listing 11-6: Handling an Attribute

```
import org.jdom.Attribute;

import javax.swing.JComponent;
import javax.swing.JPanel;
import java.awt.LayoutManager;
import java.lang.reflect.Method;


class AttributeHandler
{

    AttributeHandler(Class eltClass, JComponent component,
                     Object attrib, JPanel panel)
        throws Exception
    {
```

```
String attName = ((Attribute)attrib).getName();
String attValue = ((Attribute)attrib).getValue();


//-------Layout--------------//
if (attName.equals("Layout"))
{
   LayoutManager layoutManager =
   (LayoutManager)Class.forName
                          (attValue).newInstance();
   ((JPanel)component).setLayout(layoutManager);
}


//-------Region--------------//
else if (attName.equals("Region"))
   panel.add(component, attValue);


//-------Other---------    ----//
else
{
   Method method;
   Object[] params = new Object[1];
   final Class[] oneIntParam = {int.class};
   final Class[] oneStringParam = {String.class};

   try
   {
       params[0] = new Integer(attValue);
       method = eltClass.getMethod
                      ("set"+attName, oneIntParam);
   }
   catch (NumberFormatException e)
   {
       params[0] = attValue;
       method = eltClass.getMethod
                      ("set"+attName, oneStringParam);
   }

   method.invoke(component, params);
   }
  }

}
```

There's that magic number three again. I've divided the AttributeHandler
class (Listing 11-6) into three parts. Each part handles one of the cases
described in the previous three bullets.

The Layout attribute

Consider an attribute such as `Layout="java.awt.BorderLayout"` (in Listing 11-1). The corresponding code in Listing 11-6 has two statements.

- ✔ The first statement calls `Class.forName` to create an instance of the `java.awt.BorderLayout` class.
- ✔ The second statement calls `setLayout` to apply this `java.awt.BorderLayout` instance to a particular panel.

All in all, the code does what a statement such as

```
northPanel.setLayout(new BorderLayout());
```

does in Listing 11-2.

The Region attribute

Consider an attribute, such as `Region="West"`, in Listing 11-1. The corresponding code in Listing 11-6 has one statement. The statement adds a component to a region within a panel. When `attValue` is `"West"`, this statement does what a statement such as

```
northPanel.add(westPanel, "West");
```

does in Listing 11-2.

Property attributes

Consider attributes, such as `Text="Copy"` and `Rows="10"`, in Listing 11-1. The corresponding code in Listing 11-6 does a whole bunch of things. Instead of giving you a full blow-by-blow description, I'll describe the essential details and let you look up the rest in the Java API documentation.

First, there's this funky little class named `java.lang.reflect.Method`. An instance of this class is a Java method. (Go figure!) The point of the code is to call `getMethod`, and obtain a method such as `setText` or `setRows`. (Notice the word `set` in each of the calls to `getMethod`.)

Because of this reflection business, a description of the code in Listing 11-6 can quickly become ridiculous. You're calling the `getMethod` method in order to get the `setText` method. You could also call the `getMethod` method to get the `getMethod` method, or call the `getMethod` method method to get the `getGet` method method method. (Well, I made the last one up just to be silly, but you get the idea.)

Next, look at the `try` statement in Listing 11-6. Unlike most `try` statements, this particular `try` statement has nothing to do with errors. This `try` statement separates numeric attribute values (such as `"10"`) from non-numeric attribute values (such as `"Copy"`).

For an attribute with value "10", the Integer constructor (inside the try statement) proceeds normally. Then, when you call getMethod, the call gets a method with a single int parameter. But, for an attribute with value "Copy", the try statement's Integer constructor throws a fit. (Well, actually, it throws a NumberFormatException.) In the catch clause for the NumberFormatException, you ask for a method with a single String parameter. This use of a try statement is very sneaky, but it works.

As a final stroke of narcissistic reflection, the code in Listing 11-6 calls the invoke method. This invoke method gets something like setText or setRows running. A call to setText sets a button's text to "Copy", or to "Cut", or to something of that kind. The call to setRows (the call that gets formulated by the code in Listing 11-6) makes a text area be exactly 10 rows tall.

(Here we go again. A call to a particular method's invoke method invokes that particular method. It boggles the mind. Remember my goofy description of Russell's set of all sets back in Chapter 9? Well, what if Russell had been a Java programmer? Then Russell's set would have been "The set of all set methods that are not set methods of themselves." How about the method to set the set of all set methods' methods that are not set methods of method sets? Yikes! Is there an echo in here?)

Chapter 12

Transforming XML Data

*T*his chapter is about the XML equivalent of alchemy — the mystic discipline (or black art — opinions differ) that turns things of one kind into things of another kind. Alchemists call it transmutation; XML enthusiasts call it transformation: You start with something you like, end up with something you like even more, and maybe snag some wisdom on the way.

Of course, anything that makes such a fundamental and useful change has to come with dangers. (It's traditional.) Case in point: Alexander Sethon, an alchemist of the 1600s who managed to hide his practice from the rest of the world for years. Hanging out in Dresden, Germany, he turned worthless metals into gold (or so the story goes) — until his wife coaxed him out of hiding. She urged Sethon to capitalize on his alchemical talent and sent him to meet Christian II, the Elector of Saxony. Sure enough, the Elector believed in Sethon's powers, ordered the alchemist to become a full-time royal gold mine, and threw him in jail when he refused. (Accounts of torture and deprivation follow — not too unusual when gold is involved.)

Eventually Sethon got out of jail by convincing fellow alchemist Michael Sendivogius to bribe everyone in sight. In return for springing Sethon from the hoosegow, Sendivogius would get (you guessed it) the secret of making gold. Once out of the clinker, however, Sethon double-crossed Sendivogius by withholding the magic formula. So, after Sethon's death, Sendivogius did what anyone would do: He married Sethon's widow (who never could resist the charms of those alchemists). Sendivogius found Sethon's secrets, used them, and managed to get himself thrown in jail.

Bottom line: Sometimes the legacy system can't handle new techniques all that well. Sethon was tortured, Sendivogius was jailed, the Elector never got his gold, Sethon's wife lost one alchemist after another — and over the centuries, the whole affair may have transmuted into a tale about a princess and a rumpled elf spinning straw into gold. Finally, in 1980, scientists at the University of California managed to turn bismuth into gold. The process costs zillions of times more than the value of the gold, but the alchemists in heaven and hell must be enjoying the last laugh. Revised bottom line (take your pick):

- ✔ Timing is all (or nearly all).
- ✔ When you can make spectacular changes, be careful not to get carried away.
- ✔ Always get the right tool for the job. Which brings us to XSL, the miraculous tool that transforms XML data into something even more useful (*without* costing zillions).

Stretching and Bending Data

The whole fuss about XML comes down to one thing — the versatility of data. Suppose I have a bunch of data stored a certain way — but that way isn't good enough to meet present needs. I want my data stored a different way.

Maybe I want one program to exchange its data with another program, so the storage of the data has to be modified. Maybe I want the data on my company's computer, to be readable by another company's software. Maybe I'm just changing my own formats, and I need data translated from the old format to the new format.

Reorganizing data

Consider the following list (an abbreviated list of colleges and universities).

```
<University>
    <Name>Drew University</Name>
    <Street>36 Madison Avenue</Street>
    <City>Madison</City>
    <State>NJ</State>
    <Zip>07940</Zip>
</University>
```

After using the list for several months, I decide that each institution's name should be separate from the institution's address. I need to rework the data to reflect this change:

```
<University>
    <Name>Drew University</Name>
    <Address>
        <Street>36 Madison Avenue</Street>
```

```
        <City>Madison</City>
        <State>NJ</State>
        <Zip>07940</Zip>
    </Address>
</University>
```

Eventually, I send my list to a directory of universities. The directory's software expects attributes in place of my text. So, I rework the document a second time:

```
<University name="Drew University">
    <Address>
        <Street number="36" Name="Madison" type="Avenue"/>
        <City name="Madison"/>
        <State code="NJ"/>
        <Zip fiveDigit="07940"/>
    </Address>
</University>
```

A month later, the people who maintain the directory send letters to universities. The software creates mailing labels that look like this:

```
Drew University
36 Madison Avenue
Madison, NJ 07940
```

That's another way to represent the same data.

So, at each point in this story, the information stays the same. The only thing that changes is the way we structure and store the information.

The extensible stylesheet language

There's a very nice way to modify the structure and storage of data. It's called XSL — the eXtensible Stylesheet Language. Using XSL, you start with two files — an XML document and an XSL *stylesheet*.

- ✔ The XML document contains data, such as account information for all your customers, university names and addresses, or a list of your favorite sins.
- ✔ The stylesheet describes a way to get a brand new document from the existing XML document.

Now, we need some terminology. The terminology makes sense, so it's not too difficult to remember.

- The existing XML document is called the *source* document.
- You *apply* the XSL stylesheet to the source document.
- The computer combines the XML document with the XSL stylesheet by performing a *transformation*.
- The document that you get by applying the XSL stylesheet to the XML source document is called the *result* document (a.k.a. the *new* document or the *output* document).

All About XSL

The eXtensible Stylesheet Language is divided into three parts — XSLT, Xpath, and XSL Formatting Objects.

- **XSLT: The eXtensible Stylesheet Language Transformations**

XSLT is a set of rules for turning one XML tree into another XML tree. Take the first two University documents at the beginning of this chapter. To go from one document to the other, you apply an XSLT transformation. The transformation shifts from one XML tree to another. The shift is shown here.

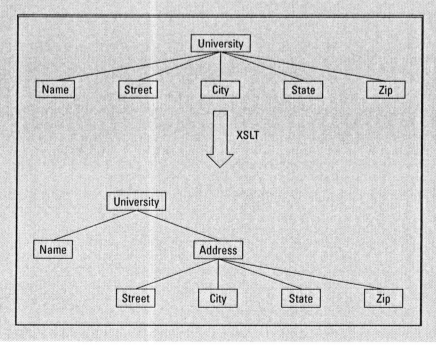

The terminology is illustrated in Figure 12-1.

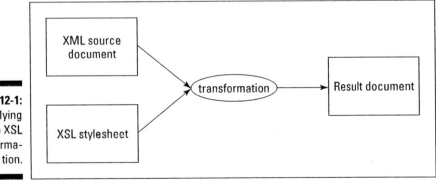

Figure 12-1: Applying an XSL transformation.

So how do you apply a stylesheet to an XML document? Well, one way is to run a Java program. Java uses classes in its `javax.xml.transform` package to apply stylesheets to XML documents. This chapter helps you with the details.

How to Get Up and Running (A Basic Example)

Let's see the code that turns an old XML document into a new XML document. First, we need an old XML document. There's a crusty old document in Listing 12-1.

Listing 12-1:   Nasty Old Data

```
<?xml version="1.0" encoding="UTF-8"?>
<!-- OldData.xml -->

<OldData>
    <Name>Burd</Name>
    <Zip>07940</Zip>
</OldData>
```

After years of painstaking research into the optimal ways for representing data, my company has decided to switch gears. Instead of having a `Name` element, my company wants a `LastName` element. (This makes sense, because Burd is a last name.) Instead of having a `Zip` element, my company prefers the more universal term — the term `PostalCode`. My company wants a document like the one in Listing 12-2.

Listing 12-2:   Bright, Shiny New Data

```
<?xml version="1.0" encoding="UTF-8"?>
<!-- NewData.xml -->
<NewData>
<LastName>Burd</LastName>
<PostalCode>07940</PostalCode>
</NewData>
```

Assume we're not talking about one tiny little XML file. My company has thousands and thousands of names and addresses in one or more files like `OldData.xml`. How do we change all the files? We have several alternatives.

✔ **Use a simple text editor.**

Do a global search, replacing `Name` with `LastName`. Then make a similar sweep changing `Zip` to `PostalCode`.

Well, give me a break. This strategy changes `Howard Namenski` to `Howard LastNamenski`, and changes `Arnold Zipf` to `Arnold PostalCodef`. Let's not even go there.

✔ **Write a DOM program, or a JDOM program, to do the work.**

In Chapters 8 and 10, I explained the process of creating a brand new XML document with Java's DOM or JDOM API. With either API, you can analyze an old document, and create a new document as you go.

DOM and JDOM are somewhat more respectable ways of solving the problem. But with XSL in the bag of tricks, there's an even better way.

✔ **Create an XSL stylesheet, and apply the XSL stylesheet to your old XML document.**

The XSL language was developed specifically for the task at hand. With XSL, we can concentrate on the content of the new document, and leave the processing logic to Java. In the next several pages, you'll see what I mean.

An XSL stylesheet

To convert from Name to LastName, and from Zip to PostalCode, we need an XSL stylesheet. There's a ready-made stylesheet in Listing 12-3.

Listing 12-3:   XSL At Its Finest

```
<?xml version="1.0"?>
<!-- old2new.xsl -->

<xsl:stylesheet
    xmlns:xsl="http://www.w3.org/1999/XSL/Transform"
    version="1.0">
  <xsl:output method="xml" indent="yes"/>

  <xsl:template match="/">
    <xsl:comment> NewData.xml </xsl:comment>
    <xsl:element name="NewData">
      <xsl:element name="LastName">
        <xsl:value-of select="//Name"/>
      </xsl:element>

      <xsl:element name="PostalCode">
        <xsl:value-of select="//Zip"/>
      </xsl:element>
    </xsl:element>
  </xsl:template>

</xsl:stylesheet>
```

I'm in luck. This isn't a book about XSL, so I don't have to describe Listing 12-3 in great detail. Instead, I can breeze over a few of the most important points.

- ✔ **Like every other XSL file, the file of Listing 12-3 is an XML document.**

  All the elements in Listing 12-3 belong to the xsl namespace. The root element is xsl:stylesheet.

- ✔ **The** xsl:output **element has a** method="xml" **attribute. So, when you apply this stylesheet, the result is an XML document.**

  When I apply the stylesheet in Listing 12-3 to the document in Listing 12-1, I get the XML document in Listing 12-2.

  As an experiment, I used Listings 12-1 and 12-3 again. But this time, in Listing 12-3, I changed method="xml" to method="text". Instead of the document in Listing 12-2, I got the following one-line text file:

```
<!-- NewData.xml -->Burd07940
```

  This makes sense. What passes for an "element" in a text file is just a word or two, scrunched right up against another word or two.

- ✔ **The template in Listing 12-3 matches any element in the document of Listing 12-1.**

  In the match attribute of Listing 12-3, the forward slash stands for any element in the source document. The computer will look for elements in Listing 12-1, and apply a template to each element. The template is the stuff between the xsl:template start and end tags in Listing 12-3.

- ✔ **The** xsl:element **tags create brand new elements.**

  Listing 12-3 has three xsl:element tags — one for NewData, another for LastName, and a third for PostalCode. And, sure enough, Listing 12-2 has three elements with those same names. Because the xsl:element tags are nested in Listing 12-3, the new XML elements are nested in Listing 12-2.

- ✔ **Each** xsl:value-of **tag in Listing 12-3 represents text from Listing 12-1.**

  Back in Listing 12-1, the text inside the Name element is Burd. So the attribute select="//Name"/ in Listing 12-3 grabs Burd, and pastes it into the result document (the document in Listing 12-2).

The code that does all the work

This section's program is very versatile. The program works with any XML file and any XSL stylesheet. Just run the program, hand the names of the files to the program, and watch the program work. The magic code is in Listing 12-4.

Listing 12-4:   Applying XSL

```java
import javax.xml.transform.TransformerFactory;
import javax.xml.transform.Transformer;
import javax.xml.transform.TransformerException;

import javax.xml.transform.stream.StreamSource;
import javax.xml.transform.stream.StreamResult;

import java.io.File;
import java.io.FileOutputStream;
import java.io.FileNotFoundException;


public class MyTransform
{
    public static void main(String[] args)
        throws TransformerException,
               FileNotFoundException


    {

        TransformerFactory factory;
        Transformer transformer;

        File oldFile, xslFile, newFile;
        StreamSource oldStream, xslStream;
        StreamResult newStream;

        factory = TransformerFactory.newInstance();

        if (args.length == 3)
        {
            oldFile = new File(args[0]);
            oldStream = new StreamSource(oldFile);

            xslFile = new File(args[1]);
            xslStream = new StreamSource(xslFile);

            newFile = new File(args[2]);
            newStream = new StreamResult(newFile);

            transformer = factory.newTransformer(xslStream);
            transformer.transform (oldStream, newStream);
        }
        else
        {
            System.out.print ("Usage: java MyTransform ");
            System.out.println("old.xml xform.xsl new.xml");
        }
    }
}
```

When you run the code in Listing 12-4, you should add three command-line arguments.

```
java MyTransform OldData.xml old2new.xsl NewData.xml
```

The first two arguments stand for source and style-sheet documents (the files in Listings 12-1 and 12-3). The third argument has the name of the result file that you're trying to create. By running the code in Listing 12-4, you get the new file shown in Listing 12-2.

How the code works

Listing 12-4 deals with three files. The filenames enter the program via the program's command-line arguments. If you issue the command line shown previously, then `args[0]` stands for `OldData.xml`, `args[1]` stands for `old2new.xsl`, and `args[2]` stands for `NewData.xml`.

The whole point of Listing 12-4 is this: Take the `old2new.xsl` stylesheet in Listing 12-3, and use it to make a *transformer*. This transformer is an instance of Java's `javax.xml.transform.Transformer` class. Once you have the transformer object, you apply that object to the source document (Listing 12-1). Here's the whole business in a bit more detail:

✔ **You convert the command-line arguments into objects that the transformer can use.**

The line `oldFile = new File(args[0])` creates a Java `File` object from a command-line argument string. Then, the line `oldStream = new StreamSource(oldFile)` creates a stream source (whatever that is) from the Java `File` object. This two-step process leads from considering the name of a file to the kind of object that a transformer can handle.

✔ **You create a transformer.**

As is the case with many of Java's XML tools, you first create a factory, and then you use the factory to create a useful object (in this case, a transformer object). Notice, in Listing 12-4, that you don't create any old transformer. The transformer that you create is specific to the XSL stylesheet that you plan to use.

✔ **You apply the transformation.**

Once you have a transformer based on your favorite XSL stylesheet, you just take the transformer and call its `transform` method. As parameters to the method, you supply references to the source document, and the result document.

You say you want to transform another document? No problem. Just reuse the transformer. Call the same `transform` method again, supplying different parameters for source document and result document.

StreamSource and StreamResult

Look at the StreamSource and StreamResult pages in Java's API documentation. You can choose from several different constructors for the StreamSource and StreamResult classes. For instance, you can call StreamSource(), StreamSource (File f), StreamSource(String systemId), StreamResult(File f), StreamResult(String systemId), and so on.

In creating Listing 12-4, I tried quite a few constructors. Some constructors worked well for one class, but not for the other class.

For instance, the argument that I used back in Listing 4-2, new File(args[0]). to URL().toString(), worked for Stream Source, but not for StreamResult. (Actually, I was able to create a StreamResult object using new File(args[0]).toURL().to String() but, later in the code's run, the transform method didn't like what it saw.)

So keep your eye on the Java documentation for the StreamSource and StreamResult classes. When you work with XSL, use the constructors that best suit each task.

Tips and Tweaks

Up to this point in the chapter, I've been doing the straightforward application of a stylesheet to a document. Well, that's the minimum you can do. Now it's time to look at more than the minimum.

Properties

Every Java XML transformer has a set of *properties*. These properties govern the way the transformer goes about its business. So what properties does a transformer have, and which properties can you set?

Well, a property's value is really an object. You can reach the object with some fancy URL notation, but you can also make use of Java's predefined strings. Look at the Java documentation for the class javax.xml.transform. OutputKeys, and you'll see what I mean.

In the documentation, one output key is named OMIT_XML_DECLARATION. When you add the statement

```
transformer.setOutputProperty
(javax.xml.transform.OutputKeys.OMIT_XML_DECLARATION, "yes");
```

to the code in Listing 12-4, you suppress the output of the line <?xml version=... in the result document. Another output key is named INDENT.

If you add

```
transformer.setOutputProperty
    (javax.xml.transform.OutputKeys.INDENT , "no");
```

to the code in Listing 12-4, then much of the result document gets squeezed onto a single line of text. The result extends much farther to the right:

```
<?xml version="1.0" encoding="UTF-8"?>
<!-- NewData.xml --><NewData><LastName>Burd</LastName><Po...
```

With an output key, you can tell the transformer when it should, and should not, create CDATA sections. For instance, let's say you start with the following simple document:

```
<MyElement>
    <![CDATA[<text>]]>
</MyElement>
```

In this tiny document, the CDATA section ensures that the angle brackets in <text> aren't taken as part of an XML tag.

Now, to your XML stew, add the following stylesheet:

```
<xsl:stylesheet
    xmlns:xsl="http://www.w3.org/1999/XSL/Transform"
    version="1.0">

    <xsl:template match="/">
        <xsl:element name="NewElement">
            <xsl:value-of select="//MyElement"/>
        </xsl:element>
    </xsl:template>

</xsl:stylesheet>
```

Run Listing 12-4 just as it is. When you do, you get this result:

```
<?xml version="1.0" encoding="UTF-8"?>
<NewElement>
    &lt;text&gt;
</NewElement>
```

In this result, the angle brackets become entities < and >. That's the default behavior. But add the following line to the code of Listing 12-4:

```
transformer.setOutputProperty
    (javax.xml.transform.OutputKeys.CDATA_SECTION_ELEMENTS,
    "NewElement");
```

Then, when you run the modified program, you get this result:

```
<?xml version="1.0" encoding="UTF-8"?>
<NewElement><![CDATA[
    <text>
]]></NewElement>
```

The CDATA_SECTION_ELEMENTS property forces the angle brackets within NewElement to be output with a CDATA section. (The same thing happens if you start with <text> in your source document.)

Java's OutputKeys strings match one-for-one with attributes that you can put in an xsl:output tag. (To see an xsl:output tag, look at Listing 12-3.)

When you add a setOutputProperty method call to the code of Listing 12-4, be sure to add it after the call to factory.newTransformer, and before the call to transformer.transform. Otherwise, the call to setOutputProperty will have no effect.

Parameters

If you're like me, then you put off making decisions until the very last minute. Don't jump to any quick conclusions. Just wait until your back is against the wall, and then fire off an answer.

Well, computers can play that game too. A program can have a variable with a meaningless value, and then get a good value when a value is needed. The Extensible Stylesheet Language, powerful as it is, can do the same thing.

Parameters in an XSL stylesheet

An XSL stylesheet can have something called a *parameter*. A parameter has a value, but that value depends on several things. One of those things can surface when you run your Java program. For a concrete example, see Listings 12-5 and 12-6.

Listing 12-5:   StoogeML

```
<?xml version="1.0" encoding="UTF-8"?>
<!-- StoogesIn.xml -->

<StoogesIn>
    <StoogeIn>Moe</StoogeIn>
    <StoogeIn>Larry</StoogeIn>
    <StoogeIn>(other)</StoogeIn>
</StoogesIn>
```

Listing 12-6: XSL with a Parameter

```xml
<?xml version="1.0"?>
<!-- in2out.xsl -->

<xsl:stylesheet
    xmlns:xsl="http://www.w3.org/1999/XSL/Transform"
    version="1.0">
  <xsl:output method="xml" indent="yes"/>

  <xsl:param name="third_stooge">Curly</xsl:param>

  <xsl:template match="/">
    <xsl:comment> StoogesOut.xml </xsl:comment>
    <xsl:element name="StoogesOut">
      <xsl:for-each select="//StoogeIn">
        <xsl:element name="StoogeOut">

          <xsl:choose>
            <xsl:when test=".='Moe'">
              <xsl:value-of select="."/>
            </xsl:when>
            <xsl:when test=".='Larry'">
              <xsl:value-of select="."/>
            </xsl:when>
            <xsl:otherwise>
              <xsl:value-of select="$third_stooge"/>
            </xsl:otherwise>
          </xsl:choose>

        </xsl:element>
      </xsl:for-each>
    </xsl:element>
  </xsl:template>

</xsl:stylesheet>
```

Listing 12-6 has two interesting elements — an XSL param element, and an XSL choose element.

✔ The param element assigns a default value, Curly, to the parameter named third_stooge. If the parameter's value doesn't change, then Curly is used in creating the transformation's output.

✔ The choose element (with its when and otherwise sub-elements) picks a value to put inside the StoogeOut element.

  • If the current StoogeIn element's text is Moe or Larry, then the resulting StoogeOut element's text is Moe or Larry. (In an XSL stylesheet, a dot stands for the current element's text.)

  • If the current StoogeIn element's text isn't Moe or Larry, then the resulting StoogeOut element's text is the value of the third_stooge parameter.

Parameters in a Java program

Take the files in Listings 12-5 and 12-6 and give them to the Java code in
Listing 12-4. With the `third_stooge` parameter's default value of `Curly`,
the resulting file is the document in Listing 12-7.

Listing 12-7:   "Nyuk, Nyuk!"

```
<?xml version="1.0" encoding="UTF-8"?>
<!-- StoogesOut.xml -->
<StoogesOut>
<StoogeOut>Moe</StoogeOut>
<StoogeOut>Larry</StoogeOut>
<StoogeOut>Curly</StoogeOut>
</StoogesOut>
```

After admiring the output in Listing 12-7, add one new line to the code in
Listing 12-4.

```
transformer.setParameter("third_stooge","Shemp");
```

Put this new line between the call to `newTransformer`, and the call to
`transformer.transform`. This line overrides the default value of the
`third_stooge` parameter. When you run the revised code, you get the result
shown in Listing 12-8.

Listing 12-8:   "Ouch!"

```
<?xml version="1.0" encoding="UTF-8"?>
<!-- StoogesOut.xml -->
<StoogesOut>
<StoogeOut>Moe</StoogeOut>
<StoogeOut>Larry</StoogeOut>
<StoogeOut>Shemp</StoogeOut>
</StoogesOut>
```

And there you have it, from alchemy to comedy — the magic of XSL.

Chapter 13

Viewing XML Data on the Web

*W*hen I first read about XML, my response was "Hey, where are the formatting tags?" I was used to creating Web pages and using HTML tags — tags like <bold>, <italic>, and <plaintext>. How do you display all the information in an XML document?

Well, it took me a while to understand one important fact — that XML is about *content*, not about making pretty displays. With XML you describe content, and that content is separate from any kind of presentation. When this idea first hit me, it was a real revelation. (Actually, it was a relief. Because I claim to know this stuff, I'm better off if I really understand it.) I carried the word forward, and became an evangelist for the XML cause. I lectured to students, spoke at conferences, and even proposed writing a book. Whenever I saw an old HTML document, I'd scoff at it. "Mixing data with display — how crude!"

Time marched on, and eventually I signed a contract to write *Java & XML For Dummies*. I wrote Chapters 1 to 12 with lightning speed, emphasizing data, not display, as the cornerstone for truth. "Display? Who needs a display? Would you judge a book by its cover? Would you judge this book by its cover? Certainly not," I say.

On and on I go. But occasionally, when I least expect it, a little voice comes up from behind. In those silent moments, the moments when I'm all alone with myself, I still ask myself the nagging question. "How *do* you display XML data?"

Going from XML to HTML

There are a variety of ways to display XML data, but one neat way is to use an XSL stylesheet. You start with an XML document, you design your sheet to output HTML tags, and you end up with an HTML document. Once you have an HTML document, you can visit the HTML document using your favorite Web browser.

Take an XML document — a University document from the start of Chapter 12. Write a stylesheet whose XSL elements express the following transformation:

```
Create an html element.
Create a center element.
Create an h2 element.
   Copy the text from the source document's Name element.
Create an address element.
   Copy the text from the source document's Street element.
   Create a br element.
   Copy the text from the source document's City element.
   Create a blank space.
   Copy the text from the source document's State element.
   Create a blank space.
   Copy the text from the source document's Zip element.
```

The transformation given here is written in English, not in XSL. To get Java to perform the transformation, you need an XSL file with tags like `<xsl:value-of select="//City"/>`.

When you apply this kind of transformation to the second University document in Chapter 12, you get the following result:

```
<html>
<center>
<h2>Drew University</h2>
<address>36 Madison Avenue<br>Madison
          NJ
          07940</address>
</center>
</html>
```

This result file is an HTML document — suitable for viewing with your favorite Web browser. In fact, if you visit this new HTML document with a Web browser, you'll get the display shown in Figure 13-1.

Figure 13-1:
A formatted
display.

> # Drew University
>
> *36 Madison Avenue*
> *Madison NJ 07940*

An XML document without a stylesheet

Let's take an XML document that's near and dear to my heart. It's an outline of this book's thirteenth chapter. The document is in Listing 13-1.

Listing 13-1: this.chapter13

```
<?xml version="1.0" encoding="UTF-8"?>
<!-- Chapter.xml -->

<Chapter
      number="13"
      title="Viewing XML Data on the Web">

   <Section title="Going from XML to HTML">
      <Subsection title=
         "An XML document without a stylesheet"/>
      <Subsection title=
         "Applying a stylesheet to create HTML code"/>
   </Section>

   <Section title="Serving Up Your XML Data">
      <Subsection title=
         "Applying a stylesheet with Internet Explorer"/>
      <Subsection title=
         "Getting the server to do the work">
         <Subsubsection>Writing a servlet</Subsubsection>
         <Subsubsection>Getting a server</Subsubsection>
         <Subsubsection>
            Putting your files on the server
         </Subsubsection>
         <Subsubsection>
            Visiting your Web site
         </Subsubsection>
         <Subsubsection>Yet another trick</Subsubsection>
      </Subsection>
   </Section>

</Chapter>
```

If you visit the file in Listing 13-1 with Microsoft Internet Explorer (version 5 or later), then you get the display shown in Figure 13-2. The display is interactive. When you click a plus sign, Explorer expands an element's sub-elements. When you click a minus sign, Explorer collapses an element's sub-elements. This is nice, but it's not user-friendly (unless the user likes seeing start tags and end tags).

Figure 13-2:
Viewing an
XML file
with
Microsoft
Internet
Explorer.

```
<?xml version="1.0" encoding="UTF-8" ?>
<!-- Chapter.xml -->
- <Chapter number="13" title="Viewing XML Data on the Web">
  + <Section title="Going from XML to HTML">
  - <Section title="Serving Up Your XML Data">
      <Subsection title="Applying a stylesheet with Internet Explorer" />
      + <Subsection title="Getting the server to do the work">
    </Section>
  </Chapter>
```

Applying a stylesheet to create HTML code

With the right kind of XSL file, you can grab the tags in Listing 13-1 and use them to create an HTML page — a page whose formats are tailored to your specific needs. To see what I mean, look at the XSL file in Listing 13-2.

Listing 13-2:   Creating an HTML File from XML Data

```
<?xml version="1.0"?>
<!-- Formal.xsl -->

<xsl:stylesheet
      xmlns:xsl="http://www.w3.org/1999/XSL/Transform"
      version="1.0">
  <xsl:output method="html"/>

  <xsl:template match="Chapter">
      <h2>
          Chapter
          <xsl:value-of select="@number"/>:
          <xsl:value-of select="@title"/>
      </h2>
      <xsl:apply-templates />
  </xsl:template>

  <xsl:template match="Section">
      <h3>
          <code>   </code>
          <xsl:value-of select="@title"/>
      </h3>
      <xsl:apply-templates />
  </xsl:template>

  <xsl:template match="Subsection">
      <code>      </code>*
      <xsl:value-of select="@title"/>
```

```
      <br/>
      <xsl:apply-templates />
   </xsl:template>

   <xsl:template match="Subsubsection">
      <code>     
                </code>-
      <xsl:value-of select="."/>
      <br/>
   </xsl:template>

</xsl:stylesheet>
```

Listing 13-2 is a mix of various things — mostly XSL tags and HTML tags. For instance, look at the tags near the word Chapter. There are two xsl:value-of tags, but there's also a pair of h2 tags. When they're viewed in a Web browser, h2 tags create a big, bold heading. That's the kind of formatting that plain old XML lacks.

The stylesheet in Listing 13-2 has another interesting feature. The stylesheet's xsl:output tag has the attribute method="html". This attribute tells the transformer to create an HTML document (as opposed to an XML document, or a plain old text document)

So here's what we'll do. Take the program in Listing 12-4. Run the program with the document in Listing 13-1, and the stylesheet in Listing 13-2. The program applies the XSL stylesheet to the XML document. What you get is a brand new document — the document in Listing 13-3.

Listing 13-3: An Automatically Generated HTML File

```
<h2>
         Chapter
         13:
         Viewing XML Data on the Web</h2>
<h3>
<code>   </code>Going from XML to HTML</h3>
<code>      </code>*
      An XML document without a stylesheet<br>
<code>      </code>*
      Applying a stylesheet to create HTML code<br>
<h3>
<code>   </code>Serving Up Your XML Data</h3>
<code>      </code>*
      Applying a stylesheet with Internet Explorer<br>
<code>      </code>*
      Getting the server to do the work<br>
<code>     
             </code>-
```

(continued)

Listing 13-3 *(continued)*

```
      Writing a servlet<br>
<code>     
            </code>-
      Getting a server<br>
<code>     
            </code>-
        Putting your files on the server
      <br>
<code>     
            </code>-
        Visiting your Web site
      <br>
<code>     
            </code>-
      Yet another trick<br>
```

Listing 13-3 is pretty ugly, even though I removed some blank lines to save space on the page. When you apply an XSL stylesheet to an XML document, you don't always get a nice-looking document. Anyway, the document in Listing 13-3 does what it's supposed to do. If you view this document with almost any Web browser, you get the display shown in Figure 13-3.

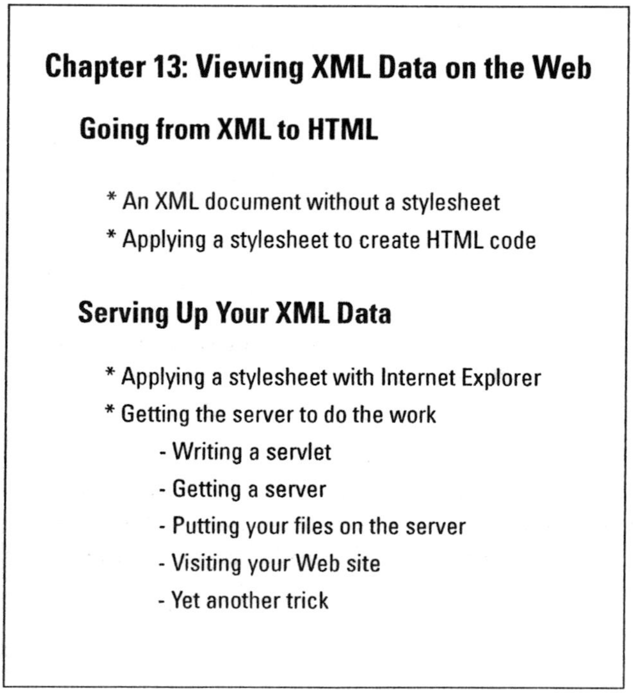

Chapter 13: Viewing XML Data on the Web

Going from XML to HTML

* An XML document without a stylesheet

* Applying a stylesheet to create HTML code

Serving Up Your XML Data

* Applying a stylesheet with Internet Explorer

* Getting the server to do the work

    - Writing a servlet

    - Getting a server

    - Putting your files on the server

    - Visiting your Web site

    - Yet another trick

Figure 13-3:
What a
beautiful-
looking
Web page!

Serving Up Your XML Data

A few paragraphs ago, I told you to run a Java program — the program in Listing 12-4. By running the program, you got the HTML page in Listing 13-3. At that point, there was one extra step. To see a nice display of XML data, you had to visit the page in Listing 13-3. This meant opening your Web browser, and typing the address of the HTML page in the browser's Address field. What a pain! The ordinary user won't do all this, and neither should you.

So the question is, how do you automate all this work? How do you create a link that combines an XML document with an XSL stylesheet, and delivers the resulting HTML page to the user's Web browser?

Applying a stylesheet with Internet Explorer

If you know in advance what browser the user has, then your work is always easier. Newer versions of Microsoft Internet Explorer can merge XML documents with their respective stylesheets. Just add the following line to the top of Listing 13-1:

```
<?xml-stylesheet type="text/xsl" href="Formal.xsl"?>
```

Then, when a user visits the document in Listing 13-1, Internet Explorer looks for the `Formal.xsl` stylesheet. Explorer applies the stylesheet to the XML data, and displays the result shown in Figure 13-3.

For industrial-strength applications, your XML and XSL files should live in different directories on the computer's hard drive. But, for testing purposes, you can put the XML and XSL files all in one directory. In fact, things go smoother when you use only one directory. So, before you test this chapter's examples, be sure that your XML source file (Listing 13-1, for instance) and your XSL file (like the one in Listing 13-2) are in the same directory on your computer's hard drive.

Of course, some people don't use the latest versions of Internet Explorer, and others don't use Internet Explorer at all. If you want to reach the widest possible audience, you better apply the stylesheet before it gets to the visitor's Web browser. To do this, you need some help from a Web server.

Getting the server to do the work

This section explains how you can run your own Web server. If you use some-one else's Web server (your company's server, or a commercial Web host's server) then many of the steps in this section still apply.

The basic steps aren't too complicated.

- ✔ You write a Java program that responds to Web page requests. A pro-gram of this kind is called a Java *servlet*.
- ✔ You find a server that can run Java servlets.
- ✔ You put your files in places where the server can find them.
- ✔ Someone clicks a link to visit your Web site.
- ✔ Your program applies a stylesheet to an XML document, and sends the resulting HTML code back to the visitor's browser.
- ✔ The visitor's browser displays a nice looking page.

In the next several pages, I cover each of these steps in more detail.

To get started with Web servers, you may want more details than I explain in this book. If so, I can recommend another book. It's an excellent book on the use of Java with Web servers. The book is *JSP: JavaServer Pages*, by Barry Burd. Buy two copies — one for your home, and another for your office.

Writing a servlet

Each visit to a Web page is a two-step process.

- ✔ **First, a user clicks a link. Clicking this link initiates an *HTTP request*.**

    A request gets sent from the user's Web browser to someone's Web server. In most cases, the browser and the server are far from each other — far enough to involve phone lines, network connections, and other Internet infrastructure things.

- ✔ **Next, the server handles the request. The server issues an *HTTP response*.**

    The server computer gets the incoming HTTP request, figures out what kind of response to send, and then sends a response back to the user's Web browser. In many instances, this response is an HTML document. When the user's browser receives the response, the browser interprets the document to create a display on the user's screen.

This request/response scenario is the essence of the HTTP protocol. The protocol supports several different kinds of requests — the most popular kind being something called a *GET* request. (The terminology makes sense. Typically, a GET request is a request to get a Web page.)

When you write a Java servlet, you can create a method to respond to a visitor's GET request. It should come as no surprise that this method is named doGet. To see a doGet method in action, look at Listing 13-4.

Listing 13-4:   A Java Servlet

```
import javax.xml.transform.TransformerFactory;
import javax.xml.transform.Transformer;
import javax.xml.transform.TransformerException;

import javax.xml.transform.stream.StreamSource;
import javax.xml.transform.stream.StreamResult;

import java.io.File;
import java.io.PrintWriter;
import java.io.IOException;

import javax.servlet.http.HttpServlet;
import javax.servlet.http.HttpServletRequest;
import javax.servlet.http.HttpServletResponse;


public class MyTransform extends HttpServlet
{

    public void doGet(HttpServletRequest request,
                      HttpServletResponse response)
        throws IOException

    {

        response.setContentType("text/html");

        String docName = request.getParameter("docName");
        String sheetName = request.getParameter("sheetName");

        TransformerFactory factory;
        Transformer transformer;

        File oldFile, xslFile;
        PrintWriter out;

        StreamSource oldStream, xslStream;
        StreamResult newStream;

        factory = TransformerFactory.newInstance();

        try
        {
            oldFile = new File(docName + ".xml");
            oldStream = new StreamSource(oldFile);
```

(continued)

Listing 13-4 *(continued)*

```
            xslFile = new File(sheetName + ".xsl");
            xslStream = new StreamSource(xslFile);

            out = response.getWriter();
            newStream = new StreamResult(out);

            transformer = factory.newTransformer(xslStream);
            transformer.transform (oldStream, newStream);
        }
      catch (TransformerException e)
        {
            System.out.println(e.getMessage());
        }
    }
}
```

Look first at the code in the middle of Listing 13-4. This is like the transformer code from Listing 12-4. In fact, there's only one difference between this code, and the transformer code in Listing 12-4. This code (in Listing 13-4) uses servlet-specific tricks to get the name of its input and output files. In Listing 12-4, all filenames came from the command line. But in Listing 13-4, the file references come from two sources:

✔ **The XML document name, and XSL stylesheet name, come from request parameters.**

A user clicks a link whose URL looks like this:

```
http://localhost:8080/examples/servlet/
MyTransform?docName=chapter&sheetName=Formal
```

Meanwhile, on the Web server, there's a Java class named MyTransform. (The MyTransform class is shown in Listing 13-4.) The previous URL gets the MyTransform class running, and sends two extra pieces of information to the MyTransform class.

- One piece of information is a parameter called docName. The value of this parameter is chapter.

- The other piece of information, a parameter called sheetName, has value Formal.

In the URL, the parameters are flagged by a question mark and an ampersand.

So, in Listing 13-4, the code makes two calls to the request's getParameter method. These calls fetch the values of the docName and sheetName parameters. Then, later in the code, these values get plugged into File constructor calls. That's how the servlet gets a document name and a stylesheet name.

You can create a link for the URL shown previously by adding the follow-ing text to a Web page: Go to <a href="http://localhost:8080/examples/servlet/MyTransform? docName=chapter&sheetName=Formal">Chapter 13</a>.

✔ **A reference to the output destination comes from the response's `getWriter` method.**

Each `doGet` method has a `response` parameter, and each `response` para-meter has a `getWriter` method. When you call `getWriter`, what you get is a destination for sending data. (My `out` variable, in Listing 13-4, points to just such a destination.) The way `getWriter` works, this output desti-nation ends up being the original user's Web browser.

When you call `transformer.transform`, and you feed the call a refer-ence to this output destination, the result of the transformation ends up in the original user's Web browser. Because the result of the transforma-tion is an HTML file, you've done what you wanted to do.

Listing 13-4 shows the code that sends an HTML file to a user's Web browser. Now you need a server to run the code in Listing 13-4.

Getting a server

Some vendors' Web servers can run Java servlets. Other vendors' Web servers cannot. Some Web hosting companies have software that can run Java servlets. Other Web hosting companies do not. To get up and running with servlets, you have to find the right venue. If you work with hosting companies, then you need a servlet-enabled company. If you run your own server, you need a server that speaks Java.

There are many Web hosting companies that can run Java servlets. For a list of such companies, visit `www.adrenalinegroup.com/jwsisp.html`. If you're a cheapskate, like I am, then check `www.mycgiserver.com`. The folks at mycgiserver.com offer free, servlet-enabled Web hosting with no banner ads. What a deal!

In this section, I'll tell you how to run your own server. For testing purposes, running a server is easier than getting a hosting company to do it for you.

A server called Tomcat is widely used for Java processing. You can download Tomcat for free, and run Tomcat on your home computer. Using Tomcat, you can test this chapter's examples without being connected to the Internet. (You can have your computer request pages from itself!)

To get started, visit `jakarta.apache.org/tomcat`. From there, you can poke around for the cat of your choice. If you're a typical reader, you want the latest stable release build (version 4). You want a binary, not a source (because you don't want to compile Tomcat on your own). You want an `exe` or `zip` file (because you run Microsoft Windows). If you don't fall into these "typical reader" categories, then you're probably used to being different, so you know exactly how to download a file for your system.

Tomcat 4 comes in two editions — a regular edition (which comes with its own XML parser), and a light edition (which has no XML parser). The edition that you choose depends on the version of Java that's installed on your computer.

✔ If you have Java 1.4 or later, download the light edition of Tomcat. Files in the light edition have the letters `LE` in their names.

✔ If you have Java 1.3 or earlier, download the regular edition of Tomcat. Files in the regular edition have no `LE` letters in their names.

After downloading Tomcat, the server's installation is a two-step process.

1. **Create a `JAVA_HOME` environment variable on your computer.**

   Make the value of `JAVA_HOME` be the directory where Java lives on your computer. For instance, set `JAVA_HOME` to `c:\ j2sdk1.4.0`. For details on creating environment variables, see Chapter 2.

2. **Run the Tomcat setup file.**

   My Tomcat setup file is named `jakarta-tomcat-4.0.3-LE-jdk14.exe`. How about yours?

Running the setup file will install Tomcat on your computer. Then, to start the server, run `startup.bat` in Tomcat's `bin` directory.

The Clash of the Parsers

Starting with version 1.4, the Java API has an XML parser built right into it. And, starting with version 4, the regular edition of Tomcat has its own XML parser. If you're stuck with that combination (Java 1.4 and Tomcat 4 regular edition), then you have a problem. When you run a servlet with both parsers in use (a Java parser and a Tomcat parser), you can get a `ClassCastException` called `Transform erFactoryImpl`. This happens because the two parsers have similarly named, incompatible classes.

When I first encountered this `ClassCastException`, I pounded on the table for several hours. Then, finally, I removed the file `xerces.jar` from Tomcat's `lib` directory. That fixed the problem. With Tomcat's Xerces parser out of the way, my servlet ran without a hitch.

One way or another, you're best off with the latest Java, and with the latest Tomcat light. Because the light edition comes with no XML parser, there are no class conflicts. And with no class conflicts, you don't get the upsetting `ClassCastException`.

To test the Tomcat installation, start up the server. Then open your Web browser, and visit `http://localhost:8080/`. If your browser displays a page with the word Jakarta in its title, then you've successfully installed the server.

Putting your files on the server

This is the hard part. I've had lots of experience with servers, and the toughest thing for me is finding the right directories for storing my files. Every vendor's server has its own favorite directories, and even different versions of a single vendor's server use different directory structures. What's worse, if you've placed a file in the wrong directory, then the error reporting by servers tends to be poor.

For the Tomcat server, try the following steps:

1. **Compile** `MyTransform.java` **— the program in Listing 13-4.**

   To do this, you'll need to have the `servlet.jar` file in your classpath. (With many versions of Tomcat, the file `servlet.jar` is in the `common\lib` directory.) Once again, you can refer to Chapter 2 for instructions on modifying the classpath.

2. **Put the compiled code,** `MyTransform.class`, **in Tomcat's** `webapps\examples\WEB-INF\classes` **directory**

   When you become experienced, you can fiddle with server directories. Until then, I recommend the `examples` directory, with its `WEB-INF\classes` subdirectory.

3. **Put the XML and XSL documents (the stuff in Listings 13-1 and 13-2) in either your main Tomcat directory, or your main Tomcat directory's** `bin` **subdirectory.**

   What an awful place to put data files! Well, for this chapter's example, it gets the job done. To find a better place, you have to tweak the server, and I don't want to open that can of worms.

   Anyway, the choice between the main directory or `bin` directory depends on the way you start the Tomcat server. Try both places, and see which place works for you.

If you place a file in the wrong directory, then most servers put error messages somewhere or other. Some servers use the browser window, others use the command prompt window, and still others use log files. (In some cases, a single server uses more than one log file. You have to poke around.) If you suspect that you've put a file in the wrong place, then check around for an error message. If you're lucky, the message will tell you where the server expected to find the file. When you find this information, you can move the file to its expected location.

Visiting your Web site

This part is easy. First, make sure that the Tomcat server is running, then type the following URL in your Web browser's Address field:

```
http://localhost:8080/examples/servlet/
MyTransform?docName=chapter&sheetName=Formal
```

When you do this, the browser sends a request to the server. The server calls MyTransform, which merges the Chapter.xml document with the Formal. xsl stylesheet. The MyTransform servlet sends an HTML document back to your browser, and the browser displays the stuff in Figure 13-3. It's wonderful!

Yet another trick

The previous paragraph ended with you viewing a lovely display in your Web browser's window. Maybe you think this is the end of the story. But, rest assured, I never run out of things to write.

Recall the scenario of the last several pages. With some URL parameters, you send two filenames to a servlet. The servlet grabs the files and creates a formatted Web page. So what?

Well, the power behind XML is the separation of data from presentation. With HTML, you're just formatting data. With XML and XSL, you're putting the data in one document, and putting the format instructions in another document. That's fantastic because either one of these things (the data or your formatting information) can change.

What if Paul Levesque tells me to rewrite Chapter 13 and change all the section headings? (Please, Paul, don't do that!) Then, to keep my Web page up to date, I can modify Listing 13-1 without touching Listing 13-2.

And what if I, with my boyish enthusiasm, want two ways to display the headings of Chapter 13? Listing 13-2 uses a formal style for displaying chapter headings. I can shift gears and try a more flamboyant style. Take, for instance, the stylesheet in Listing 13-5.

Listing 13-5: A Fancy Format

```
<?xml version="1.0"?>
<!-- Fancy.xsl -->

<xsl:stylesheet
     xmlns:xsl="http://www.w3.org/1999/XSL/Transform"
     version="1.0">
  <xsl:output method="html"/>

  <xsl:template match="Chapter">
```

```
        <center>
          <h2>
            Chapter <xsl:value-of select="@number"/>
          </h2>
          <h2>
            <xsl:value-of select="@title"/>
          </h2>
          <xsl:apply-templates />
        </center>
    </xsl:template>

    <xsl:template match="Section">
      <h3>
          <xsl:value-of select="@title"/>
      </h3>
      <xsl:apply-templates />
    </xsl:template>

    <xsl:template match="Subsection">
      <font face="Wingdings">J</font>
      <xsl:value-of select="@title"/>
      <font face="Wingdings">J</font><br/>
      <xsl:apply-templates />
    </xsl:template>

    <xsl:template match="Subsubsection">
      &#8226; <xsl:value-of select="."/> &#8226;<br/>
    </xsl:template>

</xsl:stylesheet>
```

Does Listing 13-5 look fancy to you? Well, maybe not. But try the following experiment. Put the code of Listing 13-5 (the file Fancy.xsl) into the same directory where you put Formal.xsl (Listing 13-2). Start the Tomcat Web server, then open your Web browser, and type the following URL into your browser's Address field:

```
http://localhost:8080/examples/servlet/MyTransform?
  docName=Chapter&sheetName=Fancy
```

With parameter value Fancy, the MyTransform servlet gets the stylesheet in Listing 13-5. This stylesheet takes the same old data from the XML file in Listing 13-1, and formats the data in a nice new way. Instead of the cold, drab display of Figure 13-3, your browser gives you the light-hearted dinner menu of Figure 13-4.

So there it is — the complete independence of data and presentation. I've changed the display of the information without changing the information itself. There's been no error-prone tweaking of the data. All my precious information remains untouched.

What great stuff! Aren't you glad you're learning Java and XML?

Chapter 13

Viewing XML Data on the Web

Going from XML to HTML

☺ An XML document without a stylesheet ☺
☺ Applying a stylesheet to create HTML code ☺

Serving Up Your XML Data

☺ Applying a stylesheet with Internet Explorer ☺
☺ Getting the server to do the work ☺
• Writing a servlet •
• Getting a server •
• Putting your files on the server •
• Visiting your Web site •
• Yet another trick •

Figure 13-4:
A fancy
display.

Chapter 14

Creating Custom Code for Your Document (Using JAXB)

● ●

In This Chapter
▶ What JAXB is all about
▶ An example using JAXB
▶ When you should (and should not) use JAXB

● ●

For all you rugged individualists, good news! The Association for Futuristic Studies anticipates that, in twenty years, everyone will be taking custom-made medications. No more diddling around with worthless, off-the-counter pills. At the first sign of a cold, you'll scan your cells and get a newly designed, custom cure — tailored to your personal DNA, and to the DNA of whatever virus you've contracted.

Give it forty more years, and you'll be doing the same thing with your mind. Hook your brain to a few neurosensors and neuroeffectors. The sensors decide what stimulus you need to make you as happy as possible. As the effectors feed you a calculated stimulus, the sensors monitor your brain for updates to your pleasure needs.

Early versions of this brain technology will create some deliriously happy lab rats. Then, with later versions, scientists will learn to control the flow of plea-sure. Instead of a constant gushing of joy, subjects will experience normal euphoric ups, downs, and the occasional moment of boredom. It'll be a bit like surfing the Web.

What if you can't wait for all these biological advancements? What if you won't be around to see them? Well, don't despair, because technology has given us a consolation prize. It's called *JAXB* — the *Java API for XML Binding*. You can't use it to make a custom cold cure, but you can use it to build cus-tomized code. (That's almost as good. Isn't it?) With JAXB, you take an XML document and you make a Java class file that's perfect for processing the document. I'd call it a "disposable Java class," except that the class's useful-ness lives on and on. When your needs change and the class no longer does what you want it to do, you just spawn a new subclass. It's a scene right out of science fiction. (It's a good bet Jules Verne predicted that scientists would one day create JAXB — and immediately scratched his head and muttered, *"Mais, le JAXB — qu'est-ce que c'est?"* More good news, mon ami: The next section looks closely at just what JAXB is.)

The Idea Behind JAXB

When you write SAX or DOM code, you create an XML processing program. Your program reads a document, and uses the document to do useful work — starting with something harmless like `public void startElement` or `node.getNodeName()`. Either way, your program makes no assumptions about what's inside the document. The document has a `root` element, some child elements, and that's all. Any special assumptions you make about this document actually narrow the usefulness of the code.

Versatile code versus customized code

Consider the code in Listings 7-3 and 7-4. (If you don't want to flip back to look at them, I'll tell you what they do.) The first one, Listing 7-3, scans five nodes in a document tree. Those five nodes have to be arranged a certain way, or else the program crashes. (The listing wants a `comment` and a `root` node, with at least two children directly under the `root` node.)

The code in Listing 7-4 is much more general. This code checks the document structure as it runs. When the code finds a child node, it scans the child and looks for grandchildren. If there are no grandchildren, the code looks for brothers and sisters. The code can handle any document tree — whether it has one node or a thousand nodes.

Thus Listing 7-4 is more versatile than Listing 7-3. But this versatility comes with drawbacks — including the possibility of very high overhead. The code in Listing 7-4 has to parse the entire XML document — and then put a representation of the document's tree into the computer's memory. If the document is very large, then the representation is large: Memory gets bloated with all that temporary data, and the code in Listing 7-4 slows to a crawl.

The benefits of customization

Imagine you're trying to drive to Faneuil Hall in Boston, Massachusetts. It doesn't matter where you start from; the trip will always be confusing and difficult. Anyway, you have to plan your route. You can get lost in Newton, in Waltham, in Connecticut, or in downtown Boston. Depending on your resources, you have two options:

- ✔ You can stop at a gas station and buy a map. If you do, then you may never get to Faneuil Hall. After all, you have to find where you are on the map, look for alternative routes, choose a route, and then (heaven help you) try to follow the route without getting lost again.

- ✔ You can tell your expensive, talking GPS system that you want to get to Faneuil Hall. The system will plot a customized route, and guide you, turn by turn, from whatever miserable place you're in to the optimal route that leads from there to Faneuil Hall. The route is so customized that the GPS voice says (for example), "There's no sign at this intersection, but turn left anyway." Later on, the voice says "There are two signs at this intersection, and the signs contradict each other. But turn right anyway."

Well, okay, I'm not naïve enough to expect *that* easy a time of it. I've assumed that a talking GPS system can actually help you find Faneuil Hall in Boston. (What the heck. Call it science fiction.) The point is, using the paper map takes more work (more time, effort, dexterity, and patience) than using the talking GPS. Why? Because the paper map isn't customized to your specific needs; in effect, it says, "Here's the entire Boston metropolitan area. Faneuil Hall is in there somewhere. *You* figure out what to do next."

A custom system is (as you might expect) easier to use than one that isn't tailored to your immediate situation. Thus the XML processing code of Listing 7-4 makes a huge, resource-gulping DOM tree in your computer's memory space ("Here's the tree — *you* figure out what to do next . . .") because the code isn't customized. The code works for any old document — not just the one you have on hand — and always gobbles up resources to do it.

The essence of JAXB

The idea behind JAXB is to create custom-tailored class to meet your present needs. You take the description of an XML document, run it through a special program called a *schema compiler*, and get a brand new class called the *generated class*. This generated class is streamlined to work with particular XML documents.

For example, if your XML documents have elements named `Total`, then the generated class can have `setTotal` and `getTotal` methods. If a document's element has a `fullName` attribute, then the generated class can have `setFullName` and `getFullName` methods. (See Figure 14-1.)

The connection between a part of an XML document and a part of a Java class is called a *binding*. With all these bindings, an instance of the class represents a single XML document.

So how do you connect an object with an XML document? Well, the generated class has methods named unmarshal and marshal. (See Figure 14-2.)

> ✔ The unmarshal method reads an XML file. The method gets values from the XML document, and assigns these values to variables in the Java object.

> ✔ The marshal method writes an XML file. The method gets values from the Java object, and uses these values to create the XML document.

With methods like these, you can retrieve and modify the data in an XML document.

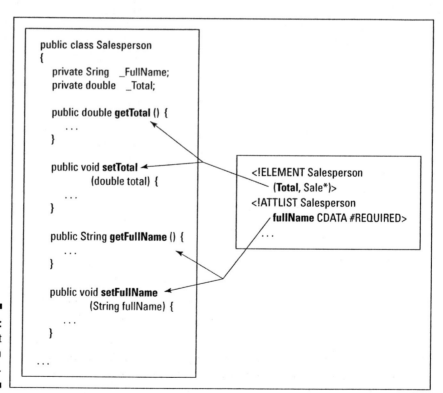

Figure 14-1:
An object represents a document.

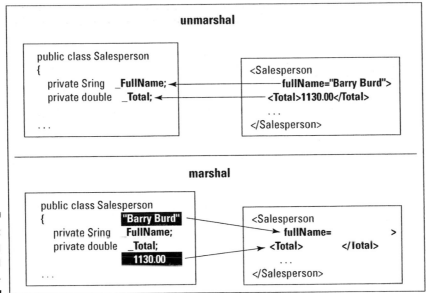

Figure 14-2:
Reading
and writing
values.

Describing a document type

Go back a few paragraphs, and notice how carefully I chose my words. "You take *the description of* an XML document, and run it through . . . a schema compiler." Exactly what kind of description do you use? Well, a DTD is a description of a document, but with JAXB, you use more than just a DTD. With JAXB you create something called a *binding schema*. This binding schema describes the way in which the Java class's values match up with data in the XML document. For example, in the binding schema, you can give the schema compiler instructions that it understands as if they were written like this:

> *"The `Total` element matches a variable with a simple type, not a class type. The variable that stores the total is of type `double`."*

Of course, the text that you put in a binding schema isn't English prose. Instead, the text consists of XML tags. (Why am I not surprised?)

So here's what you have: a DTD that describes a *type* of XML document. You also have a binding schema describing the mapping of documents into Java classes. When you apply the JAXB schema compiler, you get a generated class. Figure 14-3 illustrates the process.

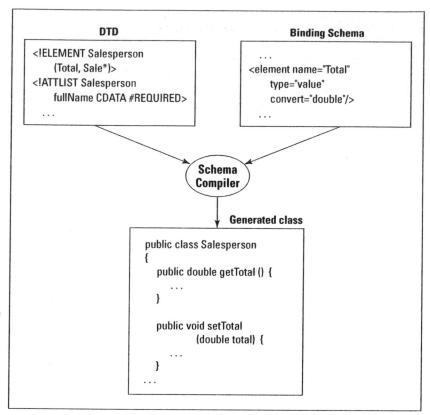

Figure 14-3:
Generating
a class with
the schema
compiler.

A generated class doesn't do anything on its own. To make use of the generated class, you write more Java code. For instance, you write a class with a main method, and have the main method call getTotal. With judicious calls to the generated class's methods, you can do all kinds of cool things to your XML documents.

Creating the Generated Class

Learning to use JAXB is a bootstrapping process. First you get the big picture, then you see the big picture in action. Next you see some details and, finally, you see the details in action. At this point in the chapter, you're up to the "big picture in action" part. I'll show you a minimal example of JAXB, and describe the steps to make the example run.

Some useful documents

Let's start with an XML document. This document describes my own personal nightmare. The document is in Listing 14-1.

Listing 14-1: Village of the Spammed

```
<?xml version="1.0" encoding="UTF-8"?>
<!DOCTYPE Nightmare SYSTEM "Nightmare.dtd">
<!-- Nightmare.xml -->

<Nightmare subject="spam" severity="high"/>
```

Now, there's an old saying: "An XML document without a DTD is like a day without chocolate." So let's look at a DTD for the document in Listing 14-1. The DTD is in Listing 14-2.

Listing 14-2: I Know What You DTD Last Summer

```
<?xml version="1.0" encoding="UTF-8"?>
<!-- Nightmare.dtd -->

<!ELEMENT Nightmare EMPTY>
<!ATTLIST Nightmare subject CDATA #REQUIRED
                    severity CDATA #REQUIRED>
```

Next, we need a binding schema. For this first example, the world's simplest binding schema (shown in Listing 14-3) does the trick.

Listing 14-3: Schema and Schema Again

```
<?xml version="1.0" encoding="UTF-8"?>
<!-- Nightmare.xjs -->

<xml-java-binding-schema version="1.0-ea">
   <element name="Nightmare" type="class" root="true"/>
</xml-java-binding-schema>
```

From this point on in the chapter, everything I write is subject to change. My version of JAXB is pre-beta. It's an early access release from Sun Microsystems. Between now and the time you read this book, the folks who develop JAXB may have changed their minds about some of the features. To keep abreast of any changes, visit Sun's Web site. The page you want is java.sun.com/xml/jaxb.

Later in this chapter, I'll tell you all about binding schemas. For now, just notice what a bare-bones schema needs to have.

- ✔ The schema needs an xml-java-binding-schema root element.
- ✔ The schema needs at least one child element.

Every binding schema has to have an element with attributes type="class" and root="true". So there's no getting around it — the document shown in Listing 14-3 is as small as it can possibly be.

Running the schema compiler

Take one more look at Figure 14-3. We need to do the stuff that's illustrated in the figure. We run the JAXB schema compiler, and get a new Java source file. The source file's name will be Nightmare.java.

I guess I can confide in you. I have a slight problem. I'm working with an early access release of JAXB. An early access release comes before a beta release. So, as JAXB migrates from early access to beta, and then to public release, I'm not sure what features will change.

One thing that will probably change is the way you invoke the schema compiler. In the early access version, you issue a command of the following kind:

```
java -jar jaxb-xjc-1.0-ea.jar Nightmare.dtd Nightmare.xjs
```

If you have a Unix system, then you can shorten this command to

```
xjc Nightmare.dtd Nightmare.xjs
```

By the time you read this book, the command will probably be something like this:

```
java -classpath jaxb.jar com.sun.tools.xjc.Main
          Nightmare.dtd Nightmare.xjs
```

(If you try this, then you should type the whole thing on one line.) Anyway, to run the schema compiler, you supply the names of the DTD and the binding schema files (Listings 14-2 and 14-3). You don't need an XML file until you want to do something productive with the generated class.

A generated class

When you run the schema compiler, the compiler creates a new file — a file named Nightmare.java. There's an abridged copy of the file in Listing 14-4.

Listing 14-4:   Nightmare on Element Street

```
/*
 * This listing is incomplete. It will not compile as is.
 * The listing has been edited to preserve your sanity.
 * To get the complete listing, run the schema compiler
 *     on Listings 14-2 and 14-3. You can also get the
 *     complete listing by visiting www.users.drew.edu/bburd.
 */


public class Nightmare
    extends MarshallableRootElement
    implements RootElement
{

    private String _Subject;
    private String _Severity;

    public String getSubject() {
        return _Subject;
    }

    public void setSubject(String _Subject) {
        this._Subject = _Subject;
        if (_Subject == null) {
            invalidate();
        }
    }

    public String getSeverity() {
        return _Severity;
    }

    public void setSeverity(String _Severity) {
        this._Severity = _Severity;
        if (_Severity == null) {
            invalidate();
        }
    }

    public static Nightmare unmarshal(InputStream in)
        throws UnmarshalException
    {
        return unmarshal(XMLScanner.open(in));
    }
}
```

The generated Nightmare code treats an XML document as if it were an instance of a Java class. For example, an XML document has a subject attribute, and the Nightmare code has methods getSubject and setSubject. In fact, the unmarshal and marshal methods create an object from a document, and create a document from an object. You'll see how this works in the next listing.

In the meantime, you need to compile Nightmare.java. If you use the command prompt, then type

```
javac Nightmare.java
```

JAXB isn't yet part of the Standard Java 2 API, so classes like MarshallableRootElement (classes that are needed for compiling Nightmare.java) aren't available without the JAXB jar file in your classpath. In my early access version, the JAXB jar file is named jaxb-xjc-1.0-ea.jar, but the name will change by the time you read this book. To review the steps for adding a file to your system's classpath, see Chapter 2.

Listing 14-4 has an unmarshal method, but the listing doesn't have a marshal method. That's because the marshal method that I'll call in this chapter's examples is inherited. It's inherited from the MarshallableRootElement superclass. If you look at the complete code for the Nightmare class, you'll find a few overridden marshal methods. But I don't use any of those marshal methods in this chapter's examples.

Making Use of a Generated Class

Don't you just love Figure 14-3? Figure 14-3 illustrates the work that we've done so far. If any picture is worth a thousand words, then Figure 14-3 certainly is. Well, Figure 14-3 tells only half of the JAXB story. You see, we have some nice code in Listing 14-4 — code created by the JAXB schema compiler. But that code has no main method. The Nightmare class in Listing 14-4 does nothing unless another piece of code calls some Nightmare class methods. To get any useful work out of JAXB, we need another piece of code. The situation is illustrated in Figure 14-4.

Methods in the generated Nightmare class can take an XML document and create a Java object from the document. We need a Java application — one that works with the object to create some useful output. That's fair enough. I've placed a Java application in Listing 14-5.

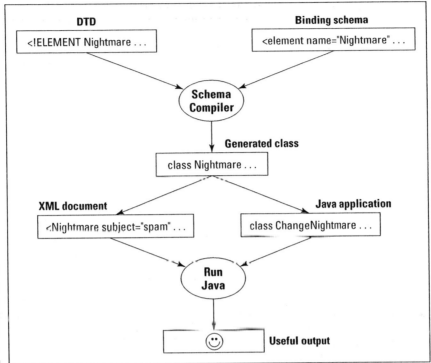

Figure 14-4:
Creating
and using a
generated
class.

Listing 14-5:   The Burds

```
import java.io.FileInputStream;
import java.io.FileOutputStream;
import java.io.IOException;
import java.io.FileNotFoundException;

import javax.xml.bind.UnmarshalException;
import javax.xml.bind.StructureValidationException;


class ChangeNightmare
{
    static Nightmare nightmare;

    public static void main(String args[])
        throws IOException, UnmarshalException
    {
        nightmare = readNightmare();

        String severity = nightmare.getSeverity();
```

(continued)

Listing 14-5 *(continued)*

```
        nightmare.setSubject("telemarketing");
        nightmare.setSeverity("very " + severity);

        writeNightmare();
    }


    static Nightmare readNightmare()
        throws FileNotFoundException, UnmarshalException
    {
        FileInputStream nightmareIn =
            new FileInputStream("Nightmare.xml");

        nightmare = Nightmare.unmarshal(nightmareIn);

        return nightmare;
    }


    static void writeNightmare()
        throws IOException, StructureValidationException
    {
        FileOutputStream nightmareOut =
            new FileOutputStream("Nightmare.xml");

        nightmare.validate();
        nightmare.marshal(nightmareOut);
    }
}
```

The code in Listing 14-5 creates a new `Nightmare.xml` file. (The code writes over everything in the existing file.) The updated `Nightmare.xml` file is shown in Listing 14-6.

Listing 14-6:   Nightmare on Extensible Markup Language Street

```
<?xml version="1.0" encoding="UTF-8"?>

<Nightmare subject="telemarketing" severity="very high"/>
```

The code in Listing 14-5 follows a familiar pattern — read a file, modify the data, and then write a file with the new data. Let's examine each of the steps in detail.

✔ **Read a file.**

   In Listing 14-5, the call to `Nightmare.unmarshal` does the bulk of the file reading work. This `unmarshal` method is a static method of the `Nightmare` class.

When you call the unmarshal method, and you feed the method a FileInputStream object, you get back an instance of the Nightmare class. In Listing 14-5, the FileInputStream object comes from an XML document — the Nightmare.xml document in Listing 14-1. The nightmare object (the object that's returned by the call to unmarshal) has its instance variables filled with data from the XML document. So, inside the nightmare object, _Subject has the value spam, and _Severity has the value high.

This potential pitfall can drive you crazy. When I first wrote my call to unmarshal, I accidentally omitted the assignment to the nightmare variable. The line Nightmare.unmarshal(nightmareIn); was an entire statement in Listing 14-5. I was calling unmarshal, but I wasn't doing anything with the method's return value. Well, the program compiled and ran, but the values inside the nightmare object were null. Instead of being very high in Listing 14-6, the severity was very null.

✔ **Modify the data.**

This is what I like most about JAXB. Once you've unmarshalled an XML document, you can treat values in the document the way you'd treat any ordinary Java variable. To get the severity value, you call getSeverity. To change the severity value, you call setSeverity. As an old-time Java programmer, this way of doing things feels very comfortable to me.

Of course, there's more to life than comfort. Compare the code in Listing 14-5 with a similar SAX or DOM program. To get the severity value in a SAX program, you have to create a startElement method, and then loop through the element's attributes. To do the same thing in DOM, you make recursive method calls. Certainly the JAXB way is more efficient, less error prone, and easier to maintain.

Calling a set method, like setSeverity in Listing 14-5, changes the value stored in a Java class variable. The call does not change the text in the XML document. To change the XML document, you have to call the marshal method. (I describe that method in the next bullet.)

✔ **Write a file.**

You have all these values in your Java nightmare object. To put the values into an XML document, you just call the marshal method. You can overwrite your original Nightmare.xml file, or create a new file containing the values. In Listing 14-5, we overwrite the original file.

Listing 14-5 has a call to nightmare.validate. Before you can marshal a class, you have to check to make sure that the class is valid. You can't marshal an invalid class. So in many situations, if you omit a call to validate, you'll get a ValidationRequiredException when you call the marshal method. In all situations, it's best to be safe and throw in a call to the validate method. In fact, you should do what I'm too lazy to do: You should enclose your call to validate in a try statement with a StructureValidationException catch clause.

When to Use the JAXB API

I hope you're not confused. My enthusiasm tends to get ahead of me, and I write what must seem to be contradictory statements. When I wrote about DOM in Chapter 7, I told you what a great tool DOM is. Then, when I wrote about JDOM in Chapter 10, I said that JDOM is an improvement over DOM. Now, in Chapter 14, I'm telling you how nice it is to break free of the DOM/JDOM tree approach, and to use the Java-class approach in JAXB.

Well, I'm always right. All these tools are useful, and each has its benefits. So, when you're putting together a project, you have to pick the right tool. The question in this section is, when do you pick JAXB?

✔ **Use JAXB for speed that's faster than DOM but slower than SAX.**

There's no doubt about it — SAX is a racehorse. That's because SAX has no clue about the document as a whole; SAX just runs through a document, looking for one event after another. With SAX, no memory is wasted, and no time is spent building a document tree.

On the other hand, DOM takes time and memory to build a holistic view of the document. With DOM, you can process the child of a child of a child. Then, if you want to go back and process the root's `start` tag, you can do it. With the whole document in memory at once, DOM can be time-consuming.

In terms of processing time, JAXB is in the middle ground between SAX and DOM. With JAXB, you unmarshal a document. This unmarshalling creates a representation of the document's data in memory. If a document is very large, then its representation in memory is large too. So JAXB can't win a race against a SAX program. (Never mind Zeno's paradox in Chapter 3. Zeno didn't know what he was talking about.)

On the other hand, JAXB creates a representation that's streamlined for a particular kind of document. With JAXB, you don't have nodes; instead you have `Nightmares` and `severities`. The JAXB in-memory representation cuts at the heart of a particular document type, and lacks some of the bulky features needed by DOM to represent all possible things in all possible documents.

A JAXB-generated class is, after all, a plain old Java class — something that's been engineered and reengineered over the past several years. Any optimizations of Java classes in general apply automatically to a JAXB-generated class. So, with JAXB, you get an internal representation of your document, along with the mature technology of Java classes.

✔ **Use JAXB when you need content validation.**

In the next chapter, I'll show you an example of JAXB content validation. Using content validation, you can insist that a particular attribute has a numeric value, or that the text inside an element is of type `boolean`.

To do content validation with SAX or DOM, you have to choose your parser wisely. But with JAXB, content validation is built right into the processing of a binding schema. When you work with JAXB, your choice of parser isn't constrained by your need for content validation. That's pretty good news.

✓ **Use JAXB to hide an XML document's eccentricities.**

The code in Listing 14-5 contains no mention of nodes, root elements, or children. But the code manages to read one XML document and write another. The whole idea behind JAXB is to shield the programmer from the document and its tree, and to present the data in a very Java-friendly way. With JAXB, everything that's specific to an XML document gets smoothed over by the binding-schema and the schema compiler.

I find JAXB easier to use than the other APIs. While using it to prepare this chapter, I spent less time creating examples — and less time debugging code — than for previous chapters in this book. Once you get the hang of the "binding schema" business, writing code for a generated class is a breeze. (You'll get more binding schema hanging if you read Chapter 15.)

Of course, the world may not be interested in what you or I find easy to program. Okay, then, let's get practical: Programmers can leverage JAXB to meet deadlines and make code more maintainable. (Speaking of deadlines, I better end this discussion and move on to writing Chapter 15.)

Chapter 15

Using JAXB to the MaxB

"**I**t's October 12, 2120, and this is reporter Sam Burd, with highlights from tonight's upcoming news stories.

"Yes, the rumors are true. The Association for Futuristic Studies reports that scientists have developed customized mates. Your partner will be fully configurable, modifiable on demand to meet your changing needs, and disposable. Estimates say the average person will change mates once a week, maybe even once a day.

"For the full story, tune in at eleven (relative to an observer in an inertial frame of reference)."

Hmm. I'd hate to be customizable or disposable. Fortunately, computer code never complains when you tweak, bash, trash, or replace it. And now, thanks to the power of binding schema, JAXB has made that whole process faster, easier, and more elegant.

Creating Generated Classes

The example that flows through most of Chapter 14 uses a one-line XML document, and a bare-bones binding schema. Well, if you read that chapter and want more than the chapter's skinny example, then this chapter is for you.

An XML document

You don't need an XML document to get started creating JAXB code. All that a schema compiler needs is a DTD and a binding schema. The schema compiler creates a generated class, and there's plenty of good Java code in a generated class.

So the most logical way to begin a JAXB example is to start with a DTD — but my mind doesn't latch onto a DTD right away. To understand a DTD, I need a sample XML document — a file in which I describe one salesperson. I won't actually *use* this XML file (shown in Listing 15-1) until several pages later, but it gives me a good foundation for thinking about the DTD to come

Listing 15-1: A Salesperson

```
<?xml version="1.0" encoding="UTF-8"?>
<!DOCTYPE Salesperson SYSTEM "Salesperson.dtd">
<!-- Salesperson.xml -->

<Salesperson fullName="Barry Burd">
    <Total>1130.00</Total>

    <Sale>
        <ItemName>Widget</ItemName>
        <UnitCost>30.00</UnitCost>
        <Quantity>2</Quantity>
    </Sale>

    <Sale>
        <ItemName>Thingamabob</ItemName>
        <UnitCost>100.00</UnitCost>
        <Quantity>1</Quantity>
    </Sale>

    <Sale>
        <ItemName>Doohickey</ItemName>
        <UnitCost>23.00</UnitCost>
        <Quantity>5</Quantity>
    </Sale>
</Salesperson>
```

Let's take a look at Listing 15-1. By January 31, Barry had sold $1130.00 in goods. Then, in February, Barry made three new sales. The first sale involved two Widgets at $30.00 per widget. Eventually, we'll have to add this $60.00 sale to Barry's total. When we do, Barry's total will increase to $1190.00.

We'll also want to add Barry's other two sales (of Thingamabobs and Doohickeys) to his running total. When we're finished, Barry's total will have increased to $1405.00. I've placed a revised document, with the new total, in Listing 15-2.

Listing 15-2:   Updated Salesperson Information

```
<?xml version="1.0" encoding="UTF-8"?>

<Salesperson fullName="Barry Burd">
   <Total>1405.0</Total></Salesperson>
```

Notice that the revised document in Listing 15-2 has no `Sale` elements. When we update an XML document, we want sales to get gobbled up by the salesperson's total. So, once we've added a sale amount to the total, we dispose of that sale information.

Describing a document

To get this chapter's example rolling, all I need is a Document Type Definition (DTD) and a binding schema.

I just happen to have a DTD for a salesperson document. The DTD is in Listing 15-3.

Listing 15-3:   What is a Salesperson?

```
<?xml version="1.0" encoding="UTF-8"?>
<!-- Salesperson.dtd -->

<!ELEMENT Salesperson (Total, Sale*)>
<!ATTLIST Salesperson fullName CDATA #REQUIRED>

<!ELEMENT Total (#PCDATA)>

<!ELEMENT Sale (ItemName, UnitCost, Quantity)>

<!ELEMENT ItemName (#PCDATA)>
<!ELEMENT UnitCost (#PCDATA)>
<!ELEMENT Quantity (#PCDATA)>
```

Any old XML document can have a DTD, but the document in this chapter needs a binding schema too. Voilá — the binding schema (Listing 15-4).

Listing 15-4:   A Binding Schema

```
<?xml version="1.0" encoding="UTF-8"?>
<!-- Salesperson.xjs -->

<xml-java-binding-schema version="1.0-ea">
   <element name="Salesperson" type="class" root="true">
      <attribute name="fullName"/>
```

(continued)

Listing 15-4 *(continued)*

```
        <content>
          <element-ref name="Total"/>
          <element-ref name="Sale"/>
        </content>
      </element>

      <element name="Total" type="value" convert="double"/>

      <element name="Sale" type="class">
        <content>
          <element-ref name="ItemName"/>
          <element-ref name="UnitCost"/>
          <element-ref name="Quantity"/>
        </content>
      </element>

      <element name="ItemName" type="value"/>
      <element name="UnitCost" type="value" convert="double"/>
      <element name="Quantity" type="value" convert="int"/>
</xml-java-binding-schema>
```

Going through the binding schema piece by piece is the best way to get at what it's doing:

✔ **The binding schema in Listing 15-4 is an XML document.**

The document's `root` element is `xml-java-binding-schema`. Notice that my version number has the letters `ea` in it. This stands for "early access." (With any luck, you're working with a real version of the product instead of an early-access release.)

✔ **The file in Listing 15-4 has an** `xjs` **extension.**

The name of the file is `Salesperson.xjs`. I guess `xjs` stands for "eXtensible Java Schema."

✔ **Listing 15-4 has several binding declarations.**

A *binding declaration* helps to connect a piece of an XML document with something in a Java class. For instance, consider the line

```
<element name="ItemName" type="value"/>
```

in Listing 15-4. This line sets things up so that `<ItemName>Widget</ItemName>` can be connected with a value of type `String`. (As it happens, `String` is the default type.) When the generated class is created, the class has declarations of the following kind:

```
private String _ItemName;
public String getItemName()
public void setItemName(String _ItemName)
```

Another line,

```
<attribute name="fullName"/>
```

helps to connect "Barry Burd" (in `<Salesperson fullName="Barry Burd">`) with a Java value of type `String`. The generated class gets declarations that look like this:

```
private String _FullName;
public String getFullName()
public void setFullName(String _FullName)
```

A typical binding schema, like the one in Listing 15-4, has several binding declarations. Sometimes, I use the nickname "declaration" when I mean "binding declaration." One way or another, it's very useful to call these things "declarations" of some kind. Without this terminology, I'd have to call everything in sight an "element." Then I'd have to write about an element whose name is `element`, or about an element whose name is `attribute`. It would be very confusing.

✔ **Listing 15-4 has six `element` binding declarations.**

Each of these `element` declarations describes an element type. The element types (`Salesperson`, `Total`, `Sale`, `ItemName`, `UnitCost`, and `Quantity`) come from the earlier listings in this chapter.

Element declarations

The code in Listing 15-4 introduces six types of elements; each element has its own characteristics. For instance, a total dollar amount shouldn't be stored as a Java `String`. If you store a dollar amount as a string, you can't do any arithmetic with the amount. So we need a way to tell the schema compiler about the `Total` element's specialized needs. We do this by adding attributes to our element's binding declarations.

The element declarations in Listing 15-4 use four attributes — `name`, `type`, `convert`, and `root`. Let's see how each attribute works:

✔ **A `name` attribute specifies the name of the element.**

In Listing 15-4, the line

```
<element name="ItemName" ... Etc.>
```

tells us that Listing 15-1 can have an `ItemName` element. Sure enough, if I look back at Listing 15-1, I see an `ItemName` element.

✔ **A `type` attribute tells the schema compiler whether it should define a new class, or not.**

Think about the `Sale` and `ItemName` declarations in Listing 15-4.

• In the `Sale` declaration

```
<element name="Sale" type="class">
```

the word `class` tells the schema compiler to create a new Java source file — a file named `Sale.java`. When you compile this new Java source file, you get `Sale.class`.

- In the `ItemName` declaration

```
<element name="ItemName" type="value"/>
```

the word `value` tells the schema compiler not to create `ItemName.java`. In the generated code, any use of an item name in the will be treated as a Java `String`. The generated code will have a line like this in it:

```
private String _ItemName;
```

In the Java API, `java.lang.String` is a class. This would lead you to believe that the `ItemName` declaration should have the attribute `type="class"` instead of `type="value"`. Well, it doesn't work that way. Because we don't want the schema compiler to create a brand new `ItemName.java` file, we specify the attribute for the `ItemName` element as `type="value"`.

✔ A convert **attribute supercedes the use of the default** `String` **class.**

In Listing 15-4, the line

```
<element name="Total" type="value"
    convert="double"/>
```

tells us that the total should be stored in a variable of type `double`. The generated code looks something like this:

```
private double _Total;
public double getTotal()
public void setTotal(double _Total)
```

Without the `type="value"` attribute, the total would be stored as a string.

You can play this game over and over again. In Listing 15-4, the `Quantity` declaration has attribute `convert="int"`. So, in the generated code, any variable storing the quantity will be of type `int`.

✔ **An element that has a** `root` **attribute, can be the root in an XML document.**

The `Salesperson` element in Listing 15-4 has attribute `root="true"`. That's good, because `Salesperson` is the `root` element in the document of Listing 15-1.

Lots of rules that govern the use of the `root` attribute. For the moment, keep these two in mind:

- Every binding schema has to have at least one declaration like this — in which an element is declared to be the root.

- A root declaration must have the attribute `type="class"`. (You can't use `type="value"` and `root="true"` in the same binding declaration.)

Now, here's a surprise. A binding schema *can* have several `element` declarations, each with attribute `root="true"`. The idea is, you can use one Java class to read or create two different XML documents. One document may have a root element named `<Chocolate>`, and the other document may have a root element named `<Vanilla>`. Both the Chocolate and Vanilla documents can come from the same DTD, and can use the same binding schema.

Doing content validation

I should make some noise about the `convert` attribute in Listing 15-4. You have two ways to validate an XML document.

✔ **You can validate the document's structure.**

A DTD describes a document's structure. With a DTD, you can check things like the absence or presence of elements, the nesting of elements, and so on. The DTD in Listing 15-3 says that a document's `Salesperson` element must have a `Total` sub-element. So, when you do *structure validation*, you check to make sure that a document's `Salesperson` element has a `Total` sub-element. If the `Salesperson` element has no `Total` sub-element, then the program makes a big fuss.

Up to this point in the book, most of the validation examples do structure validation.

✔ **You can validate the document's content.**

In Chapter 4, Listings 4-8 and 4-9 illustrate *content validation*. With content validation, you check to make sure that a document's values have the expected types. In Listing 4-8, you declare `Children` to be an integer. So, in Listing 4-9, where `Children` has value 2.5, the computer issues an error message.

The original XML specs didn't say much about content validation. So, content validation is taking its time, creeping slowly into the XML world. By the time you read this book (maybe in the year 2120, just before the book finally goes out of print), content validation will be a full-fledged part of XML processing. Until then, you have to read the fine print in each piece of software's documentation. What kind of validation (if any) does the software do?

Well, three cheers for JAXB — you can use it to do real content validation. Take the stuff in Listings 15-1 and 15-4. According to Listing 15-4, the value inside a `Total` element is to be interpreted as a `double`. So `<Total>1130.00</Total>`

is okay, but `<Total>eleven-hundred-thirty</Total>` is not okay. If you replace `1130.00` with `eleven-hundred-thirty` in Listing 15-1, and then you run this section's examples, you get a `NumberFormatException`. (Now, that's what I call progress.)

More binding declarations

I'm not finished with the tour of Listing 15-4. I still have to tell you about the things you can put inside an `element` declaration. Listing 15-4 shows three such things: `attribute` declarations, `content` declarations, and `element-ref` declarations. Each has characteristics that are worth a closer look:

 ✔ An `attribute` **declaration describes an attribute in an XML document.**

   Look again at Listing 15-4, and notice the following two lines:

   ```
   <element name="Salesperson" ... Etc.>
       <attribute name="fullName"/>
   ```

   These lines say that a `Salesperson` element has a `fullName` attribute. Sure enough, if you look at Listing 15-1, you find the following element:

   ```
   <Salesperson fullName="Barry Burd">
   ```

   When `Salesperson.java` is generated, this Java source file has lines like this:

   ```
   private String _FullName;
   public String getFullName()
   public void setFullName(String _FullName)
   ```

The `attribute` declaration in Listing 15-4 provides no new information. In fact, it's optional — the schema compiler looks at the DTD instead. To discover that a `Salesperson` element has a `fullName` attribute, you could just look in the DTD (Listing 15-3).

There are situations in which an attribute declaration isn't optional. For example, an `attribute` declaration can supersede the default `String` binding. Take a declaration like `<attribute name="fullName" convert="StringBuffer"/>`. This declaration says that the full name should be stored as a `StringBuffer`, not a `String`.

 ✔ A `content` **declaration tells you about the stuff between a start tag and its end tag.**

   The `content` declaration says, in effect, "We've finished describing attributes. Now let's talk about child elements."

 ✔ An `element-ref` **declaration describes a child element.**

In Listing 15-4, look at the following three lines:

```
<element name="Sale" type="class">
    <content>
        <element-ref name="ItemName"/>
```

The message from these three lines may look familiar if you looked at the DTD in Listing 15-3. The message says that an ItemName element is a child of the Sale element.

And what does that mean in terms of binding? Well, when the schema compiler creates Sale.java, this Java class has a variable that stores an item name, like this:

```
private String _ItemName;
public String getItemName()
public void setItemName(String _ItemName)
```

Every Sale object (every instance of the Sale class) will have its own item name.

Over time, I've made all kinds of mistakes working with content declarations. Sometimes, I forget to use a content declaration. (My element-ref declarations get to be children, not grandchildren, of the element declaration.) Occasionally, I put an attribute declaration inside of a content declaration. (That is, I accidentally turn a child into a grandchild.) In either case the schema compiler gives me an informative error message.

The generated classes

The previous section explained more than you may want to know about the declarations in a binding schema. With all that under your belt, it's time to compile the binding schema. (Some remarks about starting the schema compiler appear earlier in this chapter.)

At this point, take a look at Figure 15-1. You've written the code that's in the top two rectangles (the DTD and the binding schema). You're about to run the program in the topmost oval (the schema compiler). In this example, a run of the schema compiler creates *two* generated classes — because the binding schema in Listing 15-4 has two type="class" declarations. Both the Salesperson and the Sale declarations have type="class" attributes, so the schema compiler generates two files. One file is named Salesperson. java; the other file is named Sale.java.

The generated Java source files are about 250 lines each, but I'm not taking up ten pages to show you the generated source files. Instead, I'll show you some highlights in Listings 15-5 and 15-6.

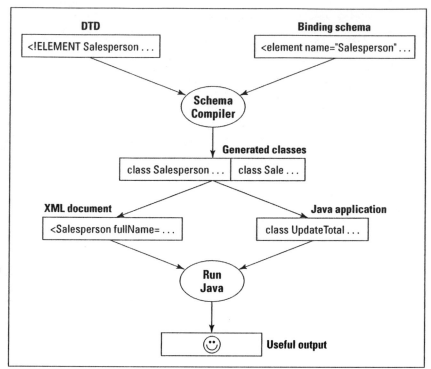

Figure 15-1:
Creating
and using
generated
classes.

Listing 15-5: Salesperson Highlights

```
/*
 * This listing is incomplete. It will not compile as is.
 * The listing has been edited to fit your television screen.
 * To get the complete listing, run the schema compiler
 *    on Listings 15-3 and 15-4. You can also get the
 *    complete listing by visiting www.users.drew.edu/bburd.
 */

public class Salesperson
    extends MarshallableRootElement
    implements RootElement
{

    private String _FullName;
    private double _Total;
    private boolean has_Total = false;
    private List _Sale =
        PredicatedLists.createInvalidating
        (this, new SalePredicate(), new ArrayList());

    public String getFullName() {
```

```java
            return _FullName;
    }

    public void setFullName(String _FullName) {
        this._FullName = _FullName;
        if (_FullName == null) {
            invalidate();
        }
    }

    public double getTotal() {
        if (has_Total) {
            return _Total;
        }
        throw new NoValueException("Total");
    }

    public void setTotal(double _Total) {
        this._Total = _Total;
        has_Total = true;
        invalidate();
    }

    public boolean hasTotal() {
        return has_Total;
    }

    public void deleteTotal() {
        has_Total = false;
        invalidate();
    }

    public List getSale() {
        return _Sale;
    }

    public void deleteSale() {
        _Sale = null;
        invalidate();
    }

    public void emptySale() {
        _Sale = PredicatedLists.createInvalidating
            (this, pred_Sale, new ArrayList());
    }

    public static Salesperson unmarshal(InputStream in)
        throws UnmarshalException
    {
        return unmarshal(XMLScanner.open(in));
    }
}
```

Listing 15-6: Sales Highlights

```
/*
 * This listing is incomplete. It will not compile as is.
 * The listing has been shortened, even though I'm expected
 *    to submit sixty more pages by Monday morning.
 * To get the complete listing, run the schema compiler
 *    on Listings 15-3 and 15-4. You can also get the
 *    complete listing by visiting www.users.drew.edu/bburd.
 */

public class Sale
    extends MarshallableObject
    implements Element
{

    private String _ItemName;
    private double _UnitCost;
    private boolean has_UnitCost = false;
    private int _Quantity;
    private boolean has_Quantity = false;

    public String getItemName() {
        return _ItemName;
    }

    public void setItemName(String _ItemName) {
        this._ItemName = _ItemName;
        if (_ItemName == null) {
            invalidate();
        }
    }

    public double getUnitCost() {
        if (has_UnitCost) {
            return _UnitCost;
        }
        throw new NoValueException("UnitCost");
    }

    public void setUnitCost(double _UnitCost) {
        this._UnitCost = _UnitCost;
        has_UnitCost = true;
        invalidate();
    }

    public boolean hasUnitCost() {
        return has_UnitCost;
    }

    public void deleteUnitCost() {
        has_UnitCost = false;
        invalidate();
```

```
        }

    public int getQuantity() {
        if (has_Quantity) {
            return _Quantity;
        }
        throw new NoValueException("Quantity");
    }

    public void setQuantity(int _Quantity) {
        this._Quantity = _Quantity;
        has_Quantity = true;
        invalidate();
    }

    public boolean hasQuantity() {
        return has_Quantity;
    }

    public void deleteQuantity() {
        has_Quantity = false;
        invalidate();
    }

    public static Sale unmarshal(InputStream in)
        throws UnmarshalException
    {
        return unmarshal(XMLScanner.open(in));
    }
}
```

The generated files have everything you need to treat a Salesperson document like a Java object. (I suppose salespeople get treated like objects all the time.)

Note, in particular, the declaration of _Sale in Listing 15-5; the _Sale variable stores a Java List. Now look back at Listing 15-1, and you'll see that a Salesperson element can have several Sale subelements. The schema compiler deals with repeatable subelements by creating a Java List.

Making Use of the Generated Classes

If you look back at Figure 15-1, you can see where we are in the overall scheme of things. The previous section gave us some generated classes — the classes described in the Salesperson.java and Sale.java files. So now we need a Java application. The application takes the generated classes, puts them to good use, and creates some worthwhile output. That Java application (in Listing 15-7) updates the total in Salesperson.xml from Listing 15-1.

Listing 15-7: **Updating the Total**

```java
import java.io.FileInputStream;
import java.io.FileOutputStream;
import java.io.IOException;
import java.io.FileNotFoundException;

import javax.xml.bind.UnmarshalException;
import javax.xml.bind.StructureValidationException;

import java.util.List;
import java.util.Iterator;


class UpdateTotal
{
    static Salesperson salesperson;

    public static void main(String args[])
        throws IOException, UnmarshalException
    {
        Sale sale;

        String fullName;
        double total, newTotal;
        String itemName;
        double unitCost;
        int quantity;

        List saleList;
        Iterator saleIterator;

        salesperson = readSalesperson();

        fullName = salesperson.getFullName();
        total = salesperson.getTotal();
        newTotal=total;

        saleList = salesperson.getSale();
        saleIterator = saleList.iterator();

        System.out.println(fullName + " sold");

        while (saleIterator.hasNext())
        {
            sale = (Sale)saleIterator.next();

            itemName = sale.getItemName();
            unitCost = sale.getUnitCost();
            quantity = sale.getQuantity();
            newTotal += unitCost*quantity;

            System.out.print("\t" + quantity);
```

```
            System.out.println(" " + itemName + "s");

        saleIterator.remove();
    }

    salesperson.setTotal(newTotal);
    writeSalesperson();
}


static Salesperson readSalesperson()
    throws FileNotFoundException, UnmarshalException
{
    FileInputStream salespersonIn =
        new FileInputStream("Salesperson.xml");

    salesperson = Salesperson.unmarshal(salespersonIn);

    return salesperson;
}


static void writeSalesperson()
    throws IOException, StructureValidationException
{
    FileOutputStream salespersonOut =
        new FileOutputStream("Salesperson.xml");

    salesperson.validate();
    salesperson.marshal(salespersonOut);
}
}
```

Listing 15-7 illustrates the enormous power of JAXB processing. If this were a DOM program, we'd be digging through a morass of recursive method calls. We'd visit the document node, make a recursive call to visit the Salesperson node, and then make another recursive call to visit the Total node. Using JAXB in Listing 15-7, we do the same thing in two lines:

```
salesperson = readSalesperson();
total = salesperson.getTotal();
```

Other parts of the document tree come just as easily. For instance, to get the item name in a sale, we issue the following call:

```
itemName = sale.getItemName();
```

If there's anything tricky in Listing 15-7, it's dealing with a list of sales. A call to salesperson.getSale returns a Java List. This is a list of Sale elements within the Salesperson root element. Although you can step through a list's entries in several ways, the most elegant is with a Java Iterator.

In Listing 15-7, we get an `Iterator` instance by calling `saleList.iterator`. Then we go into a loop, and make successive calls to the iterator's `next` method. Each call to `next` unearths another object in the list.

With an object from the list in hand, we're almost ready to call `getUnitCost` and `getQuantity`. The only hurdle is that every entry in a Java `List` is of type `Object`, not type `Sale`. So, to get the most out of the `next` method, we do a cast:

```
sale = (Sale)saleIterator.next();
```

Having a full-fledged `Sale` object means we can call `getUnitCost` and `getQuantity`. With the results of these calls, we can start updating the total.

Writing a document

The marshalling code in Listing 15-7 writes an XML document to a file. The file that gets written appears in Listing 15-2. Notice, again, that the document in Listing 15-2 has no `Sale` elements. Once we've used a `Sale` element to update the total, we want to toss that `Sale` element out the window.

In Listing 15-7, we toss a sale out the window with a call to `saleIterator.remove`. An iterator's `remove` method deletes an entry from the iterator's underlying list. So, by the time we get around to the marshalling code, the class no longer has any `Sale` elements.

Java's `List` and `Iterator` classes each have their own `remove` methods. Listing 15-7 uses the iterator's `remove` method, which is much easier to use than the list's `remove` method. With the list's `remove` method, you use an index, and it's easy to get confused keeping track of list indices. Taking away an entry makes the list shrink, so the count of entries shifts — which makes it tricky to use a loop counter in your code. In contrast, the iterator's `remove` method takes care of indices for you. A call to the iterator's `remove` method doesn't mess up a subsequent call to the iterator's `next` method (which makes the iterator's `remove` method very safe to use).

Writing to the screen

I get all excited about marshalling and creating a new XML document, so it's easy for me to forget about command prompt output. When you run the code in Listing 15-7, you get the output shown in Figure 15-2. The output values come courtesy of some methods belonging to the generated class. The methods I used in Listing 15-2 for this purpose are `getFullName`, `getQuantity`, and `getItemName`.

Figure 15-2:
Output from
Listing 15-7
to your
computer's
command
prompt.

```
Barry Burd sold
       2 Widgets
       1 Thingamabobs
       5 Doohickeys
```

Modifying a Binding Schema

The number 1405.0 in Listing 15-2 may bother you a bit. This number represents a dollar amount, but it doesn't look much like a dollar amount. (So what's happening? Is inflation so bad that pennies aren't important anymore?)

Using the string default

To change the way the total in Listing 15-2 is formatted, you can choose from among several different tricks. The brute-force trick is to go back to the binding schema (Listing 15-4), and delete convert="double" from the Total tag. Deleting convert="double" changes Total to a value of type String. But then, in Listing 15-7, you have to change total to a variable of type String. Of course, if total is a String, then you can no longer add numbers to total.

Well, by the time you're finished, you've done enough tinkering to warrant the creation of a brand new subclass like the one shown in Listing 15-8. The new, well-formatted XML output with that subclass is shown in Listing 15-9.

Listing 15-8:   Extending the UpdateTotal Class

```java
import java.text.NumberFormat;

import java.io.IOException;
import javax.xml.bind.UnmarshalException;
import java.util.List;
import java.util.Iterator;


class UpdateCurrencyTotal extends UpdateTotal
{
    public static void main(String args[])
        throws IOException, UnmarshalException
    {
        Sale sale;
```

(continued)

Listing 15-8 *(continued)*

```java
        String fullName;
        String total, newTotal;
        double doubleTotal;

        String itemName;
        double unitCost;
        int quantity;

        List saleList;
        Iterator saleIterator;

        salesperson = readSalesperson();

        fullName = salesperson.getFullName();
        total = salesperson.getTotal();
        doubleTotal = Double.parseDouble(total);

        saleList = salesperson.getSale();
        saleIterator = saleList.iterator();

        System.out.println(fullName + " sold");

        while (saleIterator.hasNext())
        {
            sale = (Sale)saleIterator.next();

            itemName = sale.getItemName();
            unitCost = sale.getUnitCost();
            quantity = sale.getQuantity();
            doubleTotal += unitCost*quantity;

            System.out.print("\t" + quantity);
            System.out.println(" " + itemName + "s");

            saleIterator.remove();
        }

        NumberFormat currency =
            NumberFormat.getCurrencyInstance();
        newTotal = currency.format(doubleTotal);
        salesperson.setTotal(newTotal);
        writeSalesperson();
    }

}
```

Listing 15-9: A Genuine Dollar Amount

```
<?xml version="1.0" encoding="UTF-8"?>

<Salesperson fullName="Barry Burd">
  <Total>$1,405.00</Total></Salesperson>
```

Converting to a class type

Listing 15-8 has a lot of conversion code. In the listing, you go from the String value total to the double value doubleTotal, and then back to a String value (newTotal). Maybe there's a way to simplify this ping-pong motion of values in the code before somebody gets a sore neck.

Well, the unmarshal and marshal methods do some conversions behind the scenes. All you need is a Java type that converts gracefully between numeric and string representations.

The type that you seek is called java.math.BigDecimal. This type has some very nice features:

✔ When you construct a BigDecimal object from a string, the constructor remembers the number of digits of accuracy in the string. For example, if you construct a BigDecimal object from "1130.00", then the object remembers two digits beyond the decimal point.

✔ You can do arithmetic with methods belonging to the BigDecimal class. You don't have to convert from String to double, or from double back to String.

That settles it — gotta get a look at an example featuring the BigDecimal class. The first thing to do is to inform the binding schema that I intend to use BigDecimal; Listing 15-10 shows the revised binding schema.

Listing 15-10: Converting to BigDecimal

```
<?xml version="1.0" encoding="UTF-8"?>
<!-- Salesperson.xjs -->

<xml-java-binding-schema version="1.0-ea">
    <element name="Salesperson" type="class" root="true">
        <attribute name="fullName"/>
        <content>
            <element-ref name="Total"/>
            <element-ref name="Sale"/>
```

(continued)

Listing 15-10 *(continued)*

```
        </content>
    </element>

    <element name="Total" type="value" convert="BigDecimal"/>

    <element name="Sale" type="class">
        <content>
            <element-ref name="ItemName"/>
            <element-ref name="UnitCost"/>
            <element-ref name="Quantity"/>
        </content>
    </element>

    <element name="ItemName" type="value"/>
    <element name="UnitCost" type="value" convert="double"/>
    <element name="Quantity" type="value" convert="int"/>

    <conversion name="BigDecimal"
                type="java.math.BigDecimal"/>
</xml-java-binding-schema>
```

Listing 15-10 contains a newly discovered declaration. It's called a *conversion declaration*. With a conversion declaration, you indicate the full name of a Java class. In Listing 15-10, you indicate that `BigDecimal` is a nickname for `java.math.BigDecimal`. (You could also indicate that `FishStick` is a nickname for `java.math.BigDecimal`. But why would you want to do that?)

One conversion declaration holds for an entire binding schema. For instance, in Listing 15-10, if you want to convert both `Total` and `UnitCost` to `BigDecimal`, you can do it with just one conversion declaration. After the conversion to a `BigDecimal`, the code that updates the total is sleek as silk.

The code appears in Listing 15-11. The resulting Salesperson.xml document is in Listing 15-12.

Listing 15-11:   Using the BigDecimal class

```
import java.text.NumberFormat;

import java.io.IOException;
import javax.xml.bind.UnmarshalException;
import java.util.List;
import java.util.Iterator;

import java.math.BigDecimal;
```

```
class UpdateBigDecimal extends UpdateTotal
{
   public static void main(String args[])
      throws IOException, UnmarshalException
   {
      Sale sale;

      String fullName;
      BigDecimal total, newTotal;
      String itemName;
      double unitCost;
      int quantity;

      List saleList;
      Iterator saleIterator;

      salesperson = readSalesperson();

      fullName = salesperson.getFullName();
      total = salesperson.getTotal();
      newTotal=total;

      saleList = salesperson.getSale();
      saleIterator = saleList.iterator();

      System.out.println(fullName + " sold");

      while (saleIterator.hasNext())
      {
         sale = (Sale)saleIterator.next();

         itemName = sale.getItemName();
         unitCost = sale.getUnitCost();
         quantity = sale.getQuantity();
         newTotal =
            newTotal.add(new BigDecimal(unitCost*quantity));

         System.out.print("\t" + quantity);
         System.out.println(" " + itemName + "s");

         saleIterator.remove();
      }

      salesperson.setTotal(newTotal);
      writeSalesperson();
   }
}
```

Listing 15-12:   Marshal's Delicious Mystery Appetizer

```
<?xml version="1.0" encoding="UTF-8"?>

<Salesperson fullName="Barry Burd">
  <Total>1405.00</Total></Salesperson>
```

Listing 15-11 reduces the clumsy conversion code to just one statement —
which adds unitCost*quantity to newTotal. For this run of good code, we
owe thanks to Java's BigDecimal class. But we also owe thanks to JAXB.
With the JAXB binding schema, we can move seamlessly from an XML document to the most convenient, most natural Java class. (Ah, progress.)

Part III

Special-Purpose Tools for the Web-Services Revolution

The 5th Wave   By Rich Tennant

"Well, this is festive—a miniature intranet amidst a swirl of Java applets."

In this part . . .

*1*f you want to make money with Java and XML, then don't skip this part of the book. Everyone is excited about Web services, and this part of the book has the tools to help you get started. You can create services, use services, and find other peoples' services.

The first of the chapters goes deep into Web-service techniques and gets dirty with the details; and the remaining two chapters use broad, bold strokes. Either way, you're working with Web services — the next big wave in information technology.

Chapter 16

Sending SOAP Messages with JAXM

* * *

In This Chapter

▶ Sending messages across the Net

▶ Finding businesses

▶ Answering queries about businesses

* * *

This chapter is dedicated to my Aunt Nettie, who was good at helping people find things. If you'd lost your keys, Nettie would know exactly what questions to ask. When do you remember having them? Where have you been today? Where do you usually keep them? If anyone could help you find your keys, Nettie could.

I suppose she could help search for intangible things too. What kind of fact do you need for your homework report? Where was your friend when she mysteriously disappeared? Which vendors' parsers support the latest version of SAX?

If Nettie was still around, then we'd have no need for UDDI queries that search lists of businesses. Do you need a business that offers an online stock quote ticker? Just formulate your need as a UDDI query. Want a service that tracks packages for your online store? Send a query to a registry, and get a list of matching services.

Nettie wouldn't view UDDI as a form of competition. She'd understand the need for fast, efficient searches in today's busy marketplace. She'd appreciate the way UDDI speeds the transition from concept to production. She'd view UDDI as an important part of today's Web-services paradigm. Besides, if you ever lost your car keys, you'd still need my Aunt Nettie.

Sending and Receiving Messages

So you want to make a million bucks, heh? And you want to do it quickly. Well, just jump on the big Web services bandwagon. These days, Web services are all the rage. Among the companies investing heavily in Web services are Microsoft, Microsoft, and Microsoft. (With its .NET framework, Microsoft is betting the farm on the demand for Web services tools.) Using Web services, companies can share data and applications without batting their corporate eyebrows. So it's time you looked into this hot new technology.

There's a primer on Web services in Chapter 1. The basic idea is that a *Web service* is a shared application. Company A makes a service available on the Web, and Company B incorporates that service into its own online processing routines. This incorporation takes place with little human intervention, because standards and tools are targeted for the task.

Web services represent the next leap in shared, distributed computing. With Web services, companies can automate the process of building sophisticated software applications. No longer do you ship expensive software from one location to another, or download an independent copy of a software product. Instead, you use software that's in a central repository. This software plugs into your own code as if it was meant to live there, and the transfer of commands and data is fully automated.

Standards, standards, standards

Web services involve sharing data *and tasks* over the Internet. So the big question is how to do all this sharing. We need standards of all kinds — for sharing bits, for sharing raw data, and for sharing high-level commands.

Fortunately, there's no shortage of standards. Three nice ones exist that can help bring Web services to life:

✓ **UDDI: Universal Description, Discovery, and Integration**

With XML-based UDDI standards, companies list their services in centralized registries. These registries store information about businesses along with descriptions of the Web services that the businesses offer.

When you're hunting for a particular kind of service, you don't have to surf a registry's Web site. Instead, you automate the search process by sending UDDI queries to the registry server. If your company has high-volume processing needs, then the automated search is of enormous benefit.

✓ **WSDL: The Web Services Description Language**

Once you've decided to use a particular Web service, you have to plug that service into your existing software structure. Traditionally, getting software products to work together has been a pain in the career end. One product runs on Windows; the other on Linux. One product uses an Access database; the other an Oracle database. One product is written in Java; the other in COBOL. Neither product is well documented. (Each product's developers are busy defending their turf.)

Here comes WSDL to the rescue. With WSDL, the vendor of a Web service describes the exact interfaces presented by the service. To make use of the service, all your company has to do is to interpret the WSDL code. And interpreting the WSDL code can be done programmatically. By running software, you can use the WSDL description of a Web service to create calls to that service.

By the way, what markup language do you think WSDL is based on? Let's see. Could it possibly be XML?

✔ **SOAP: The Simple Object Access Protocol**

SOAP is a standard for sending data and commands along Internet lines. Using SOAP, you can send UDDI messages, WSDL messages, or almost any other kind of message.

With SOAP, you wrap data in an XML document. You send that document to another user, to another company, or to a droid in another galaxy. When the receiver unwraps the SOAP message, the receiver interprets and acts on the SOAP data. Because SOAP is standardized, the information in the SOAP message is interpreted correctly.

Most SOAP messages travel across the Internet the way Web pages travel to your computer's Web browser. These messages use the Web's HTTP protocol. So, as with everything else having to do with networks, the set of protocols you use with Web services are layered.

The layers are illustrated in Figure 16-1. The development of Web services relies on UDDI and WSDL, which relies on SOAP, which in turn relies on HTTP, and so on.

Development of Web Services	
UDDI	WSDL
SOAP	
HTTP	
The Internet infrastructure	

Figure 16-1:
The layering
of protocols.

SOAP

Both UDDI and WSDL are based on SOAP. So the fundamental task in the next few chapters is to compose, send, and unwrap SOAP messages. This isn't too difficult, because a SOAP message is primarily an XML document. But a SOAP message has a special structure, as illustrated in Figure 16-2.

A SOAP Message

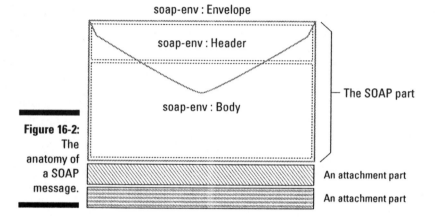

soap-env : Envelope

soap-env : Header

soap-env : Body

The SOAP part

An attachment part

An attachment part

Figure 16-2:
The
anatomy of
a SOAP
message.

For most purposes, the terms "SOAP message" and "SOAP document" are interchangeable. The words "SOAP message" emphasize the conveying of content, and the term "SOAP document" reminds us that it's all just XML text. Don't read too much into my use of one term versus another. (Occasionally, I switch back and forth for the sake of variety.)

A SOAP message has a *SOAP part* and *attachment parts.* The SOAP part is the part that's most interesting to us — the XML fanatics. The SOAP part consists of just one thing — an XML document called a *SOAP envelope.* The document's root element is named Envelope.

```
<Envelope xmlns="http://schemas.xmlsoap.org/soap/envelope/">
...
</Envelope>
```

A SOAP document must have a namespace. The document cannot have a DOCTYPE declaration or processing instructions. The document's innards consist of two elements — a *header* and a *body.*

 ✔ **The optional header contains information about the handling of the SOAP message.**

Does this message really come from user Barry Burd? Does Barry want all the message data to be processed at once (or is part of the processing optional)? To what account will Barry charge the processing of the data? These concerns, and more, can be described in a SOAP message's header.

✔ **The body contains text data.**

Data that can be efficiently represented with text go into a SOAP message's body. For instance, a salesperson's totals, or the ingredients for a greasy Philly cheese steak can be transmitted in the body of a SOAP message. Anything in an ordinary XML document can be turned into a SOAP message's body.

If a SOAP message has any attachment parts, then each attachment is a piece of binary data. Because an attachment isn't text, an attachment can be anything you want it to be. It can be an image, a Word document, a *For Dummies* chapter, or whatever. Most of the time, I send SOAP messages that have no attachments.

Listing 16-1 contains a short SOAP message. This message has no attachments, so the entire message is a single XML document. The message starts with the Envelope tag, and has both Header and Body elements.

Listing 16-1:   A SOAP message

```
<soap-env:Envelope xmlns:soap-env=
    "http://schemas.xmlsoap.org/soap/envelope/">
  <soap-env:Header/>
  <soap-env:Body>
      <find_business xmlns="urn:uddi-org:api" generic="1.0">
          <name>Computer</name>
      </find_business>
  </soap-env:Body>
</soap-env:Envelope>
```

For more information on the SOAP standard, visit www.oasis-open.org/cover/soap.html. You can also visit www.w3c.org/2002/ws.

Composing and Sending a UDDI Query

Our goal is to write code that sends a SOAP message. In fact, the message that we'll be sending is shown in Listing 16-1. This particular SOAP message happens to be a UDDI query. The query asks for a list of businesses with the string Computer in their names.

If you send this message to a UDDI registry, then the registry sends another SOAP message back to you. The message you receive lists businesses that are stored in the registry's database.

The many releases of JAXM

The code in this chapter uses JAXM — the *Java API for XML Messaging*. As I write these words, the JAXM API is in *early-access release*. That means the software isn't even a beta product yet. Of course, the difference between early-access and beta is whatever you want it to be. I've seen beta products that weren't nearly as polished as this early-access release of JAXM.

In any case, the JAXM developer forum has postings with remarks like "This class has been deprecated since early-access release 0.0001," and "We plan to add a method that accepts string arguments." Things change rapidly between early-access and final public release. So the stuff in this chapter is a moving target. If you try to run my code, and you get an evil-looking error message, then check the JAXM API documentation. Maybe a method name has changed, and you can fix it very quickly. You can also check for updates on my Web site: `www.users.drew.edu/bburd`.

Setting up your computer to use JAXM

The JAXM packages aren't part of the core Java API. So to run this chapter's examples, you'll need to download JAXM. You can download the API by visiting `java.sun.com/xml/jaxm`.

When you download the product, and look at the documentation, you may find the discussion to be a bit intimidating. In the release that I have, the documentation starts with seven or eight steps on installing a Web server and copying files among directories. The good news is, you may not have to do all that.

> ✔ **To send a UDDI query to an existing registry, you can do a minimal software setup.**
>
> The first big example in this chapter sends a query to a public registry at ibm.com. To query the registry, you just run the code in Listing 16-3. Of course, running the code may have some prerequisites. For instance, you may have to set the system classpath to point to one or more of the following JAR files: `jaxm.jar`, `jaxm-client.jar`, `mail.jar`, `activation.jar`, `dom4j.jar`, `log4j.jar`.
>
> The JAR files that you need come with the JAXM download. To learn more about setting your system's classpath (something I always dislike doing), see Chapter 2.

✔ **To respond to a query, you need a heftier setup.**

This chapter's second big example composes a response to a UDDI query. To do this, the code needs to receive the query, and the usual channel for receiving such queries is the World Wide Web. So you need a mini Web server to run the second example in this chapter.

Chapter 13 describes the download and installation of a server called Tomcat. Once you have the Tomcat setup file, you no longer need an Internet connection. (You can send queries from your own computer to your own computer. I do it all the time.) Anyway, you should check to see if JAXM has any of its own requirements for running Tomcat. In the JAXM early-access release, I have to copy some files to Tomcat's `common/lib` and `webapps` directories. Fortunately, the JAXM documentation is very thorough.

A UDDI response

Take another look at the SOAP message in Listing 16-1. This message is a UDDI query. The query asks for all businesses whose names have the string `"Computer"` in them. When I compose this query, and I send it to `http://www-3.ibm.com/services/uddi/testregistry/inquiryapi`, then I get back the response shown in Listing 16-2.

Listing 16-2:   A Response from a UDDI Registry

```
<?xml version="1.0" encoding="UTF-8"?>
<Envelope xmlns="http://schemas.xmlsoap.org/soap/envelope/">
   <Body>
      <businessList generic="1.0" xmlns="urn:uddi-org:api"
      operator="www.ibm.com/services/uddi"
      truncated="false">
         <businessInfos>
            <businessInfo businessKey=
            "0FB2B330-00D2-11D6-8C49-0004AC49CC1E">
               <name>Computer Hardware</name>
               <description xml:lang="en">Real Time
               Procurement of Computer Hardware via Internet
               </description>
               <serviceInfos/>
            </businessInfo>
            <businessInfo businessKey=
            "29064E10-36C3-11D6-83CD-000C0E00ACDD">
               <name>ComputersToYou</name>
               <description xml:lang="en"/>
               <serviceInfos>
                  <serviceInfo serviceKey=
                  "348B5E00-36CE-11D6-83CD-000C0E00ACDD"
```

(continued)

Listing 16-2 *(continued)*

```
              businessKey=
              "29064E10-36C3-11D6-83CD-000C0E00ACDD">
                  <name>DomainRegistrationService</name>
              </serviceInfo>
              <serviceInfo serviceKey=
      ... Etc.
```

Well, to be truthful, I get a response that's bigger than the one in Listing 16-2. And the real response isn't nicely indented or line wrapped. Anyway, I've marked the element names in bold so that the response's structure stands out. Please notice a few important things:

✔ **The response in Listing 16-2 is a SOAP message.**

The response has an envelope, and a body. Take my word for it, this response follows all the other rules and regulations that SOAP messages are supposed to follow.

✔ **The response lists several businesses, each in its own** businessInfo **element.**

All the businessInfo elements are children of one big businessInfos element. The words businessInfo and businessInfos are part of the UDDI standard.

Listing 16-2 has businesses named Computer Hardware and ComputersToYou. A complete listing may yield hundreds, maybe thousands, of businesses.

✔ **The response has two different kinds of** name **elements.**

I highlight this fact only because it tends to confuse people. Each business has a name, each business lists one or more services, and each service has a name. So the business with name ComputersToYou offers a service with name DomainRegistrationService. That's why you see

```
<businessInfo ... >
    <name>ComputersToYou</name>
    <serviceInfos>
        <serviceInfo ... >
            <name>DomainRegistrationService</name>
```

in Listing 16-2. Because the name DomainRegistrationService is buried within a serviceInfo element, the name DomainRegistrationService plays no role in this UDDI query. (A business's serviceInfo element can impact other UDDI queries, but not the query as it's stated in Listing 16-1.)

For more information on the UDDI standard, visit www.uddi.org. There's also an excellent set of UDDI reference pages at www.zvon.org/xxl/uddiReference/Output.

Making a UDDI query

I have a program that composes a query (a SOAP message), and sends the query to a UDDI registry. This is one of those programs that started off being ten lines long. The code expanded to twenty times its original size when I divided it into classes. Fortunately, each class is a fairly digestible chunk. You can read about each chunk in turn, or gloss over some of the chunks. It's up to you.

The program to send the query starts in Listing 16-3. When I run the program, I call it with the following command:

```
java AskUDDIquery Computer
    http://www-3.ibm.com/services/uddi/testregistry/inquiryapi
```

I get the output shown Figure 16-3.

Listing 16-3: Creating and Sending a UDDI Query

```java
import javax.xml.soap.SOAPConnectionFactory;
import javax.xml.soap.SOAPConnection;
import javax.xml.soap.SOAPMessage;
import javax.xml.soap.SOAPException;

import javax.xml.messaging.URLEndpoint;
import java.io.IOException;


public class AskUDDIquery
{
    static SOAPConnection connection;
    static URLEndpoint endpoint;


    public static void main(String args[])
        throws SOAPException, IOException
    {
        SOAPMessage request, response;
        MyRequestMaker maker = new MyRequestMaker();
        MyDisplayer displayer = new MyDisplayer();

        request = maker.createRequest(args[0]);

        System.out.println("Sending the following message:");
        displayer.displayOnConsole(request);

        doNetworkPlumbing(args[1]);
        response = connection.call(request, endpoint);

        System.out.println("Received the following message:");
```

(continued)

Listing 16-3 *(continued)*

```
        displayer.displayOnConsole(response);

        System.out.println("Matching business names:");
        displayer.displayBusinessNames(response);

        connection.close();
    }


    static void doNetworkPlumbing(String urlEndpoint)
        throws SOAPException
    {
        SOAPConnectionFactory connFactory;

        endpoint = new URLEndpoint (urlEndpoint);
        connFactory = SOAPConnectionFactory.newInstance();
        connection = connFactory.createConnection();
    }
}
```

```
Sending the following message:
<soap-env:Envelope xmlns:soap-env="http://schemas.xmlsoap.org/soap/envelope/"><s
oap-env:Header/><soap-env:Body><find_business xmlns="urn:uddi-org:api" generic="
1.0"><name>Computer</name></find_business></soap-env:Body></soap-env:Envelope>

Received the following message:
<?xml version="1.0" encoding="UTF-8" ?><Envelope xmlns="http://schemas.xmlsoap.o
rg/soap/envelope/"><Body><businessList generic="1.0" xmlns="urn:uddi-org:api" op
erator="www.ibm.com/services/uddi" truncated="false"><businessInfos><businessInf
o businessKey="0FB2B330-00D2-11D6-8C49-0004AC49CC1E"><name>Computer Hardware</na
me><description xml:lang="en">Real Time Procurement of Computer Hardware via Int
ernet</description><serviceInfos></serviceInfos></businessInfo><businessInfo bus
inessKey="29064E10-36C3-11D6-83CD-000C0E00ACDD"><name>ComputersToYou</name><desc
ription xml:lang="en"></description><serviceInfos><serviceInfo serviceKey="348B5
E00-36CE-11D6-83CD-000C0E00ACDD" businessKey="29064E10-36C3-11D6-83CD-000C0E00AC
DD"><name>DomainRegistrationService</name></serviceInfo><serviceInfo serviceKey=
"9C1A9190-3795-11D6-83CD-000C0E00ACDD" businessKey="29064E10-36C3-11D6-83CD-000C
0E00ACDD"><name>DomainRegistrationQueriesService</name></serviceInfo></serviceIn
fos></businessInfo><businessInfo businessKey="5A9136D0-DCC2-11D5-9094-0004AC49CC
1E"><name>computer</name><description xml:lang="zh">???????</description><service
Infos><serviceInfo serviceKey="87C5D380-DCC3-11D5-9094-0004AC49CC1E" businessKey
="5A9136D0-DCC2-11D5-9094-0004AC49CC1E"><name>PC</name></serviceInfo></serviceIn
fos></businessInfo></businessInfos></businessList></Body></Envelope>

Matching business names:
Computer Hardware
ComputersToYou
computer
```

Figure 16-3:
A run of the
program in
Listing 16-3.

The basic outline of Listing 16-3 consists of just three steps.

✔ **Create a request.**

I create a request by calling a method in my own `MyRequestMaker` class. (See the first bold line in Listing 16-3. The code for the `MyRequestMaker` class comes later in Listing 16-4.) The `MyRequestMaker` object creates a request message (a.k.a. SOAP message, a.k.a. UDDI query) from a Java string.

Just before Listing 16-3, I call the code with command-line argument `Computer`. So the `createRequest` call in Listing 16-3 has the following effect:

```
request = maker.createRequest("Computer");
```

✔ **Create a connection.**

The second bold line in Listing 16-3 calls method doNetworkPlumbing. In method doNetworkPlumbing, I create a SOAPConnectionFactory, and from the factory, I create a connection. The connection goes from my network card to a particular *endpoint*. In this section's example, the endpoint is www-3.ibm.com/services/uddi/testregistry/inquiryapi.

✔ **Send the request along the connection; get back a response.**

This step is the third bold line in Listing 16-3. The connection's call method sends the request message to the endpoint, and returns a response from the endpoint's UDDI registry. Once I have a response, I can display it on the screen, parse it, use it to choose a Web service, or do whatever else I want with it. In Listing 16-3, the calls to System.out.println display the message and some of its data.

Creating and composing a request

The next stop in your tour is the MyRequestMaker class. The code is in Listing 16-4.

Listing 16-4:   Creating a SOAP Message

```
import javax.xml.soap.SOAPMessage;
import javax.xml.soap.SOAPEnvelope;
import javax.xml.soap.SOAPElement;
import javax.xml.soap.Name;
import javax.xml.soap.SOAPException;


class MyRequestMaker
{
    SOAPMessage request;
    MyMessageHelper helper = new MyMessageHelper();


    SOAPMessage createRequest(String businessName)
        throws SOAPException
    {
        request = helper.createMessageObject();
        composeRequest(businessName);
        return request;
    }
```

(continued)

Listing 16-4 *(continued)*

```
void composeRequest (String businessName)
    throws SOAPException
{

    SOAPEnvelope envelope;
    SOAPElement element;
    Name name;

    envelope = helper.getMessageEnvelope(request);
    element = helper.getMessageBody(request);

    element = element.addChildElement
        ("find_business", "", "urn:uddi-org:api");

    name = envelope.createName("generic");
    element.addAttribute(name, "1.0");

    element = element.addChildElement("name");
    element.addTextNode(businessName);

    request.saveChanges();
  }
}
```

The work in Listing 16-4 comes in two parts — creating a request object, and filling the request object with XML elements (what I call "composing the request"). Fortunately, we can put off the study of request object creation until later in this section. (I do the request creation details inside the MyMessageHelper class, which you'll see in Listing 16-5.) For now, let's assume that we've created a blank request object, and just worry about composing a useful UDDI request.

Listing 16-4 doesn't compose any old request. The code composes a request for all businesses with a certain string in their names. An outline describing the composeRequest method looks like this:

```
Get the request object's body.
To the body, add a child element with name find_business
    and namespace urn:uddi-org:api.
To the find_business element, add a generic="1.0" attribute.
To the find_business element, add a name child element.
To the name element, add the text Computer.
```

There are a few things to notice about the composeRequest method in Listing 16-4:

✓ Statements of the form

```
element = element.addChildElement(JavaString);
```

take an existing element, create a child, and then make the element variable point to that new child.

✔ All the elements created in this `composeRequest` method are required as part of a UDDI query. Even the `generic="1.0"` attribute is part of the UDDI standard.

✔ In the early-access release of JAXM, I can't create an attribute without first creating an XML `Name`. An instance of the `javax.xml.soap.Name` interface has a prefix, a URI, a qualified name, and all that other good stuff. So, to create an attribute, I have to make a name from a SOAP envelope, and then create an attribute with the new name.

It's a big rigmarole, which may be different by the time you write your own JAXM code. (It's safe to say you'll still have *some* rigmarole.)

✔ The call to `saveChanges` isn't absolutely necessary. Calling `saveChanges` does two things — it updates the SOAP message and gathers any of the message's attachment parts. Well, all that stuff gets done automatically with the `call` method in Listing 16-3. Even so, it doesn't hurt to call `saveChanges` as soon as you've composed the message. Besides, I like being thorough.

My little helper

The code in Listing 16-4 makes several references to a helper — an instance of a `MyMessageHelper` class. Well, it's time to sit down and take a look at the `MyMessageHelper` class. The class is shown in Listing 16-5.

Listing 16-5:   Working with a SOAP Message

```
import javax.xml.soap.MessageFactory;
import javax.xml.soap.SOAPMessage;
import javax.xml.soap.SOAPPart;
import javax.xml.soap.SOAPEnvelope;
import javax.xml.soap.SOAPBody;
import javax.xml.soap.SOAPElement;
import javax.xml.soap.SOAPException;

import java.util.Iterator;


class MyMessageHelper
{

    SOAPMessage createMessageObject()
        throws SOAPException
    {
        MessageFactory messFactory =
            MessageFactory.newInstance();
        return messFactory.createMessage();
    }
```

(continued)

Listing 16-5 *(continued)*

```
SOAPEnvelope getMessageEnvelope(SOAPMessage message)
    throws SOAPException
{
    SOAPPart soapPart;

    soapPart = message.getSOAPPart();
    return soapPart.getEnvelope();
}


SOAPBody getMessageBody(SOAPMessage message)
    throws SOAPException
{
    SOAPPart soapPart;
    SOAPEnvelope envelope;

    soapPart = message.getSOAPPart();
    envelope = soapPart.getEnvelope();
    return envelope.getBody();
}


static SOAPElement findSubelement(SOAPElement element,
                                  String targetQualName)
{
    String qualName;
    Iterator iter;

    do
    {
        iter = element.getChildElements();
        element = (SOAPElement)iter.next();
        qualName =
            element.getElementName().getQualifiedName();
    }
    while (!qualName.equals(targetQualName));

    return element;
}
}
```

Listing 16-5 has three kinds of methods — a `create` method, some `get` methods, and a `find` method. Sure, I can make up any method names I want but, in this case, I really have three kinds of methods:

> ✔ Method `createMessageObject` makes a brand new SOAP message. As usual, the method first creates a factory, and then uses the factory to create a message.

✔ Methods `getMessageEnvelope` and `getMessageBody` are what some people call "convenience" methods. I got tired of writing `getSOAPPart` in all my other code, when I knew darn well that the SOAP part was just a steppingstone to other message items. So I created these `get` methods.

✔ Method `findSubelement` performs a useful service. The method starts at a certain point in a SOAP message, and then digs downward until it finds a particular element (a `businessInfos` element, a `name` element, or whatever element you want the method to find).

Method `findSubelement` is another example of an I-got-tired-of-rewriting-it method. You haven't seen any sub-element finding in the listings so far, but you'll see some examples in the next several pages. As it turns out, this sub-element finding business is tricky and prone to error, so it's a good thing that I created a trusty method for the task.

Displaying messages and message data

The code in Listing 16-3 creates the output in Figure 16-3. The code does this by calling on a `MyDisplayer` class. This `MyDisplayer` class (another home-grown piece of code) is shown in Listing 16-6.

Listing 16-6:   Displaying Information

```java
import javax.xml.soap.SOAPMessage;
import javax.xml.soap.SOAPElement;
import javax.xml.soap.SOAPException;

import java.io.IOException;
import java.util.Iterator;


public class MyDisplayer
{
   MyMessageHelper helper = new MyMessageHelper();


   void displayOnConsole (SOAPMessage message)
      throws SOAPException, IOException
   {
      message.writeTo(System.out);
      System.out.println();
      System.out.println();
   }


   void displayBusinessNames(SOAPMessage message)
      throws SOAPException
   {
```

(continued)

Listing 16-6 *(continued)*

```
        SOAPElement element;
        Iterator iter;

        element = helper.getMessageBody(message);
        element =
            helper.findSubelement(element, "businessInfos");

        iter = element.getChildElements();
        while (iter.hasNext())
        {
            element = (SOAPElement)iter.next();
            element = helper.findSubelement(element, "name");
            System.out.println(element.getValue());
        }
    }
}
```

Figure 16-3 shows two SOAP messages — the message that gets sent to the IBM registry, and the message that comes back from the IBM registry. Back in Listing 16-3, both the sent and the received messages get displayed with a call to displayOnConsole. In Listing 16-6, this displayOnConsole method calls a message's writeTo method, and adds a few extra println calls for good measure.

The displayBusinessNames method in Listing 16-6 performs a very specific task. The method hunts down all the name entries in the response's businessInfo tags. To do this, the method performs an intricate search-within-a-search loop.

- ✔ First the code finds the response's businessInfos element.

- ✔ Then, the code makes a list of all businessInfo elements (all children of the big businessInfos element).

- ✔ Finally, for each businessInfo element, the code finds the name element, and displays the name element's text.

The result is the last few lines in Figure 16-3.

Responding to a UDDI Query

Have you ever wondered what goes on inside your refrigerator while the appliance door is closed? Is a little man hiding behind the mayo, waiting to turn on the light? Are your vegetables getting drunk on oil and vinegar, and throwing a wild party?

Questions like these can drive you crazy. You can also go crazy wondering how a UDDI request gets answered. So, as a public service, and to help you maintain your precious sanity, I'm going to show you what happens when you make a UDDI request.

An overview

In the rest of this chapter, you'll be putting together the software to respond to a UDDI query. It's not hard work, but it involves gathering resources from a few different places. To help guide your work, I've created a summary of the steps that you're about to follow.

1. **Download a Web server, if you don't already have one.**
2. **Install the Web server.**
3. **If JAXM requires configuration changes to your Web server, then make the changes.**
4. **Put the code from Listings 16-5, 16-7, and 16-8 in your server's servlets directory.**
5. **Make sure that your system classpath includes the JAXM JAR files, and the** servlet.jar **file that comes with your Web server.**
6. **Compile the code from Listings 16-5, 16-7, and 16-8.**
7. **Start up your server.**
8. **Run the code from Listing 16-3.**

The rest of this chapter covers all the details, step by step.

Setting up your Web server

Here's the scenario. You take the code in Listing 16-3 — code to formulate and send a UDDI request. You run the code, and send the UDDI request to your own server on your own computer. To do this, you issue the following command:

```
java AskUDDIquery Jennie
    http://localhost:8080/Know-it-all/servlet/AnswerUDDIquery
```

You're looking for businesses with Jennie in their names, so you send a request to a place called http://localhost:8080/Know-it-all/servlet/ AnswerUDDIquery. This URL points to your own computer (localhost), and to a place on your computer that's named Know-it-all/servlet/ AnswerUDDIquery. Of course, to make this work, you have to have a place on your computer named Know-it-all/servlet/AnswerUDDIquery. If you're running Apache Tomcat, then just follow these steps:

1. **In your Tomcat directory, look for a subdirectory named** webapps.

2. **In the** webapps **directory, create a subdirectory named** Know-it-all.

3. **In the** Know-it-all **directory, create a subdirectory named** WEB-INF.

4. **In the** WEB-INF **directory, create a subdirectory named** classes.

5. **In the** classes **directory, put the code from this section's listings (the files** AnswerUDDIquery.java, MyResponseMaker.java, **and** MyMessageHelper.java).

6. **Compile the source code that you put in the** classes **directory.**

Before you try to compile the code in this section, be sure to set your system's classpath. Point to the .jar files that come with the JAXM API download. In addition, you should point to the servlet.jar file that comes with your Java enabled server. (With Apache Tomcat, you're likely to find servlet.jar in the common/lib directory.)

After making any changes to the source code in the webapps/Know-it-all/WEB-INF/classes directory, be sure to stop and restart the Tomcat server. If you don't, then your changes may not take effect.

If you're not using Tomcat, then you'll have to do the unthinkable. You'll have to read your server's documentation, and figure out where the server wants your servlets to be placed. Each server has its own favorite directories, so you need to poke around and find out what the server expects you to do. In any case, you should remember two things:

✔ The use of port 8080 is special to Tomcat. So, to get this section's code running, you may issue a command of the following kind:

```
java AskUDDIquery Jennie
    http://localhost/Know-it-all/servlet/... Etc.
```

With localhost instead of localhost:8080, the command defaults to the usual HTTP port number 80.

✔ Your server's documentation probably won't tell you where to put a JAXM program. But, as long as the server is Java enabled, the documentation tells you where to put a servlet. Treat this section's examples as if they're ordinary Java servlets.

• Put the .class files where the server expects you to put servlets.

• Call the .class files with whatever URL the server uses for servlets.

For example, if servlets normally get called without any subdirectories in the URL, then run this section's code with a call of the following kind:

```
java AskUDDIquery Jennie http://localhost/AnswerUDDIquery
```

The code that responds to a query

You're sitting in front of the computer, minding your own business. You've placed the required code (the code in Listings 16-5, 16-7, and 16-8) in your Tomcat directories. You start running a Java-enabled server, perhaps Apache Tomcat. You go back to the directory that has Listing 16-3 in it, and you run the listing by typing the following command:

```
java AskUDDIquery Jennie
   http://localhost:8080/Know-it-all/servlet/AnswerUDDIquery
```

Now Tomcat takes over and runs your `AnswerUDDIquery` program. The program is shown in Listing 16-7.

Listing 16-7:   Answering a UDDI Query

```
import javax.xml.soap.SOAPMessage;
import javax.xml.soap.SOAPException;

import javax.xml.messaging.JAXMServlet;
import javax.xml.messaging.ReqRespListener;


public class AnswerUDDIquery extends JAXMServlet
    implements ReqRespListener
{

    public SOAPMessage onMessage(SOAPMessage request)
    {
        try
        {
            SOAPMessage response;
            String businessName;

            MyResponseMaker maker =
                new MyResponseMaker(request);

            response = maker.createResponse();

            return response;
        }
        catch(SOAPException e)
        {
            e.printStackTrace();
            return null;
        }
    }
}
```

What a lazy piece of software! The code in Listing 16-7 hands most of the work over to the MyResponseMaker class. The only work this code does without assistance is to catch the SOAP request and then fling back a response.

Of course, catching an incoming request is no small matter. Listing 16-7 catches a request by implementing the onMessage method. (The onMessage method is part of the javax.xml.messaging.ReqRespListener interface.)

Forming a UDDI response

The real work in this example gets underway when the code in Listing 16-7 calls createResponse. The createResponse method is something that I defined in the MyResponseMaker class. That class, in all its glory, is shown in Listing 16-8.

Listing 16-8:   Creating a Response

```
import javax.xml.soap.SOAPMessage;
import javax.xml.soap.SOAPEnvelope;
import javax.xml.soap.SOAPElement;
import javax.xml.soap.Name;
import javax.xml.soap.SOAPException;


class MyResponseMaker
{
    SOAPMessage request, response;
    MyMessageHelper helper = new MyMessageHelper();


    MyResponseMaker (SOAPMessage request)
    {
        this.request = request;
    }


    SOAPMessage createResponse ()
        throws SOAPException
    {
        String businessName;

        response = helper.createMessageObject();
        businessName = getBusinessName();
        composeResponse(businessName);
        return response;
    }
```

```
String getBusinessName()
   throws SOAPException
{
   SOAPElement element;

   element = helper.getMessageBody(request);
   element = helper.findSubelement(element, "name");
   return element.getValue();
}


void composeResponse(String businessName)
   throws SOAPException
{
   SOAPEnvelope envelope;
   SOAPElement element;
   Name name;

   envelope = helper.getMessageEnvelope(response);
   element = helper.getMessageBody(response);

   element = element.addChildElement
      ("businessList", "", "urn:uddi-org:api");
   name = envelope.createName("generic");
   element.addAttribute(name, "1.0");

   element = element.addChildElement("businessInfos");

   element = element.addChildElement("businessInfo");
   name = envelope.createName("businessKey");
   element.addAttribute(name, "000A00-A000");

   element = element.addChildElement("name");
   element.addTextNode
      (businessName + "'s Turing Machine Repair Service");
}
}
```

Ah, yes! Listing 16-8! Now there's a real workhorse. In the listing's
createResponse method, I've set three statements in bold. Each of these
three statements triggers its own important action:

✔ **The first bold statement gets a blank SOAP message.**

The statement gets a SOAP message by calling method
createMessageObject. (The method's declaration is in Listing 16-5.)
Eventually, this SOAP message will become the program's UDDI response.
But at this point, it's not a response — it's just a blank message.

Because the code in Listing 16-8 uses a method from the MyMessageHelper class, you better make Listing 16-5 available to your server. The easiest way to do this is to plunk a copy of Listing 16-5 into the same server directory as the code in Listing 16-8. It's crude, but it gets the job done.

✔ **The second bold statement fishes for a business name.**

The statement looks for the name in the original requesting SOAP message. If you run Listing 16-3 with the command `java AskUDDIquery Jennie ... Etc.`, then the business name is `Jennie`.

Of course, to find a business name, the createResponse method passes the buck to another method in Listing 16-8. And this other method, the getBusinessName method, falls back on our faithful MyMessageHelper class from Listing 16-5. The only independent statement in this part of the code is the call to element.getValue at the end of the getBusinessName method. The method getValue, part of the JAXM API, retrieves text from between an element's start and end tags.

✔ **The third bold statement uses the business name to compose the response.**

At this point, Barry cheats. Method createResponse calls method composeResponse, and method composeResponse makes up a fake UDDI response. A real composeResponse method would search a database and find all business names containing the string Jennie. Instead, the method in Listing 16-8 just adds `Jennie's Turing Machine Repair Service` to what is otherwise a carefully crafted UDDI message.

Look back at Listing 16-2; recall that a UDDI response has elements like businessList, businessInfos, businessInfo, and name. Well, the code in method composeResponse piles on these same elements. As in Listing 16-4, the code uses envelope.createName to add the required generic attribute. (According to the UDDI specs, a response's businessInfo element also has a required businessKey attribute.)

When the response is fully formed, it looks like the document in Listing 16-9. (The only difference is, the real response has no line breaks or indentation.)

Listing 16-9: Another UDDI Response

```
<soap-env:Envelope xmlns:soap-env=
    "http://schemas.xmlsoap.org/soap/envelope/">
  <soap-env:Header/>
  <soap-env:Body>
    <businessList xmlns="urn:uddi-org:api" generic="1.0">
      <businessInfos>
```

```
                <businessInfo businessKey="000A00-A000">
                    <name>
                        Jennie's Turing Machine Repair Service
                    </name>
                </businessInfo>
            </businessInfos>
        </businessList>
    </soap-env:Body>
</soap-env:Envelope>
```

Finally, when you run this section's code, you get the output shown in Figure 16-4.

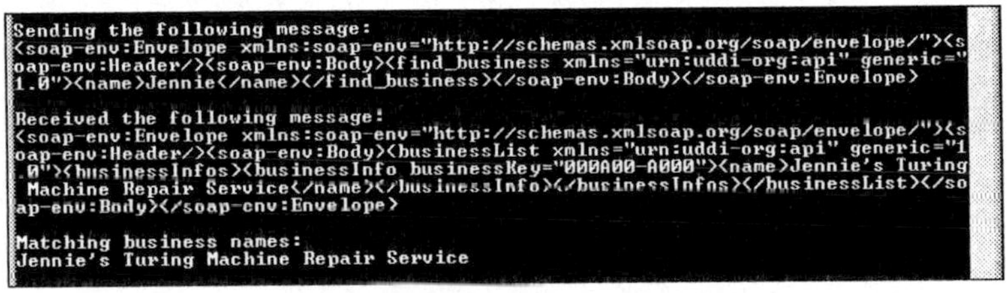

Figure 16-4:
Another
run of the
program in
Listing 16-3.

```
Sending the following message:
<soap-env:Envelope xmlns:soap-env="http://schemas.xmlsoap.org/soap/envelope/"><s
oap-env:Header/><soap-env:Body><find_business xmlns="urn:uddi-org:api" generic="
1.0"><name>Jennie</name></find_business></soap-env:Body></soap-env:Envelope>

Received the following message:
<soap-env:Envelope xmlns:soap-env="http://schemas.xmlsoap.org/soap/envelope/"><s
oap-env:Header/><soap-env:Body><businessList xmlns="urn:uddi-org:api" generic="1
.0"><businessInfos><businessInfo businessKey="000A00-A000"><name>Jennie's Turing
 Machine Repair Service</name></businessInfo></businessInfos></businessList></so
ap-env:Body></soap-env:Envelope>

Matching business names:
Jennie's Turing Machine Repair Service
```

Wow! Besides sending and answering a useful UDDI query, I've managed to write this entire chapter without making any cheap SOAP puns.

Chapter 17

Working with XML Registries

*I*t's your big day. You're speaking at the company's annual meeting of sales representatives. You're reporting on the company's new marketing initiative. "We're telling the whole world about our business," you say. "Our services are being posted on several UDDI registries."

One of the regional sales managers interrupts with a question. "I'm interested in sending you an updated list of services. Can you tell me about the process you use for posting services to the registry?" You smile and start reciting Chapter 16 of *Java & XML For Dummies*. "This chapter is dedicated to my Aunt Nettie, who was good at helping people find things . . ."

"No," says the sales manager. "Spare us the details. Tell us about the most important steps in the process." So you start explaining the ideas in Chapter 16 — things like SOAP envelopes, message bodies, and XML elements. You explain the find_business element and its name child element.

Well, that's much better. Isn't it? You've been asked about adding the business to a registry, and you're answering with ideas about SOAP and XML. You're immersed in this stuff because of the tools in Chapter 16. With these tools, you stay very close to the ground. You work with small details, and combine details to create larger processes. The classes in Chapter 16 give you fine-grained control but, for this control, you pay a price. You must micromanage your communications with the UDDI registry, and this micromanaging slows you down.

The sales manager follows up with another batch of questions. "Don't you ever get tired of composing SOAP messages? Can't you just type 'Publish this,' and have the software do the rest for you? Aren't there times when you don't need fine-grained control?"

Well, the sales manager has a good point. Sometimes you need SOAP messages for very individualized tasks. But much of the time, your SOAP messages do routine things. Find businesses, post businesses, find services, and post services. So you need another API. The new API floats above things like SOAP and XML. With this API, you do as the sales manager suggests — you type "Publish this," and the software does the rest for you.

This wondrous API is called *JAXR*. It's the *Java API for XML Registries*. It replaces some of the painstaking tasks in Chapter 16 with high-level classes and methods.

So let's return to the sales reps' meeting. "Can't you just type 'Publish this,' and have the software do the rest for you?" asks the regional sales manager. "As a matter of fact, I can," you say. "Let me depart from Chapter 16, and quote a few words from Chapter 17 instead."

You clear your throat, and then you begin: "It's your big day. You're speaking at the company's annual meeting of sales representatives . . ." (A high-pitched, eerie guitar riff starts to play. A dapper man with a cigarette appears, grins ironically, and remarks, "Presented for your approval. . . .")

UDDI Registries

Using JAXR is like dreaming that you can fly. You're not walking along the streets, dealing with XML elements. Instead, you're hovering above a city, seeing the grand plan all at once. Look west; there's a search for a needed Web service. Off to the east; there's the name of your business. When you use JAXR, you're working with business issues, not with the nitty-gritty details of SOAP and XML.

In fact, there isn't a single XML tag in this chapter. You'll see plenty of Java code, but no reference to elements or attributes. So what's this chapter doing in a *Java & XML* book? Well, the code in this chapter works with UDDI registries, and UDDI registries are based on SOAP and XML. The code in this chapter does the same kinds of things that the code in Chapter 16 does, but all under the hood.

All about registries

Let's make sure that we agree on the terminology. A registry is a list of things, and each thing in the list is called an *entry*. The entries can be team names, pet feeding instructions, or any other kind of data. But typically, the entries are related to businesses and other organizations. (In the world of registries, the words "business" and "organization" are almost synonyms.)

One entry is a business, another entry is one of the business's services, and a third entry is some business contact information. These entries are related to one another, so it helps to represent registry data hierarchically. Of course, we already have an excellent way to represent data hierarchically. We represent data with XML documents.

There are two popular standards for representing registry data with XML documents. In this book, I emphasize the UDDI standard. Another emerging standard is called *ebXML* — the *electronic business eXtensible Markup Language*.

There are several things you can do with a registry, and several ways to do each thing. You can *query* a registry, as we do in Chapter 16. You can also *update* a registry. Doing an update can involve adding entries, changing entries, or deleting entries. When you add an entry, you can also say that you're *posting* the entry, or *publishing* to the registry.

Working with a registry

How do you query or update an XML registry? Two ways come to mind.

- ✔ **You can run your favorite Web browser, and visit the registry's Web site.**

    The registry's Web site has pages with buttons labeled Add Business, Add Service, Delete Business, and so on. When you click these buttons, you're using the registry's *Web interface*.

- ✔ **You can run Java programs that send SOAP messages to the registry.**

    You send SOAP messages in Chapter 16, and again in this chapter. You're using the registry's *SOAP interface*.

A registry's SOAP interface has two different URLs. One is called the *inquiry URL*, and the other is called the *publishing URL*.

- ✔ To get information from the registry, you send a SOAP message to the registry's inquiry URL.

- ✔ To update the registry, you send a SOAP message to the registry's publishing URL.

You can find examples of the two kinds of URLs later in this chapter.

Getting information about a UDDI registry

Some registries allow access via Web interface only — which means you can't query or update the registry's entries by running a JAXR program. If you try running this chapter's code on any such registry, the code simply doesn't work.

So how do you recognize an evil registry that has no SOAP interface? Well, I have a very roundabout technique. Each registry has a Web site with a helpful, informative home page. The page has useful information about the registry, and has links to important documentation. The page also has links to the registry's Web interface.

Go fishing at a registry's Web site, looking for documentation that gives the *inquiry URL* and the *publishing URL*. If you've fished for a long time, and you can't find any documentation about these two URLs, then the registry probably doesn't support SOAP messages. That's how you tell.

There's a difference between a registry's Web-interface pages and its home page. The Web-interface pages are for interacting with the registry; they have buttons for querying and updating the entries in the registry. In contrast, the registry's home page has useful information about the registry, links to other documentation pages, and probably links to the registry's Web-interface pages. (For examples, see Figure 17-1.)

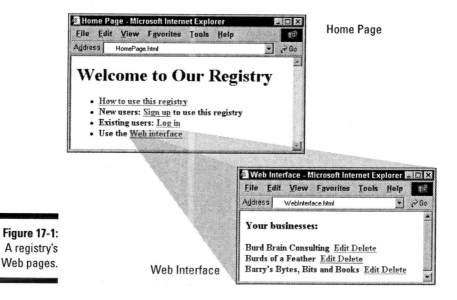

Figure 17-1:
A registry's
Web pages.

Preparing to Use JAXR

How do you run the code in this chapter's examples? Well, there are two possibilities.

  ✔ **You're sending a query to a UDDI registry.**

  You're running the code in Listings 17-1 and 17-2. Maybe you want a list of businesses with the word "Burd" in their names. (Doesn't everybody?)

  The information in the registry is for public consumption, so you don't need any special privileges to send a query. All you need is the JAXR API. This API doesn't come with the core Java 2 download, so you have to get the API by visiting java.sun.com/xml/jaxr.

  Once you've downloaded the API, just point your system's classpath to all the .jar files that come with the download. (With my early-access release of the JAXR API, almost all the .jar files are in a subdirectory named lib.) For help in setting your system's classpath, see Chapter 2.

  ✔ **You're updating information in a UDDI registry.**

  You're running the code in Listings 17-3, 17-4, and 17-5. You're adding a business to the registry, changing the description of one of your business's services, or deleting entries from the registry. You can't do this unless you're a bona fide user of a UDDI registry. So, before you run the code in the latter half of this chapter, you have to sign up with a registry.

Fortunately, signing up with a UDDI registry isn't difficult.

  ✔ Visit a registry's home page, and look for the New User page.

  ✔ Enter your name, e-mail address, mother's maiden name, and blood type.

  ✔ Click the Submit button.

At this point, the registry may send you a confirmation e-mail message. Once you reply to the confirmation message, you can run the code in Listings 17-3, 17-4, and 17-5.

Finding a registry

Before you can sign up to use a registry, you have to find the registry. So where are all these registries, and how do you choose among the registries that are available?

Well, you have a few things to consider. For instance, there are test registries and production quality registries. The test registries are for your trial-and-error efforts. The production quality registries are for publishing your company's services.

There are other differences among registries. Most have Web interfaces, but many offer no SOAP interface. If you're signed up to use a registry that has no SOAP interface, then you can't use the code in this chapter's examples. My advice is, find yourself a registry with a SOAP interface. (For advice on finding a soapy registry, flip back a few pages to the section entitled "Getting information about a UDDI registry.")

Of course, each registry has its own special features, and many of these features are not documented. For instance, one registry ignores my request for case-sensitive searches. Another registry lists all business names as `null`. So I switch back and forth between registries, depending on which registry implements features that I want to use. A bit awkward, but it works.

My recommendations

For testing the code in this chapter, I have three useful Web sites. Each site is the starting point for one or more registries.

- **✓ IBM**

   IBM has test registries and production quality registries. To see the home page for the IBM registries, visit `www-3.ibm.com/services/uddi`. This home page tells you how to get a username and password. The page also has links to the Web interface for each registry.

   To send SOAP messages to the IBM test registry, you use the registry's inquiry and publishing URLs. The inquiry URL is `http://www-3.ibm.com/services/uddi/testregistry/inquiryapi`, and the publishing URL is `https://www-3.ibm.com/services/uddi/testregistry/protect/publishapi`. (For examples of the use of inquiry and publishing URLs, see Listings 17-2 and 17-4.)

- **✓ Microsoft**

   The home page for Microsoft's test registry is `test.uddi.microsoft.com`. The home page for Microsoft's production quality registry is `uddi.rte.microsoft.com`.

- **✓ Systinet**

   To see the home page for Systinet's test registry, visit `www.systinet.com/web/uddi`. The registry's inquiry URL is `http://www.systinet.com:80/wasp/uddi/inquiry/`, and the registry's publishing URL is `https://www.systinet.com:443/wasp/uddi/publishing/`. (For examples of how to use inquiry and publishing URLs, see Listings 17-2 and 17-4.)

If you're gung-ho about UDDI registries, you can try downloading and installing your own registry. The registry server software at www.systinet.com is free for development and testing purposes. (To make the software work, you'll need to run your own database.) Another no-cost registry server comes with certain versions of JAXR. In the early access release, it's called the *Java WSDP Registry Server*. (The acronym *WSDP* refers to Sun's *Web Services Developer Pack*.)

Performing a Query

Listing 17-1 has a program that queries a UDDI registry. As usual, the listing relies on some helper code to make it work. Anyway, Listing 17-1 gives you the big picture, and a later listing has the helper-code details.

Listing 17-1: Sending a Query to a UDDI Registry

```
import javax.xml.registry.BusinessQueryManager;
import javax.xml.registry.BulkResponse;
import javax.xml.registry.JAXRException;

import java.util.Vector;


public class DoQuery
{
    public static void main(String[] args)
        throws JAXRException
    {
        MyBusinessHelper helper;
        BusinessQueryManager manager;
        Vector names;
        BulkResponse response;


        helper = new MyBusinessHelper();
        helper.createConnection();

        manager = helper.createBusinessQueryManager();

        names = new Vector();
        names.add("%Burd%");
        response = manager.findOrganizations
            (null, names, null, null, null, null);

        helper.displayResults(response);
    }
}
```

I'm working with an early-access release of JAXR. Some of the things I do in this chapter won't be current by the time the product is released for general public use. If you run my code, and things don't go the way you want them to go, you may try visiting my Web site (`users.drew.edu/bburd`) for updates to this chapter's code. You can also fiddle around on your own with the JAXR documentation. (That's always fun.)

Dissecting the code

The heart of the code in Listing 17-1 is the call to the `findOrganizations` method. Everything else in the listing is mere detail. Sample output from a run of Listing 17-1 appears in Figure 17-2.

Figure 17-2:
Running a
UDDI query.

```
Organization: Burd Brain Consulting
        Service: Java Training
Organization: Burds of a Feather
        Service: Family Genealogy
```

Listing 17-1 begins by calling a `createConnection` method — a method whose code is buried in one of my famous helper classes. (The code for my helper class is in Listing 17-2. But don't peek yet. If you do, you'll spoil the fun of anticipation.)

After making a connection, the listing creates a big Java vector to hold the word `"%Burd%"`. You see, the `findOrganizations` method is built to withstand any kind of querying. (The call to `findOrganizations` is the big bold statement in Listing 17-1.) The method's six parameters represent different kinds of constraints that you can put on your query. You can fill all or some of the parameters with values that narrow your search. (For any parameter, the value `null` means that you're not using a particular kind of constraint.)

Take, for instance, the second parameter in the call to `findOrganizations`. Whatever you put in this position constrains the name of the company that you're searching for. If you put `"%Burd%"` in this position, then you find companies with the string `Burd` in their names.

The percent signs act as wildcards, so you find company names of the form
any-characters`Burd`*any-other-characters*

Of course, none of the `findOrganizations` parameters are plain old strings. Instead, each parameter is a collection of strings, and each string in a collection constitutes a separate constraint. Suppose I change Listing 17-1 as follows:

```
names = new Vector();
names.add("Do%");
names.add("Re%");
names.add("Mi%");
response = manager.findOrganizations
    (null, names, null, null, null, null);
```

Then the query looks for names containing any of the three syllables — Do, Re, or Mi. My search turns up companies like Dot's Restaurant, Real Estate Brokers' Anonymous, and Michigan Society for Fifes and Flugelhorns.

Each UDDI registry has its own idiosyncratic behavior. One registry coughs up a big error message when I send it a query with the collection "Do%", "Re%", "Mi%".

Some gossip about the findOrganizations method's parameters

The findOrganizations method has six parameters. There's a description of each findOrganizations parameter in Table 17-1.

Table 17-1   The Parameters of the findOrganizations Method

Position	JAXR Name	UDDI Name	Meaning
1	findQualifiers	findQualifiers	Effects things like sort order, case-sensitivity, and exact match versus "contains" match
2	namePatterns	[none]	Specifies a string for matching with company names
3	classifications	categoryBag	Narrows in on industry types, product and service types, or geographical locations

(continued)

Table 17-1 *(continued)*

Position	JAXR Name	UDDI Name	Meaning
4	specifications	tModelBag	Narrows in on certain technical specifications of a company's software offerings
5	externalIdentifiers	identifierBag	Narrows in on certain standard assigned company numbers
6	externalLinks	overviewDoc	Specifies links to information that's outside of the registry

A few items in Table 17-1 need some explaining.

✔ The table's first column refers to a position in the findOrganizations method's parameter list. For instance, in the findOrganizations method call in Listing 17-1 parameter number 2 contains the variable names. Parameters 1, 3, 4, 5, and 6 contain null values.

✔ Most findOrganizations parameters have two names. One name is used in the JAXR documentation, and another name is used in the UDDI documentation. Table 17-1 shows both names.

✔ The first findOrganizations parameter affects the way the other parameters behave. For instance, the value FindQualifier.CASE_SENSITIVE_MATCH in the first parameter makes searches case-sensitive. The value FindQualifier.SORT_BY_NAME_DESC in the first parameter lists results in reverse alphabetical order.

There's a real cute item among the first parameter's options. It's called FindQualifier.SOUNDEX. With this value in your collection, the search looks for names that sound like the name in your search string. A search for "%Burd%" may turn up Joe's House of Snakes and Birds.

✔ The fifth parameter lists numbers that represent particular organizations. For instance, many businesses have nine-digit Dun & Bradstreet D-U-N-S numbers. With a D-U-N-S number in this fifth parameter, the query is narrowed to a particular organization. (Two organizations can have the same name, but no two organizations have the same D-U-N-S number.)

The helper class

Listing 17-1 relies on the `MyBusinessHelper` class, so it's time we looked at that class's code (Finally! Some help on the way!) in Listing 17-2.

Listing 17-2: A Helper Class

```
import javax.xml.registry.Connection;
import javax.xml.registry.ConnectionFactory;
import javax.xml.registry.RegistryService;
import javax.xml.registry.BusinessQueryManager;
import javax.xml.registry.BulkResponse;
import javax.xml.registry.JAXRException;

import javax.xml.registry.infomodel.Organization;
import javax.xml.registry.infomodel.Key;
import javax.xml.registry.infomodel.Service;

import java.util.Properties;
import java.util.Collection;
import java.util.Iterator;


class MyBusinessHelper
{
   Connection connection;
   RegistryService registryService;


   void createConnection()
      throws JAXRException
   {
      Properties properties;
      ConnectionFactory factory;

      properties = new Properties();
      properties.setProperty
         ("javax.xml.registry.queryManagerURL",
          "http://www.systinet.com:80/wasp/uddi/inquiry/");
      properties.setProperty
         ("javax.xml.registry.factoryClass",
          "com.sun.xml.registry.uddi.ConnectionFactoryImpl");

      factory = ConnectionFactory.newInstance();
      factory.setProperties(properties);

      connection =  factory.createConnection();
      registryService = connection.getRegistryService();
```

(continued)

Listing 17-2 *(continued)*

```
    }


    BusinessQueryManager createBusinessQueryManager()
        throws JAXRException
    {
        return registryService.getBusinessQueryManager();
    }


    void displayResults(BulkResponse response)
        throws JAXRException
    {
        Collection organizations;
        Organization organization;
        Collection services;
        Service service;
        Iterator orgIterator, servIterator;

        organizations = response.getCollection();

        orgIterator = organizations.iterator();
        while (orgIterator.hasNext())
        {
            organization = (Organization) orgIterator.next();

            System.out.print("Organization: ");
            System.out.println
                (organization.getName().getValue());

            services = organization.getServices();
            servIterator = services.iterator();
            while (servIterator.hasNext())
            {
                service = (Service) servIterator.next();

                System.out.print("\tService: " );
                System.out.println
                    (service.getName().getValue());
            }
        }
    }
}
```

A quick march through the methods in Listing 17-2 looks like this:

✔ `createConnection`

This method builds a tie between your computer and a particular registry service. As always, we use a factory to help us forge the connection.
If there's anything unusual about this factory, it's that we tweak the
factory's settings with a collection of Java properties.

A Java property is like an XML attribute. A property has a name and a value.

- In Listing 17-2, the first property's name is `javax.xml.registry.queryManagerURL`. The property's value, `http://www.systinet.com:80/wasp/uddi/inquiry/`, is an inquiry URL. You can read more about inquiry URLs in the section entitled "Working with a registry" (earlier in this chapter).

- The second property, with name `javax.xml.registry.factoryClass`, points to the class that will be used to create a connection. Fortunately, the class `ConnectionFactoryImpl` comes as part of the JAXR API download.

  Listing 17-2 blazes a twisty trail from the abstract class `ConnectionFactory`, to the real class `ConnectionFactoryImpl`, to the `connection` object itself. (Sorry, that's just the way it's done.)

✔ `createBusinessQueryManager`

With JAXR, you don't just fling a request to a registry. You hand the request to a manager, and the manager issues the request on your behalf. In Listing 17-2, we get a `RegistryService` object from the connection, and then we get a manager from the `RegistryService` object.

✔ `displayResults`

How many companies do we get from our query? And how many services are associated with each company? If the answers to these questions were always "one," then we wouldn't need collections and iterators in the `displayResults` method. Unfortunately, life is never so simple. A query can return many businesses, and each business can have several services.

So a `BulkResponse` object is indeed bulky. To extract information from the `BulkResponse` object, you call methods like `getCollection` and `getServices`. These methods return Java collections, which get pulled apart using iterators.

This iterator stuff isn't new. I started using iterators in Listing 15-7, and I haven't stopped since then.

In Listing 17-2, the output created by the `displayResults` method is just the tip of the UDDIceberg. In addition to calling `getServices`, you can call `getUsers`, `getTelephoneNumbers`, `getParentOrganization`, and a host of other `get` methods. For details see the `Interface Organization` page in the JAXR documentation.

Publishing to a Registry

You're the CEO of a huge corporation, and you're interested in promoting the corporation's services. Because you're very smart, you consider listing the corporation on a UDDI registry.

But with all the mergers, sell-offs, and new projects, the corporation's list of businesses and services is constantly changing. You can hire someone to sit in front of a computer all day, clicking buttons in the registry's Web interface. But button-clicking gets boring, and tasks that are boring get done very poorly.

The answer is automation. Use Java code to publish data about your company's services. Feed information to the Java code from terminals all around the world. Keep the Java code running so that your company's listings are always current.

Many test registries have restrictions that limit each user to just one business listing at a time. So, to test a publishing program several times, you have to run another program between each pair of publishing runs. The other program deletes the registry entry that you create in your publishing run. My own publishing program is in Listing 17-3, and my deleting program is in Listing 17-5.

Seeing the code

This section's example publishes data to a UDDI registry. The task is a little bit trickier than querying a registry, but not much trickier. The big difference is, you can't add or modify a registry entry without first logging in.

In this context, "logging in" may not be interactive. One program can feed a username and password to another program, and that's precisely how this section's example works. Of course, as you pass a sensitive password from one place to another, you shouldn't expose the password for everyone to see. But that's a security issue, not an XML issue. The programs in this section don't hide passwords from plain view — but you'd best address that security issue before you work with them on the Internet.

Like some earlier examples, this section's example comes in two parts — a main program and a helper class. The main program is in Listing 17-3. There's no visible output from a run of the main program. This program just runs, does its publishing work, and then stops.

Listing 17-3:   Publishing to a Registry

```
import javax.xml.registry.BusinessLifeCycleManager;
import javax.xml.registry.JAXRException;

import javax.xml.registry.infomodel.Organization;
import javax.xml.registry.infomodel.Service;

import java.util.Vector;


public class DoPublish
{
    public static void main(String[] args)
        throws JAXRException
    {
        MyBusinessCycleHelper helper;
        BusinessLifeCycleManager manager;
        Organization organization;
        Service service;
        Vector organizations;


        helper = new MyBusinessCycleHelper();
        helper.createConnection();
        helper.addCredentials();

        manager = helper.createBusinessLifeCycleManager();

        organization = manager.createOrganization
                            ("Burd Brain Consulting");
        service = manager.createService("Java Training");
        organization.addService(service);

        organizations = new Vector();
        organizations.add(organization);

        manager.saveOrganizations(organizations);
    }
}
```

On the surface, Listing 17-3 looks a heck of a lot like Listing 17-1. But there's something important that you should notice. Both Listings 17-1 and 17-3 get assistance from helpers, but the helpers in the two listings come from different classes.

In Listing 17-1, the `helper` variable points to a `MyBusinessHelper` object, and in Listing 17-3, the `helper` variable points to a `MyBusinessCycleHelper` object. The reason for this is simple. The code in Listing 17-3 needs more help. It takes more code to publish than it takes to query.

So, as you read through the next several paragraphs, keep in mind that some details are hidden in yet another helper class. This helper class is like the helper in Listing 17-2, but fatter. (If you insist on looking ahead, then you'll find the helper for Listing 17-3 in Listing 17-4. Just don't tell anyone else about the surprise ending.)

Dissecting the code

The processing in Listing 17-3 has five phases. Here's the whole scoop:

✔ **Creating a connection**

As is the case in Listing 17-1, you have to connect with a registry before you can talk to the registry. So, on a superficial level, the connections in Listings 17-1 and 17-3 look identical. But to publish to a registry, you need a meatier connection than the connection that queries a registry. That's why the createConnection call in Listing 17-3 goes to the MyBusinessCycleHelper class, not the MyBusinessHelper class. (You can read more about that when you get to Listing 17-4.)

✔ **Adding credentials to the connection**

This is where you plug your username and password into the connection. Again, we push the dirty details into some helper code (in Listing 17-4).

✔ **Getting a** BusinessLifeCycleManager **object**

The JAXR API has several manager interfaces. These manager interfaces are defined in the package javax.xml.registry.

Back in Listing 17-1, we use the BusinessQueryManager to ask for companies with the word Burd in their names. That makes sense, because asking for companies' names constitutes a query. Well, in Listing 17-3, we need something to manage our requests for registry updates. So we call on a BusinessLifeCycleManager object.

Now what does the term "life cycle" suggest? A life cycle manager is meant to stick with you for life. In Listing 17-3, we create a company entry with a BusinessLifeCycleManager object. Later in this chapter, we'll use a BusinessLifeCycleManager object to delete a company entry. So that's what "life cycle" means. You use a manager of this kind from the cradle to the grave.

✔ **Preparing the data**

This part of the story may seem familiar by now. In Listing 17-3, you don't just create an organization. You create a collection of organizations. (The class java.util.Vector is a subclass of java.util.Collection.) You do this even if you're publishing only one organization's data.

✔ **Publishing the data**

With all this preparation, the actual publishing step in Listing 17-3 is anticlimactic. You call the manager's `saveOrganizations` method, and you hand your collection of organizations to the method. That does it. Your organization is now published.

The helper class

What this world needs is another helper class — a class that assists in the publishing and updating of a UDDI registry. There's a class of that kind in Listing 17-4. The class fills in the details that were missing from Listing 17-3.

Listing 17-4: Helping to Update a Registry

```
import javax.xml.registry.Connection;
import javax.xml.registry.ConnectionFactory;
import javax.xml.registry.RegistryService;
import javax.xml.registry.BusinessLifeCycleManager;
import javax.xml.registry.JAXRException;

import java.net.PasswordAuthentication;

import java.util.Properties;
import java.util.HashSet;


class MyBusinessCycleHelper extends MyBusinessHelper
{

    void createConnection()
        throws JAXRException
    {

        Properties properties;
        ConnectionFactory factory;

        properties = new Properties();
        properties.setProperty
            ("javax.xml.registry.queryManagerURL",
            "http://www.systinet.com:80/wasp/uddi/inquiry/");
        properties.setProperty
            ("javax.xml.registry.lifeCycleManagerURL",
            "https://www.systinet.com:443/" +
            "wasp/uddi/publishing/");
        properties.setProperty
            ("javax.xml.registry.factoryClass",
            "com.sun.xml.registry.uddi.ConnectionFactoryImpl");

        factory = ConnectionFactory.newInstance();
```

(continued)

Listing 17-4 *(continued)*

```
        factory.setProperties(properties);

        connection = factory.createConnection();
        registryService = connection.getRegistryService();
    }


BusinessLifeCycleManager createBusinessLifeCycleManager()
    throws JAXRException
{
    return registryService.getBusinessLifeCycleManager();
}


void addCredentials()
    throws JAXRException
{
    PasswordAuthentication authentication;
    HashSet credentials;

    char[] password =
        {'s','w','o','r','d','f','i','s','h'};
    authentication =
        new PasswordAuthentication("myUsername", password);

    credentials = new HashSet();
    credentials.add(authentication);

    System.setProperty("java.protocol.handler.pkgs",
        "com.sun.net.ssl.internal.www.protocol");
    System.setProperty("javax.net.ssl.trustStore",
        "C:\\JavaPrograms\\.keystore");

    connection.setCredentials(credentials);
}

}
```

Listing 17-4 has everything that Listing 17-2 had, and more. That's because the class in Listing 17-4 is a subclass of the MyBusinessHelper class from Listing 17-2. So Listing 17-4 automatically has variables Connection and RegistryService, and method createBusinessQueryManager. That's good because we use all these things when we publish to a registry. We also use the three things that are newly declared in Listing 17-4.

These are the new things in Listing 17-4: a connection, a manager, and some credentials. (See the lines marked in bold in the listing.)

✔ **Creating a beefier connection**

Back in Listing 17-2, where we query a registry, we call `setProperty` to enter the inquiry URL. Here in Listing 17-4, we enter two URLs — an inquiry URL and a publishing URL. This publishing URL is the value of the property named `javax.xml.registry.lifeCycleManagerURL`. You can read more about publishing URLs in the section entitled "Working with a registry" (earlier in this chapter).

Each registry has a home page. The home page points to documentation containing the registry's inquiry and publishing URLs. You use these inquiry and publishing URLs in your `setProperty` calls.

Before you can call the `createConnection` method, you must always set the `queryManagerURL` property. You must do this even if your program doesn't perform a query. (As far as I can tell, the value of the `queryManagerURL` property can be any string at all. The `queryManagerURL` value doesn't have to be a real URL, unless you're actually performing a query.)

✔ **Creating a** `BusinessLifeCycleManager`

Look at my poor little method in the middle of Listing 17-4. The method's name is almost as long as the rest of the method's code. This method serves the same purpose as the `createBusinessQueryManager` method in Listing 17-3. The only difference is, the method in Listing 17-4 creates a manager that can update a registry. (With the `BusinessQueryManager` in Listing 17-2, you can only query a registry.)

✔ **Adding credentials to the connection**

Adding credentials can be the stickiest, most troublesome part of the whole endeavor. How are passwords transmitted? How is information encrypted? Which pieces of the puzzle are public, and which are private? Security is a big topic, and it gets bigger with every security breech.

In this example, I leave all the tough issues to the Java security experts. I'm just happy to have permission to publish on the registry. As you can see in Listing 17-4, my username and password are in full public view. I'm focusing on the mechanics of sending authentication information, and not on the technical or political questions surrounding security.

In Listing 17-4, the `addCredentials` method takes me two steps closer to the use of the registry. In the first step, the method readies my username and password. The username and password get stored in a `java.net.PasswordAuthentication` object, and this object gets added to a set of credentials.

The username and password in Listing 17-4 are fakes. There's no one called `myUsername` on the Systinet UDDI registry, and no one with any sense uses `swordfish` for a password. (A password like `swordfish` is too easy to guess.) Before you can run the code in Listing 17-4, you have to visit a registry's Web site and get your own username and password. For details, see the section entitled "Preparing to Use JAXR" (lurking nearby in this chapter).

After setting up a username and password, the code in Listing 17-4 makes calls to `setProperty`. These calls look for a file named `C:\JavaPrograms\.keystore`, and make the content of that file available to your connection.

Inside a Java string, you represent a single backslash by writing two side-by-side backslashes. That's why, in Listing 17-4, there are pairs of backslashes in the string `"C:\\JavaPrograms\\.keystore"`.

Using a keystore

A *keystore* is a collection of authentication items. A keystore from Systinet contains data that allow you to update the Systinet registry. If this keystore isn't associated with your connection, then any requests that you make to update the Systinet registry are refused. In essence, this keystore is like an extra password for the registry.

Unlike an ordinary password, the stuff inside a keystore file is encrypted. This means that you can't examine or forge the material in the keystore. You can watch someone type a password on the keyboard, but if you try to examine the authentication data in a keystore, then all that you see is garbled bits.

Getting a Keystore File

The name `.keystore`, starting with a dot, is not uncommon for a file of this kind. The trouble is, some Web browsers get confused when you try to download a file named `.keystore`. I've tried several browsers, and have gotten several different results.

✔ My Linux browsers have no problem downloading the `.keystore` file.

✔ When I single-click in Netscape Navigator for Windows, the program doesn't offer to download the file. Instead, the program displays the file's incomprehensible bits on my screen.

When I right-click and choose Save As, Navigator downloads a file. But the file is twelve times the normal `.keystore` file size. This bloated monster isn't a valid keystore file.

✔ On Windows, Microsoft Internet Explorer saves a file named `[1].keystore`. I rename the file by typing `rename [1].keystore .keystore` in my command prompt window. (Windows Explorer's point-and-click interface won't let me change the file's name to `.keystore`.)

The truth is, you can give this file any name that you want to give it. You can call it `duckDip` instead of `.keystore`. Just make sure that the last `setProperty` call in Listing 17-4 has whatever name you've given to the file.

✔ Most browsers do a decent download if I hold down the Shift key and click the left mouse button at the same time.

I'm sure you'll deal with your own browser's distinctive behavior, whatever that behavior may be.

Because a keystore doesn't contain ordinary text, you don't type the keystore's contents into your code. Instead, you make calls to the `setProperty` method. This is what I do in Listing 17-4.

If your registry requires you to use a keystore, then you must call the keystore `setProperty` methods before you call `connection.setCredentials`. If you first call `setCredentials`, and later call the keystore `setProperty` methods, then the keystore `setProperty` methods will have no effect. You won't get connected to the registry.

Some registries do not use a keystore. Others do.

✔ If you're working with a registry that doesn't use a keystore, then be sure to remove the calls to `setProperty` in the `addCredentials` method of Listing 14-4. You'll have no luck updating a registry if you're using a keystore that doesn't belong there.

✔ If you're working with a registry that uses a keystore, then you can probably download the keystore from a page at the registry's Web site. Just download the file, and put the file in a known place on your computer's hard drive. Then change the last `setProperty` call in Listing 14-7 so that it points to the keystore file on your computer's hard drive.

Deleting Registry Entries

Anything that goes up must come down. Anyone who goes into business eventually goes out of business. All black holes decay to nothing in the long run. And any entry that you make in a UDDI registry eventually needs to be removed.

The publish/query/delete cycle

In the JAXR API, the `BusinessLifeCycleManager` class has several `delete` methods. You can `deleteServices`, `deleteObjects`, and delete all kinds of unwanted things. In this section's example, we'll delete an entire organization. You'll find the code handy when you're testing the other programs in the chapter. In fact, my usual testing cycle is as follows:

```
Do a query to find organizations with Burd
    in their names. (Listing 17-1)
Publish a new entry, such as Burd Brain Consulting.
    (Listing 17-3)
Do a query to verify that Burd Brain Consulting is
    in the registry. (Listing 17-1)
```

```
Delete organizations with Burd in their
    names. (Listing 17-5)
Do a query to verify that Burd Brain Consulting is
    no longer in the registry. (Listing 17-1)
```

But wait just a darn minute! I search for organizations with the word Burd in their names. Sure, I'll find "Burd Brain Consulting," but I'll also find "Burdette's Bookstore" and "Burdensome Business Associates." I don't want to delete these other companies. And even if I don't mind making casual deletions, I don't have the credentials to delete anyone's listings but my own.

This section's code has two features that keep me from trying to delete the wrong registry entries.

- ✔ The code makes a query that does not retrieve other peoples' organizations.
- ✔ The code's delete method does not refer to any organizations by name.

The code, with its most relevant lines marked in bold, is in Listing 17-5.

Listing 17-5: Deleting Registry Entries

```java
import javax.xml.registry.BusinessQueryManager;
import javax.xml.registry.BusinessLifeCycleManager;
import javax.xml.registry.BulkResponse;
import javax.xml.registry.JAXRException;

import javax.xml.registry.infomodel.Organization;

import java.util.Collection;
import java.util.Vector;
import java.util.Iterator;


public class DoDelete
{
    public static void main(String[] args)
        throws JAXRException
    {
        MyBusinessCycleHelper helper;
        BusinessQueryManager queryManager;
        BusinessLifeCycleManager cycleManager;
        BulkResponse response;
        Organization organization;
        Collection organizations;
        Vector keys;
        Iterator iterator;
```

```
      String orgName;


      helper = new MyBusinessCycleHelper();
      helper.createConnection();
      helper.addCredentials();

      queryManager = helper.createBusinessQueryManager();
      response = queryManager.getRegistryObjects();


      organizations = response.getCollection();
      iterator = organizations.iterator();
      keys = new Vector();

      while (iterator.hasNext())
      {
         organization = (Organization)iterator.next();
         orgName = organization.getName().getValue();
         System.out.print(orgName);

         if (orgName.indexOf("Burd") != -1)
         {
            keys.add(organization.getKey());
            System.out.print(" is being DELETED,");
         }
         else
         {
            System.out.print(" is NOT being deleted.");
         }

         System.out.println();
      }

      if (!keys.isEmpty())
      {
         cycleManager =
            helper.createBusinessLifeCycleManager();
         cycleManager.deleteOrganizations(keys);
      }
   }
}
```

Listing 17-5 does a query, followed by a deletion. The query method,
getRegistryObjects, returns only the entries that belong to me. Let's
say I've posted Burd Brain Consulting, but not General Motors or
Burdette's Bookstore. Then neither General Motors nor Burdette's
Bookstore comes back from the query.

Fingering organizations

Once you've queried a registry, and found some organizations that you'd like to delete, you have to mark these organizations for deletion. Your first idea is to mark organizations by name. Well, names are useful in everyday speech, but names work terribly in automated processing. A quick search for "Joe's Diner" turns up restaurants in the United States, in England, and in Germany. (The search also unveils a place in a *Simpsons* episode, and the URL for a very active chat room.) The name "Joe's Diner" doesn't identify only one business or organization.

So business names aren't the answer. You can try to delete Geneva Miters, and delete General Motors instead. The best way to identify businesses is to give each business its own number. Think of all the advantages you have when you assign numbers to businesses.

✔ You can make sure that no two businesses have the same number.

✔ You can assign numbers by groups of businesses.

✔ You can make sure that similar businesses have dissimilar numbers.

The last advantage is very important. If business A is similar to business B, and it's easy to confuse businesses A and B, then the two businesses should have very different numbers.

Well, you're in luck. When you list a business in a UDDI registry, the listing gets assigned a number. This number is called a *UUID key*, where "UUID" stands for "Universally Unique IDentifier" (and "key" stands for "key!"). The key is a huge 128-bit number that gets assigned when you list your business.

The acronym "UUID" has nothing to do with the acronym "UDDI." The word "key" in "UUID key" has nothing to do with last section's security keystore. In summary, nothing has anything to do with anything else.

To assign a UUID key, the registry combines a number from its own network hardware with a number from its internal clock. So, both the time and place of a listing matters.

✔ You can list a business, delete the business, and then list the same business again. The business's key is different each time.

✔ You can list a business with two different registries. The two listings have two different keys.

With a unique key, you can unambiguously identify a business's listing in a registry. You can target that business's listing for deletion from the registry, and then remove that business without removing any other businesses (businesses with similar names, for instance).

To see an organization's UUID key, put a statement like `System.out.println(organization.getKey().getId())` in your code.

In Listing 17-5, I make use of UUID keys.

- ✔ I query the registry and find businesses that I intend to delete.
- ✔ I find the key for each such business.
- ✔ I use the key to delete the business from the registry.

To delete registry entries, I call `deleteOrganizations`. This call removes the entire listing of any business in the `keys` collection.

If I call `deleteOrganizations`, and the `keys` vector in the method's parameter has just one key that I'm not permitted to delete, then the entire call to `deleteOrganizations` fails. The call doesn't even delete the entries that I'm entitled to delete. (It doesn't help if the entries that I'm entitled to delete come earlier in the list than the entries that I'm not entitled to delete. Even in that situation, nothing at all gets deleted.)

When I run the code in Listing 17-3, I get output of the kind shown in Figure 17-3.

Figure 17-3:
Deleting
Burd Brain
Consulting.

```
Burd Brain Consulting is being DELETED.
Barry's Bytes, Bits and Books is NOT being deleted.
```

If, for some reason, you can't run this section's code, then you can always use the registry's Web interface to delete an organization.

I've run the code in Listing 17-5, and I want to check to make sure that Burd Brain Consulting is no longer in the registry. So I run Listing 17-1 one more time. The code in this listing looks for businesses with the word Burd in their names, and there are no such businesses in the registry. Alas! When I do the query, I get the output shown in Figure 17-4.

Figure 17-4:
An example
of Jean-
Paul Sartre's
nothingness.

Chapter 18

Automating Web-Service Processes (Using JAX-RPC)

⁂ ⁂

In This Chapter
- ▶ Taking another look at Web services
- ▶ Serving up software
- ▶ Using a Web service

⁂ ⁂

*P*icture this scenario. My company sells werbledooks at ten dollars a piece. I have a large supply of werbledooks that I advertise at my Web site (Werbledooks come in all shapes, sizes, and colors. Best of all, they're almost odor free!) When someone buys a werbledook, I get your shipping company to deliver the thing. Because you have a Web site, I point my customers to your site for up-to-the-minute package tracking information. (Werbledooks don't keep very well in dry weather, so shipping time is critical.)

I want to keep customers at my Web site as long as possible. So I get a brilliant idea. I can have the package tracking information appear on my own Web page. Not only is this good marketing, it also makes things easy for the customer. Instead of visiting your Web site and starting from scratch, the customer logs in at my site, gets a list of werbledooks purchased, and clicks a link to see tracking data. (The government's werbledook inspectors can track the shipments too!)

So the question is, how do I get the data from your Web site to my own Web site in real time? There are several possibilities.

✔ One possibility: Copying software components

In this scenario, I buy software from your company. The software reads tracking data from your system, and makes the data available to my own software systems. I integrate your software with mine, and hope for the best.

There are at least a hundred reasons why this plan is doomed to failure. Here are a few reasons:

- My program is reaching into your system's database. Next thing you know, I'll be reaching into your bank account.

- I may have to work hard to integrate your software into my system.

- You lose control of your software. If I use my copy improperly or illegally, you never know about it. And if you happen to find out about it, then there's not much you can do about it. (You can send me a registered letter, or take me to court, but you're in business to ship packages, not to become a guest on the Judge Judy show.)

- I have to maintain your component as part of my own code. If that component breaks, then I'm on the phone to your tech support people (who put me on hold for an hour and a half). For high volume business, the whole tech support issue is troublesome. Your folks may not know much about my proprietary software environment.

- I lose contact with the software's source. If you update the software, then I have to download a new copy. I don't get updates in real time.

✔ **Another possibility: Screen scraping**

The term *screen scraping* refers to any process that grabs characters or other content from a Web page. For instance, I can take the tracking number for a werbledook shipment, and send the number to your Web site. When I get back a Web page, I don't send the page to my customer's browser. Instead, I do wasteful, unreliable text filtering to find tracking data on the page. I paste the tracking data into my own Web page, and send my page to my customer's browser.

Heaven help me if you ever change the format of your Web page. And what happens to all the images on your Web page? I just toss these images into my virtual recycling bin. For my purpose, the images add unneeded bloat to the transmission of data. They do this every time I request tracking information.

✔ **Your best bet: Calling Web services with SOAP**

Compared with the previous awful scenarios, a Web service is a life-saver. You create a Java method of the following kind:

```
public TrackingData getData(TrackingNumber num)
```

You make this method available to the world. To call the method, all I have to do is to send a SOAP message to a URL. Maybe the URL looks like this:

```
http://my-car-rier.biz/jaxrpc-tracking/jaxrpc
```

SOAP is a standard. So my method call, and the tracking data returned by the method, can be interpreted without hassle at both ends. The tracking information is reliable because it isn't bundled with other garbage on a consumer-oriented Web page. And, because you send only the tracking data, the response is concise and efficient.

That settles it. We'll use a Web service with SOAP. To see how it works, take a look at Figure 1-1 (in Chapter 1). You run a package tracking service, and I make use of the package tracking service. The service's software runs on your computer. When my software needs tracking information, my software sends a message over the Internet to your software. My software gets back a message with tracking information, and I use that information to compose my Web page. In the meantime, both companies are doing what they do best. Your company's software is tracking packages, and my company's software is selling werbledooks.

Let's take the process one step further. We can automate the configuring of my system, so that my system accepts your software's data. After all, you offer me a getData method. That method's existence is a fairly straightforward fact. Instead of sending my programmers into their cubicles for twelve months, maybe I can run some software and have the software generate calls to the getData method.

Well, the software to generate calls has a name. The software is part of *JAX-RPC* – the *Java API for XML-based Remote Procedure Calls*. And the "straightforward fact" of the getData method's existence can be encoded in an XML document. This XML document conforms to a standard named *WSDL* — the *Web Services Description Language*.

So let's investigate this Web-services stuff. The rest of this chapter shows you some rock-solid examples. The examples belong to the JAX-RPC API. You can download the API from java.sun.com/xml/jaxrpc.

How rock-solid can an example be if the example is based on an early-access release? In this chapter, I don't have the luxury of writing about a real product. My version of JAX-RPC isn't even a beta version yet. Well, depending on how you view things, you'll think that I'm a hero or a fool. I'm a hero for writing about software that isn't stable yet, or I'm a fool for writing about ideas that are bound to change. One way or another, you can check on changes to JAX-RPC by visiting this book's Web site. The URL is users.drew.edu/bburd.

Getting a Handle on the Details

In this chapter, I do some serious name-dropping. I drop several filenames, and tell you where these files belong on various computers. The situation isn't too complicated as long as you have a roadmap for all the filenames. So, I put a roadmap in Figure 18-1. The map separates files on the client from files on the server.

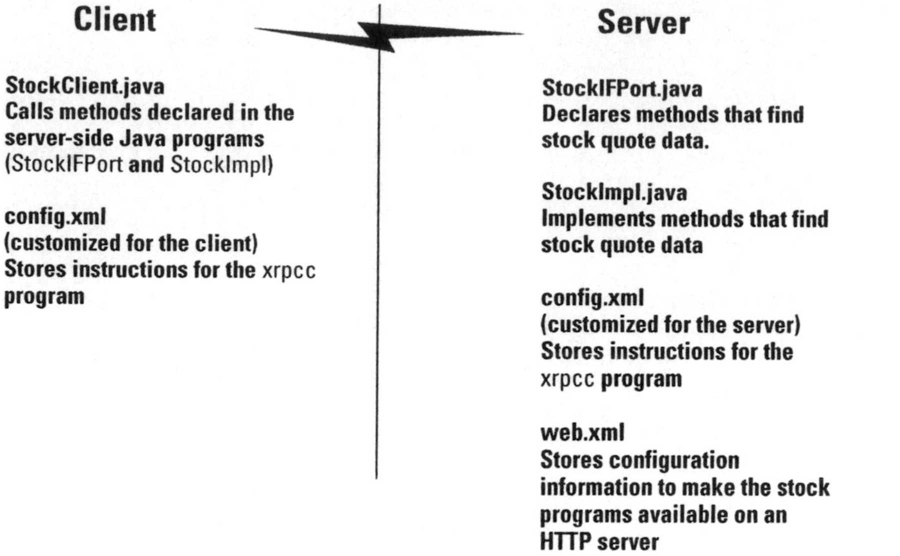

Client

Server

**StockClient.java
Calls methods declared in the
server-side Java programs
(StockIFPort and** StockImpl**)**

**StockIFPort.java
Declares methods that find
stock quote data.**

**StockImpl.java
Implements methods that find
stock quote data**

**config.xml
(customized for the client)
Stores instructions for the** xrpcc
program

**config.xml
(customized for the server)
Stores instructions for the**
xrpcc **program**

Figure 18-1:
Client files
and server
files.

**web.xml
Stores configuration
information to make the stock
programs available on an
HTTP server**

- The *server* has programs that provide a service. In this chapter's big example, the server programs provide stock-quote information. In the werbledook example (mentioned previously), your server programs provide package tracking information.

- The *client* has programs that use a service. In this chapter's big example, the client program requests stock-quote information from the server programs. In the werbledook example (mentioned previously), my program requests tracking information from your server programs.

Usually the two computers (client and server) belong to two different companies.

In this chapter, you can find examples of all the files named in Figure 18-1. The basic idea is that StockClient.java calls methods in StockImpl.java. To do this, the client computer has to reach out from its own Java Virtual Machine to the Java Virtual Machine on the server computer. This reaching is harder than you may think. There has to be additional code on both the client and server computers. (See Figure 18-2.)

- On the client computer, we need code that forwards method calls to the server. This code is called the *stub*.

- On the server computer, we need code that receives incoming method calls. This code is called the *tie*. The tie code relays method calls to the StockImpl program in Figure 18-2. When the StockImpl program returns a value, the tie relays that value back to the client.

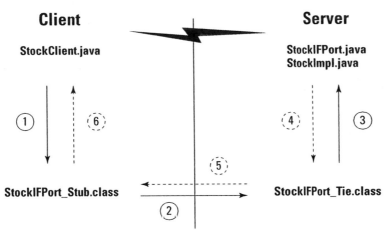

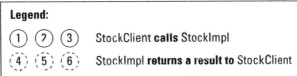

Figure 18-2:
Making a
remote
method call.

With all the stubs and ties in Figure 18-2, it looks as if everyone has to write a lot of code. And we call this "progress?" What ever happened to all those automated, easy-to-use Web services?

Well, the stubs and ties don't need to be touched by human hands. We can get software to write all that code for us. We use a program called xrpcc. (The name is an acronym for "XML-based RPC Compiler.") This xrpcc program is part of JAX-RPC. Depending on the content of a configuration file, the xrpcc program works in either of two ways. One way is for the server; the other way is for the client. (See Figure 18-3.)

✔ **On the server**, the xrpcc program takes StockIFPort.java and StockImpl.java and uses them to create ties. The program also creates a WSDL document, which contains useful information (including the following):

- The WSDL document contains the names, parameter lists, and return types of the methods in the server's StockIFPort and StockImpl programs.

- The WSDL document contains URLs on the server where these methods are available for calling.

✔ **On the client,** the xrpcc program takes the WSDL document, and uses it to create stubs.

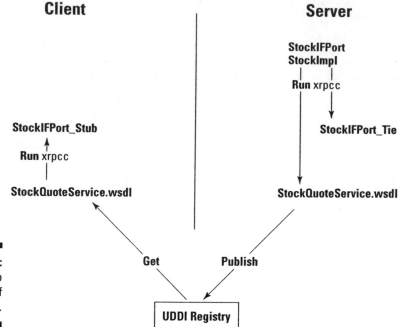

Figure 18-3:
The two
faces of
xrpcc.

So, the xrpcc program completes the Web services loop. Here's what the folks who run the server do:

- ✔ They start with Java code whose methods are to be made available as a Web service.
- ✔ They run xrpcc to create ties and a WSDL document.
- ✔ They publish the WSDL document on a UDDI registry. (See Chapter 17.)

And here's what the folks who run the client do:

- ✔ They get a copy of the WSDL document from the UDDI registry.
- ✔ They run xrpcc to create stubs.
- ✔ They run Java code that calls the server's methods.

In the rest of this chapter, I describe the six steps in detail. Keep a bookmark on this page, and you'll always know where you are in the grand scheme of things.

The Server Side of the Story

In this section, you're a big-time financial wizard. You provide financial data for the worldwide business community. (Don't you love *Java & XML For Dummies*? By reading this book, you've become an instant success.)

Writing Web-service code

Your company offers a Web service that provides real time stock quotes. The backbone of the service lives inside two Java source files. The files appear in Listings 18-1 and 18-2. The first file describes two methods available to anyone who wants to get stock quotes. The second file tells a computer what to do when someone calls either method.

Listing 18-1: A Stock-Quote Interface

```
package stock;

import java.rmi.Remote;
import java.rmi.RemoteException;

public interface StockIFPort extends Remote
{
    public double getQuote(String s) throws RemoteException;

    public String getSymbol(String s) throws RemoteException;
}
```

Listing 18-2: Implementing the Stock-Quote Interface

```
package stock;

public class StockImpl implements StockIFPort
{
    public double getQuote(String company)
    {
        if (company.equals("SUNW"))
            return 17.5300;
        else
            return 8.6600;
    }

    public String getSymbol(String company)
    {
        if (company.equals("Sun"))
            return ("SUNW");
```

(continued)

Listing 18-2 *(continued)*

```
        else
            return "other";
    }
}
```

Listings 18-1 and 18-2 follow a pattern that's familiar to many Java programmers. The pattern is especially familiar to programmers who work with Java RMI — *Remote Method Invocation*. Using RMI, you can have the code running on one computer call code running on another computer. In fact, RMI isn't only for computer-to-computer method calling. With RMI, you can have two copies of the Java Virtual Machine running on a single computer. The code running in one JVM can call code running in the other JVM.

It's not difficult to run two copies of the Java Virtual Machine on one computer. Just open up two command prompt windows, and type `java some-class-name` in each window.

Interface and implementation

Listings 18-1 and 18-2 illustrate the separation of interface from implementation. Let's say that you're running a client program that makes use of stock quotes. The program doesn't generate any information on its own. The program just calls the `getSymbol` and `getQuote` methods in Listing 18-2.

Now, what does the client program need to know in order to call the `getSymbol` and `getQuote` methods? The client needs to issue method calls such as

```
getSymbol("Sun Microsystems");
```

and

```
getQuote("SUNW");
```

The client program needs to know the stuff in Listing 18-1 — the names of the methods, the type of parameter that each method takes, and the type of value returned by each method. The client doesn't need to know what statements are executed when methods `getSymbol` and `getQuote` are called. In other words, the client doesn't need to know the stuff in Listing 18-2. The stuff in Listing 18-2 runs on a server computer.

So, with bandwidth in short supply and safe programming practices in even shorter supply, it's best to show code to the client computer on a need-to-know basis. Don't waste resources trying to send Listing 18-2 to the client. Instead, keep Listing 18-2 on a server computer, and send the *information* in Listing 18-1 to a client.

Now this is an important point. We don't send Listing 18-1 (the `.java` source file) to the client. We don't even send the bytecode `.class` file from Listing 18-1 to the client. That's the whole point of Web services. We don't send Java files because we don't know if the client runs Java, C#, or Werbledook++. All ye know on earth is that the client understands SOAP and WSDL. (That's all ye need to know.)

We don't send Java files to the client. Instead, we send WSDL documents wrapped in SOAP envelopes.

Of course, this book has *Java* in its title, so in this chapter, the client's code is written in Java. In a sense, the client will reconstruct Listing 18-1 from the information received in a WSDL document.

Some observations

You may notice that the class in Listing 18-1 extends `java.rmi.Remote`. The `Remote` interface is part of Java's remote method invocation API. Any interface whose methods can be called by code from another computer (or another Java Virtual Machine running on the same computer) must implement this `Remote` interface.

By the way, you're not going crazy. The code in Listing 18-2 is vaporware, and that's intentional. This code handles only one company at one moment in time. A real stock quote program would parse its input, query a database, and send back an honest result. Listing 18-2 just responds to a message with any data that it can toss out. If you want a more realistic look at databases, you'll have to read *JDBC(tm) 3.0: Java(tm) Database Connectivity* by Bernard Van Haecke.

Creating ties and a WSDL document

Here's the plan: We take Listings 18-1 and 18-2 (programs on the server), and run them through the JAX-RPC `xrpcc` program. When we do this, the `xrpcc` program magically creates some tie code on the server. The program also creates a WSDL document. (Earlier in this chapter, I described the action of the `xrpcc` program in more detail.) We don't look at the code inside the `xrpcc` program, because we don't need to. As far as we're concerned, `xrpcc` is a black box.

What I call "the `xrpcc` program" is really a combination of things. If you work in Windows, there's a script named `xrpcc.bat`. This script calls the code in a Java package, and the name of the package is `com.sun.xml.rpc.tools.xrpcc`. You can also call the code with a build tool such as Unix `make` or Apache Ant.

To run the `xrpcc` script, you type a command of the following kind:

```
xrpcc.bat config.xml
```

I'm not being very specific, because there are a million variations depending on things like your operating system, the day of the week, and the wind direction. But if you follow the documentation that comes with JAX-RPC, you should be okay. The main thing to notice is that `xrpcc` takes a configuration file. The configuration information (written in XML, of course) tells `xrpcc` what to do, what to do it with, where to do it, and how to do it for less.

The configuration file

The configuration file comes in two flavors — vanilla for the server, and chocolate for the client. A free sample of the vanilla flavored version is in Listing 18-3.

Listing 18-3:   The Server-Side Configuration for xrpcc

```xml
<?xml version="1.0" encoding="UTF-8"?>
<!-- config.xml (server version) -->

<configuration
    xmlns="http://java.sun.com/jax-rpc-ri/xrpcc-config">

    <rmi name="StockQuoteService"
        targetNamespace="http://stock.org/wsdl"
        typeNamespace="http://stock.org/types">

        <service name="StockQuote" packageName="stock">
            <interface name="stock.StockIFPort"
                servantName="stock.StockImpl"/>
        </service>
    </rmi>

</configuration>
```

The document in Listing 18-3 has a big `rmi` element, and that's important to notice. It's important because `rmi` is short for the command to "examine and use the code that extends `java.rmi.Remote`." (The code that extends `java.rmi.Remote` is in Listing 18-1.) Only the server has the original copy of Listing 18-1, so the server can run `xrpcc` with an `rmi` configuration file. (When you get to the client's version of `config.xml`, you'll see that the client's `config.xml` has no `rmi` element.)

Running `xrpcc` with Listings 18-1, 18-2, and 18-3 creates a whole bunch of new files. Most of them are `.class` files, like `StockIFPort_Tie.class`. These tie files relay method calls from a client to the server code in Listing 18-2. You can't read the code in these files, because they're not Java source files. (They're bytecode files.) But that's all right. You don't need to look at the stuff in these files. Just leave them where the xrpcc script puts them, and they'll do what they're supposed to do.

Despite what I wrote in the previous paragraph, there are times when you want to peek at the code created by xrpcc. (Maybe something isn't running correctly, and you need to do some detective work.) To decipher the code in .class files, you need to convert them back to Java source files. There's a neat program, called DJ Java Decompiler, that does this for you. To download the decompiler, visit members.fortunecity.com/neshkov/dj.html.

The new WSDL document

Along with some new .class files, a run of xrpcc on the server creates a WSDL file. The WSDL file created by my early-access release is shown in Listing 18-4.

Listing 18-4:   A WSDL Document

```
<?xml version="1.0" encoding="UTF-8"?>

<definitions name="StockQuoteService"
    targetNamespace="http://stock.org/wsdl"
    xmlns:tns="http://stock.org/wsdl"
    xmlns="http://schemas.xmlsoap.org/wsdl/"
    xmlns:soap="http://schemas.xmlsoap.org/wsdl/soap/"
    xmlns:xsd="http://www.w3.org/2001/XMLSchema">

    <types/>

    <message name="getQuote">
        <part name="String_1" type="xsd:string"/>
    </message>
    <message name="getQuoteResponse">
        <part name="result" type="xsd:double"/>
    </message>
    <message name="getSymbol">
        <part name="String_1" type="xsd:string"/>
    </message>
    <message name="getSymbolResponse">
        <part name="result" type="xsd:string"/>
    </message>

    <portType name="StockIFPort">
        <operation name="getQuote">
            <input message="tns:getQuote"/>
            <output message="tns:getQuoteResponse"/>
        </operation>
        <operation name="getSymbol">
            <input message="tns:getSymbol"/>
```

(continued)

Listing 18-4 *(continued)*

```
            <output message="tns:getSymbolResponse"/>
        </operation>
    </portType>

    <binding name="StockIFBinding" type="tns:StockIFPort">
        <operation name="getQuote">
            <input>
                <soap:body encodingStyle=
                    "http://schemas.xmlsoap.org/soap/encoding/"
                    use="encoded"
                    namespace="http://stock.org/wsdl"/>
            </input>
            <output>
                <soap:body encodingStyle=
                    "http://schemas.xmlsoap.org/soap/encoding/"
                    use="encoded"
                    namespace="http://stock.org/wsdl"/>
            </output>
            <soap:operation soapAction=""/>
        </operation>
        <operation name="getSymbol">
            <input>
                <soap:body encodingStyle=
                    "http://schemas.xmlsoap.org/soap/encoding/"
                    use="encoded"
                    namespace="http://stock.org/wsdl"/>
            </input>
            <output>
                <soap:body encodingStyle=
                    "http://schemas.xmlsoap.org/soap/encoding/"
                    use="encoded"
                    namespace="http://stock.org/wsdl"/>
            </output>
            <soap:operation soapAction=""/>
        </operation>
        <soap:binding transport=
            "http://schemas.xmlsoap.org/soap/http"
            style="rpc"/>
    </binding>

    <service name="StockQuote">
        <port name="StockIFPort" binding="tns:StockIFBinding">
            <soap:address location=
"http://localhost:8080/jaxrpc-stock/jaxrpc/StockIFPort"/>
        </port>
    </service>

</definitions>
```

To be perfectly frank, I (gasp!) edited the file in Listing 18-4 before I pasted it onto the page. The file created by xrpcc had some very long lines, so I added lots of line breaks. If you're curious, then you'll be happy to know that the example in this chapter works with my modified version of Listing 18-4.

You don't compose Listing 18-4 on your own, so I won't explain the listing line by line. Just notice that the listing includes familiar things — things like StockIFPort, getQuote, and service. The listing describes the methods made available by the code in Listings 18-1 and 18-2, and describes the way in which a computer can call these methods.

In the early-access release of JAX-RPC, the WSDL document that's created by running xrpcc isn't designed for round tips. And what do I mean by this? You can start with a file named StockIF.java, and end up with a WSDL document that applies to StockIFPort.java. It's not a big problem because the names of files on the client and server don't have to match in every respect. Even so, it's nice to keeps things consistent. That's why, in creating Listing 18-1, I chose StockIFPort for the name of my class.

Doing the routine stuff

With all this talk about generating a WSDL file, it's easy to forget the basics. In addition to running xrpcc, you have to compile your Java code, and install the code on a Web server. Many JAX-RPC fans use the Apache Tomcat server, and the JAX-RPC documentation has lots of advice about installing code on Tomcat. So to install the code on Tomcat, follow these steps:

1. **Find the configuration files for the examples that come with the JAX-RPC documentation.**

2. **Change any example-specific references so that they refer to this chapter's stock-quote example.**

3. **Follow the directions in the JAX-RPC documentation for installing code onto Tomcat.**

For instance, to install this chapter's examples, I looked at the web.xml file for the documentation's Hello World example. I did a Replace All, changing HelloWorld to StockQuote. With that modified web.xml configuration file, I was ready to install this chapter's examples on Tomcat. It worked like a charm.

Publishing the WSDL document

As I say in Chapter 17, a UDDI registry can have at least two interfaces — a Web interface, and a SOAP interface. Using either interface, you can upload a WSDL file to a UDDI registry.

Of course, you can transfer a file without a UDDI registry. You can call the client company, and say "Hey, Joe, come over and get this diskette with a WSDL file on it." Or, as you'll see in the next section, you can copy a file from one place to another on your computer's hard drive.

Please read on.

The Client Side of the Story

If you've made it to this point in Chapter 18, then you've read all about creating a Web service. You've seen a simple service that provides stock quotes, and read about xrpcc — a program that generates ties and WSDL files.

Now it's time to become a client for the Web service. In this section, you pretend that you're using a different computer, and you call methods in Listing 18-2. This pretending won't work unless a Web server is running, so start up your server, and get ready for good times!

Getting the WSDL document

In real life, your first client-side action would be to get the service's WSDL file. (That's the document in Listing 18-4. Running the xrpcc program on the server is what creates this file.) As a client, you'd probably get the WSDL file from a UDDI registry. Well, to test the code in this chapter's example, you don't need no stinkin' UDDI registries. All you do is copy the file named StockQuoteService.wsdl from your server directory to your client code's directory.

If you don't already have a directory for your client code, then just create one. Here's a list of files that you need in your client directory:

✔ You need the .wsdl file that was created by running xrpcc earlier in this chapter. (See Listing 18-4.)

✔ You need a configuration file to run xrpcc on the client side. (See Listing 18-5, later in this section.)

✔ Eventually, you'll need a program that requests stock quotes from the Web service. This program makes calls to the methods in Listing 18-2.

Of all the stuff in your client computer directory, the program that requests stock quotes wins the honor of being called the *client program*. Other programs in the client directory support this client program. This client program appears later in this section, in Listing 18-6.

✔ You need any other files that are required by the JAX-RPC documentation.

> For instance, there's a tutorial that comes with JAX-RPC. The tutorial uses a build tool called Apache Ant, and Ant needs its own configuration file (a file named `build.xml`) in order to run. Strictly speaking, you can use JAX-RPC without Ant or the Ant configuration file. But life is easier when you follow the official documentation's recommendations.

If you create a new client directory, don't forget to add that directory to your system's classpath. For help on setting the classpath, see Chapter 2.

You don't need the client program on your hard drive until you're ready to request a stock quote. That's interesting. You can run `xrpcc` and create stock-quote stubs before the client has any hand-written stock-quote code. When you run `xrpcc`, the program recreates the code Listing 18-1. You can examine that code to discover the kinds of method calls to write in your client program.

Separating the Client from the Server

Software like JAX-RPC is designed to run on two computers — a client dancing the tango with a server. If you don't use two computers, then you can separate your work into two different directories. But when people create sample code for this kind of software, they often bundle all the sample code in combined directories.

For instance, in the JAX-RPC tutorial, the Hello World example uses two directories — a directory named `hello`, and another named `common`. But both the `hello` and `common` directories contain client and server files. The assumption is, when you're testing code, you don't care if the client files are separate from the server files. Besides, if the files are in combined directories, then it's easier to test the code.

Well, I agree that combined directories make testing easier. And if you're not sure how a new API works, then you don't want to stray from the tutorial's instructions. You're best off using the tutorial's ready-made directory structure.

But I like to test the code's split personality. When I run this kind of code in combined directories,

I'm often lulled into a false sense of security. So I start by testing the code in combined directories. The code runs, and I'm happy. Then I ask myself which files would normally live on the server, and which would live on the client. (After all, the "R" in "JAX-RPC" stands for "Remote.") Sometimes, when I try moving some files to a separate directory, the tools stop working. This means that I don't really understand the cooperation between the client and the server. Often, the documentation is of little help.

So here's what I recommend. If the tutorial's example files come all bunched together, then work with the combined directory structure first. Once you have the code running correctly, make a backup copy of your work. Then look at Figure 18-1, and try moving files to separate directories. If things like `xrpcc` no longer work, or if the resulting code fails to run, then reconsider your choice of file locations.

P.S. Don't start moving files on a day when the kids want you to drive them to the mall.

Creating stubs

You've placed a `.wsdl` file into your client directory. You're about to run `xrpcc` to create stubs for the client. But wait! The `xrpcc` program needs a configuration file, and the file must be tailored for the client's needs. You can't use the `config.xml` file from Listing 18-3. That file isn't designed to use a WSDL document. (That file is designed to create a WSDL document.)

You need a chocolate-flavored file like the one in Listing 18-5. The `wsdl` element in Listing 18-5 distinguishes this file from the file in Listing 18-3. The `wsdl` element tells `xrpcc` to start by examining `StockQuoteService.wsdl`. So, when you run `xrpcc`, the computer generates stub code from the information that it finds inside `StockQuoteService.wsdl`. (The file `StockQuoteService.wsdl` is in Listing 18-4.)

Listing 18-5: **The Client-Side Configuration for xrpcc**

```
<?xml version="1.0" encoding="UTF-8"?>
<!-- config.xml (client version) -->

<configuration xmlns=
        "http://java.sun.com/jax-rpc-ri/xrpcc-config">

    <wsdl name="StockQuoteService"
          location="StockQuoteService.wsdl"
          packageName="stock">
    </wsdl>

</configuration>
```

When you run `xrpcc` with the configuration file in Listing 18-5, you get a bunch of new files on your hard drive. These files include `StockQuote_Impl.class`, `StockIFPort_Stub.class`, `GetQuote_RequestStruct.class`, and lots of other goodies.

Writing and running the client code

A client program calls the methods that are declared in Listing 18-2. To see a client program, look at Listing 18-6.

Listing 18-6: **A Stock-Quote Client**

```
package stock;

import java.rmi.RemoteException;

public class StockClient
```

```
{
   public static void main(String[] args)
      throws RemoteException
   {
      String symbol;
      double quote;

      StockIFPort_Stub stub = (StockIFPort_Stub)
         (new StockQuote_Impl().getStockIFPort());

      symbol = stub.getSymbol("Sun");
      quote = stub.getQuote(symbol);

      System.out.println("Sun Microsystems: " + quote);
   }
}
```

The action in Listing 18-6 has two phases.

✔ **Create a stub object.**

Both Listings 18-3 and 18-4 have tags that start with `<service name=`
`"StockQuote"` .... These tags give the name `StockQuote` to the Web
service provided by Listings 18-1 and 18-2. So, when the client runs `xrpcc`,
the `xrpcc` program creates a file named `StockQuote_Impl.class`.

In Listing 18-6, you use the `StockQuote_Impl` class to create a new
`StockQuote_Impl` object. Then, from the `StockQuote_Impl` object,
you get a stub object by calling `getStockIFPort`.

✔ **Call the Web service's methods.**

Here's the good part: Once you have a stub object, you just use the stub
to call the Web service's methods. So Listing 18-6 contains the calls
`stub.getSymbol("Sun")` and `stub.getQuote(symbol)`. There's no
special syntax. A programmer writing this part of the code doesn't have
to know about Web services or remote method invocation. In fact, the
programmer doesn't have to know that any other computer, or any
other Java Virtual Machine, is involved at all.

Now remember that the server computer runs the code in Listing 18-2.
When the client calls `getSymbol` and `getQuote`, the server computer
may be halfway around the globe. It doesn't matter. The intermediary
classes (shown in Figure 18-2) relay SOAP messages between the client
program and the code in Listing 18-2.

You'll find a run of Listing 18-6 depicted in Figure 18-4. The listing's
`System.out.println` call displays a company name and an up-to-the-minute
stock quote. (There must be minutes now and then when the value of Sun's
stock is 17.53. You have to run my program at one of those minutes.)

Figure 18-4:
Running
the code in
Listing 18-6.

Sun Microsystems: 17.53

Part IV
The Part of Tens

The 5th Wave   By Rich Tennant

Re·al Pro·gram·mers

INVALID CODE
YOU @*^!*
WALNUT BRAIN!

Real Programmers strive to insult users
with error messages.

In this part . . .

You're near the end of the book, and the time has come to sum it all up. This part of the book is your slam-bam, two-thousand-words-or-less resource for Java and XML. What? You didn't read *every word* in the chapters before this one? That's okay. You can pick up a lot of useful information in this Part of Tens.

Chapter 19

Ten Important Web Sites

I visited a search engine, and looked for sites that deal with Java and XML. I got 11,600,000 hits. So I examined all 11,600,000 sites. Believe me, it took almost an hour.

Of the 11,600,000 Web sites, I chose ten of my favorites to feature in this chapter. Due to space limitations, I had to omit about seven million excellent sites. (The remaining 4,599,990 sites are just fair, in my opinion.)

So, here are my ten favorites. I hope you enjoy them.

✔ java.sun.com

This Web site is "theeee place to look" for information about Java. Pages of particular interest to me are java.sun.com/j2se (for the Java™ 2 Platform Standard Edition) and java.sun.com/xml (for Sun's XML-related products).

I also like the discussion section at forum.java.sun.com. That's where I post questions to the Java developer community.

✔ www.jdom.org

The JDOM initiative isn't represented in any official way at Sun's Web site. So to get the last word on JDOM, you have to take a side trip. This JDOM Web site features source code, class files, API documentation, the formal JDOM specification, and an active mailing list.

✔ www.w3.org

The official standards documents are housed at this site. It's the main page of the esteemed World Wide Web Consortium. Many documents at this site are difficult to read, but that's okay. After all, they're official. Treat them as reference materials for checking facts and settling arguments.

By the way, while you're visiting this site, you should swing by www.w3.org/XML.

- `www.xml.org`

  This is a huge collection of links and resources on XML. My favorite part is the registry of XML schemas. You can find schemas for accounting, manufacturing, real estate property tracking, classroom planning, cave mapping, poem indexing, and more. There's a link to the registry on the main page, or you can go directly to the registry by visiting `www.xml.org/xml/registry.jsp`.

  While you're visiting this Web site, be sure to check the xml-dev mailing list and its archives. Follow the link from the main page, or visit `www.xml.org/xml/xmldev.shtml`.

- `xml.coverpages.org`

  Managed by Robin Cover, this Web site is a comprehensive list of links and resources on XML. Believe me, anything having to do with XML is referenced somewhere on this site.

  I'm especially fond of the articles that are posted here. The articles tend to be long. They use full paragraphs rather than bullets and links. It isn't flashy the way most Web sites are, but it's extremely useful.

- `www.uddi.org`

  This Web site is the starting place for information about UDDI. For me, the site's most useful resources are the online technical papers. In addition to these papers, you can find FAQs, forums, and links to special events.

- `The UDDI registries`

  To publish your services, or to test UDDI software, visit any of the following sites: `www.systinet.com/web/uddi`, `www-3.ibm.com/services/uddi`, `uddi.microsoft.com`, `www.xmethods.com`, `udditest.sap.com`, `https://uddi.hp.com/uddi`.

- `www.zvon.org`

  Never before have I seen reference materials that were so well organized. The tutorials' multi-frame interface puts other online training sites to shame. If you have a quick technical question, or you want a guided tour of a particular XML topic, then this Web site is the first place to look.

- `sourceforge.net`

  Many ongoing projects involving Java and XML are the work of independent groups, publishing their software as open-source code. This site is a repository for open-source activities.

  You can find all kinds of software goodies at this site — things you can't get from the official Sun APIs. You can become a participant by joining a discussion or helping to write software. It's a great way to become part of the open-source community.

✔ groups.google.com

It's two in the morning, and Paul wants Chapter 25, polished and proofread, by noon. The trouble is, my code doesn't work. I can make up some nonsense to cover up what I don't understand, or I can go to the Google Web site.

Certainly someone has encountered this problem before. They've posted a question, and received several replies. I can search the site for relevant keywords, and read postings about fixes for my stubborn problem. If I don't find a solution, then I can post my own question. I'll probably have some responses within 24 hours.

Who knows? Maybe I'll meet that noon deadline after all.

Chapter 20

Ten Ways to Avoid Mistakes

. . . .

In This Chapter

▶ Skirting SAX pitfalls

▶ Dodging DOM hazards

. . . .

*T*o write this chapter, I combed my manuscript for the top ten mistakes that people tend to make. Oddly enough, the mistakes aren't evenly distributed among chapters. In fact, they're all clumped around a few sections of this book.

All ten involve SAX and DOM — the first two topics in the book. In a way, it makes sense. Both SAX and DOM are primitive and powerful. Both let you micromanage the processing of an XML document. Both force you to take all the responsibility. You have lots of power, but you can easily goof things up.

Six SAX Snags

My big list of mistakes includes six SAX snafus. Of the six, five involve the characters between tags.

✔ **For one string of characters, a SAX parser can call the** characters **method several times. (See Chapter 3.)**

In the following code, my SAX parser reads the stuff between the MyThreeSins tag and the Sin tag.

```
<MyThreeSins>
   <Sin rank="favorite" ... Etc.
```

At this point, my parser makes three calls to the characters method. The first call has no characters in it, the second call contains the line feed after the <MyThreeSins> tag, and the third call contains three blank spaces (the indent before the <Sin> tag).

✔ **The characters method's first parameter can contain irrelevant characters. (See Chapter 3.)**

In some instances, the parameter contains an entire XML document. To zoom in on the relevant characters, you apply the method's second and third parameters.

For instance, when my parser handles the following Sin element, the characters method's first parameter contains all 140 characters in the XML document.

```
<Sin rank="favorite">sloth</Sin>
```

The second parameter is 79 (pointing to the 79th character in the document; namely, the s in sloth). The method's third parameter is 5 (for the 5 letters in the word sloth).

✔ **Different SAX parsers exhibit different behaviors. (See Chapter 3.)**

So, you think you've figured out how a SAX parser calls its characters method. You write a program whose code depends on a certain kind of behavior. You send your program to a customer, and the customer crashes the program. What went wrong? The program crashed because the customer's parser and your parser make different calls to the characters method.

So what do you do to prevent this fiasco? First, you test your code with whatever parser the customer plans to use. Next, you test your code with several parsers (if the code needs to be very robust). Finally, you make no assumptions about the way the characters method gets called. You always apply the characters method's second and third parameters, and you test resulting content to make sure that it contains the text that you expect.

✔ **A SAX parser behaves differently for documents that have, and don't have, DTDs. (See Chapter 5.)**

If a document has a DTD, then the parser can call both the characters and the ignorableWhitespace methods. If a document has no DTD, then the parser does not call the ignorableWhitespace method. Without a DTD, all text that would be handled by the ignorableWhitespace method gets handled by the characters method instead.

✔ **Line breaks don't separate character method calls from one another. (See Chapter 6.)**

Someone hands you a document that uses line breaks for separators; it looks like this:

```
<MyFourSins>
    Micromanaging
    Robbing a bank
    Having a Chip on your shoulder
    Earning too much money
</MyFourSins>
```

Don't depend on SAX to separate the items for you. Instead, create your own lexical parsing code. You'll find Java's `StringTokenizer` class to be very useful.

✔ **SAX suffers from amnesia. (See Chapter 6.)**

When it stops executing the `startElement` method, the parser forgets about the element's attributes. When it stops executing the `characters` method, the parser forgets about the text. Neither the attributes nor the text gets saved for methods like `endElement` and `endDocument`.

If you need attributes or text near the end of an element's processing, then you have to save these pieces of information in instance variables. But sometimes, simple variables aren't sufficient. For nested elements, you may have to save several versions of the attributes or the text — in which case, use a stack.

Those Darn DOM Dangers

Both SAX and DOM have potential stumbling blocks. This section covers a few of the surprises that you can encounter in DOM programs.

✔ **A DOM tree doesn't start with an XML element. (See Chapter 7.)**

The root of a DOM tree is an entire XML document. Under that document node comes the content of the document.

The content's outermost items can include things other than elements. For instance, the following document has a comment node directly beneath its document node.

```
<?xml version="1.0" encoding="UTF-8"?>
<!-- Yum! -->
<ChocolateLoversClub>
    <ILoveChocolate/>
</ChocolateLoversClub>
```

The comment and `ChocolateLoversClub` nodes are siblings in the DOM tree.

I've made this same mistake many times. I feed a DOM tree to a method that expects an element node. The method blows up because the tree is a document, not an element. To fix the problem, I dig the `root` element out of the DOM tree, and pass the `root` element to the method.

✔ **The meaning of `nodeName` and `nodeValue` vary with the type of node. (See Chapter 7.)**

It's difficult to keep one pattern in your mind to remember node names and node values. Take, for instance, the line

```
<Sin rank="favorite">sloth</Sin>
```

In this line, the element's name is `Sin`, but the text node's name is `#text`. The element's value is `null`, but the text node's value is `sloth`. The element has no value, but the element has attributes. No other types of nodes have attributes.

Before you use methods like `getNodeName`, `getNodeValue`, and `getAttributes`, be sure to check Table 7-1 in this book.

✔ **DOM is slow. (See Chapter 7.)**

DOM takes an entire XML document, and uses it to form a data structure. This structure gets held in your computer's memory. With small XML documents, the use of memory isn't significant. But with large documents, you have all the problems of any memory-hogging program. Other running programs have to share their memory, and your hard drive chirps while chunks of memory get passed back and forth.

Even if memory isn't an issue, the computer still takes a lot of time to traverse a big DOM data tree. If you're working with large documents, and processing time is important to you, don't use DOM.

✔ **To create a new DOM node, you need an existing DOM document. (See Chapter 8.)**

You don't get a DOM node out of the blue. First, you create a DOM document with code like this:

```
DocumentBuilderFactory factory =
    DocumentBuilderFactory.newInstance();
DocumentBuilder builder =
    factory.newDocumentBuilder();
Document doc = builder.newDocument();
```

Then you use the document to create a node:

```
Node eltNode = doc.createElement("Item");
```

Finally, you hang the node onto your DOM document tree with a command like this one:

```
doc.appendChild(eltNode);
```

It's confusing for two reasons. First, you can forget that a node comes from a document. Second, you can forget that creating a node from a document doesn't place the node on the document tree. Placing the node on the tree requires an `appendChild` method call.

And there you have it: a set of gotchas for both SAX and DOM. Keep 'em handy.

Index

• E •

● *F* ●

● *G* ●

• *X* •

Z

Java™ & XML For Dummies®

Cheat Sheet

Java Program Excerpts

SAX (Chapters 3, 4, 5, and 6)

```java
SAXParserFactory fact = SAXParserFactory.newInstance();
SAXParser saxParser = fact.newSAXParser();
XMLReader xmlReader = saxParser.getXMLReader();
xmlReader.setContentHandler(new MyContentHandler());
xmlReader.parse(new File("MyDoc.xml").toURL().toString());
public void startDocument()
public void startElement(String uri, String localName,
                         String qualName, Attributes attribs)
public void characters(char[] charArray,
                       int start, int length)
public void endElement(String uri, String localName,
                       String qualName)
public void endDocument()
```

DOM (Chapters 7, 8, and 9)

```java
DocumentBuilderFactory fact =
    DocumentBuilderFactory.newInstance();
DocumentBuilder builder = fact.newDocumentBuilder();
Document doc = builder.parse
    (new File(args[0]).toURL().toString());
new MyTreeTraverser (doc);
Node child = node.getFirstChild();
while (child != null) {
    new MyTreeTraverser (child);
    child = child.getNextSibling();
}
NamedNodeMap attribs = node.getAttributes();
for (int i = 0; i < attribs.getLength(); i++) {
    System.out.println(attribs.item(i).getNodeName());
    System.out.println(attribs.item(i).getNodeValue());
}
```

JDOM (Chapters 10 and 11)

```java
SAXBuilder builder = new SAXBuilder(false);
Document doc=builder.build
    (new File(args[0]).toURL().toString());
new MyEltTraverser (doc.getRootElement());
List children = element.getChildren();
for (int i=0; i<children.size(); i++) {
    Element child = (Element)children.get(i);
    new MyEltTraverser(child);
}
```

For Dummies: Bestselling Book Series for Beginners

Java™ & XML For Dummies®

Cheat Sheet

Java Program Excerpts (continued)

XSLT (Chapters 12 and 13)

```
TransformerFactory fact = TransformerFactory.newInstance();
StreamSource oldStream = new StreamSource(new File(args[0]));
StreamSource xslStream = new StreamSource(new File(args[1]));
StreamResult newStream = new StreamResult(new File(args[2]);
Transformer transformer = fact.newTransformer(xslStream);
transformer.transform (oldStream, newStream);
```

JAXB (Chapters 14 and 15)

```
FileInputStream nightmareIn=new FileInputStream("Nite.xml");
Nightmare nightmare = Nightmare.unmarshal(nightmareIn);
String severity = nightmare.getSeverity();
nightmare.setSeverity("very" + severity);
FileOutputStream nightOut=new FileOutputStream("Nite.xml");
nightmare.validate();
nightmare.marshal(nightOut);
```

JAXM (Chapter 16)

```
URLEndpoint endpoint = new URLEndpoint (urlEndpoint);
SOAPConnectionFactory connFactory =
    SOAPConnectionFactory.newInstance();
SOAPConnection connection = connFactory.createConnection();
MessageFactory messFactory = MessageFactory.newInstance();
SOAPMessage request = messFactory.createMessage();
SOAPPart soapPart = request.getSOAPPart();
SOAPEnvelope envelope = soapPart.getEnvelope();
SOAPElement elt = envelope.getBody();
elt=elt.addChildElement
    ("find_business", "", "urn:uddi-org:api");
Name name = envelope.createName("generic");
elt.addAttribute(name, "1.0");
elt = element.addChildElement("name");
elt.addTextNode(businessName);
SOAPMessage response = connection.call(request, endpoint);
```

For Dummies: Bestselling Book Series for Beginners